The Surrealist Mode in Spanish Literature

The Surrealist Mode in Spanish Literature

An Interpretation of Basic Trends
from Post-Romanticism
to the Spanish Vanguard

by

Paul Ilie

Ann Arbor
THE UNIVERSITY OF MICHIGAN PRESS

This book was made possible by grants from
the John Simon Guggenheim Memorial Foundation
and the Horace H. Rackham Foundation.

FOR PEGGY

*who sees clearly
into reality and beyond*

Contents

Introduction

The purpose of this book is to define the nature and scope of the surrealist mode in Spanish literature on the basis of an analysis of representative works. Similar studies have been made in connection with French literature, but so far nothing on a comparable scale has been done for Spain.[1] One reason for this is the lack of any real historical development of surrealism as a movement in Spain. There were no self-proclaimed exponents of surrealism, either as a "school," as imitators of the French, or as independent writers.[2] This does not mean, of course, that surrealist practices were not cultivated by Spanish writers. The proof of these practices lies not only in various anthologies but in the fact that critics dealing with the Generation of 1927 have often had recourse to the word surrealism as the only term suitable for identifying much of the poetry written by that group.

Nevertheless, it is difficult to document the history of these surrealist manifestations. Unlike the situation in France, no manifestos or statements of purpose describing the theory behind literary surrealism were produced in Spain. Nor did any group of writers organize a movement in order to chart the direction of their experimental practices. And yet, many poets and novelists were aware of surrealism as a creative force of great aesthetic value. They explored its artistic implications with subtle originality, devising new methods which extended the scope of surrealism beyond the implications of André Breton's manifesto of 1924.

In this book, however, I will not attempt to give a complete historical account of Spanish surrealism. Instead, I will try to examine the basic trends in the evolution of an aesthetic mode, leaving future critics with the task of evaluating the roles of Larrea, Cernuda, and others in the complex vanguard upheaval of which surrealism was a part. Since this represents the first book-length venture into this aspect of peninsular Spanish literature, it will be enough to discover the broad outlines of an aesthetic which could not be expected to be devoid of national influences or precedents. Hispanists should not be surprised, therefore, to find Antonio Machado and Juan Ramón Jiménez represented here, since their early poetry supplies the bridge between Romanticism and the Generation of 1927. And the general reader should not be surprised to find Federico García Lorca occupying a good deal of our time, for his is the best that Spanish surrealism has to offer. By drawing upon these and other contemporaries, I hope to trace the development of forms and motifs that constitute the surrealist mode in Spain without regard to the question of a French-linked school.

The fact that Spain lacked a well-defined surrealist school was, in any case, due more to the nature of her literary vanguard than to any failure to exploit the possibilities of the new aesthetic. Spanish writers were not inclined to collective efforts, and they preferred to channel their energies into a wide variety of individual art forms. This is why very few works are totally identifiable as surrealistic, or, for that matter, as exclusively the product of any literary fashion popular at the time. This is, of course, a tribute to the synthetic genius of modern Spanish literature, which has continually eschewed dogmatic precept in favor of a pluralistic view of art theory. However, the scant material available in the way of external surrealist history has created a gap with consequences for Hispanic scholarship that have been unfortunate. For one thing, it has caused critics to overlook an important alternative to the historical approach to literary criticism: the method of arriving at aesthetic principles inductively by textual analysis. For another, it has made critics like Guillermo de Torre and Dámaso Alonso either negative or apologetic about the use of the term surrealism in connection with the Spanish vanguard.[3] And finally, it has distracted everyone from the real issue of literary criticism, namely, whether the usage of words like Baroque, Romantic, and surrealist is at all meaningful, and whether the broad basis for defining terminology should be external influences or, rather, the intellectual and aesthetic structure of the work of art.[4]

At the root of these difficulties is a more serious problem, one which appears in the form of a scholarly fait accompli: virtually everything written about literary surrealism deals with the French movement. Since the men who first called themselves surrealists were French, or were associated with the Parisian school, it was only natural that critical studies should have defined surrealism exclusively in terms of French theory and practice. The trouble is that this definition has solidified in the absence of scholarship devoted to other surrealist literatures. Thus, what French criticism says about the surrealists in France has become the official standard by which all other claims to the title of surrealism are currently judged. Unless critics are convinced that similar ideas and art forms cannot develop independently of each other in different countries at the same time, they can only resist the imposition of such a dogma. But, if so convinced, then critics must be prepared to reserve the word surrealism exclusively for the Parisian school of writers and painters, or to use it only where their influence is explicitly demonstrated.[5]

This book rejects the thesis that writers are surrealists only when they consciously imitate the original French group, or that a work may be called surrealistic only if it conforms to the aesthetic pronouncements of André Breton and his associates. Not that any French critic has ever affirmed such a thesis, but its tacit acceptance has, as I have said, inhibited the use of the term in Spain, as well as any detailed study of the writers who practiced the surrealist mode. The problem, then, is to arrive at a working definition of surrealism that will assure the recognition of those Spanish works which are the most suitable for examination in this limited study. At the end of the book, there will be an opportunity to review some of the scholarly interpretations of French surrealism, as it compares with its Spanish counterpart. For the moment, however, the best approach is to seek an objective view of the subject.

Perhaps the most balanced discussion of surrealism is that presented by Renato Poggioli in his *Teoria dell'arte d'avanguardia* (Bologna, 1962). Thinking in broad yet meaningful terms, he places Dadaism and surrealism third in a series of aesthetic waves that swept across Europe after the decline of naturalism. Poggioli points out the importance of expressionism as a precursor of surrealism, but while he limits the former to Germany, he makes no attempt to restrict the latter to one country or group of artists. Rather, he suggests that the primary characteristic of surrealism is internal: the cultivation of dream states, stream of consciousness, and psychic violence of all types.

Poggioli's view of surrealism is equally balanced when he discusses particular traits and techniques. For example, he regards the theoretical principle of automatic writing—proposed by Breton— as a metaphorical way of suggesting many diverse methods of psychological release and expression. He also speaks of the "biological and psychic vitalism" of the surrealists and expressionists, a concept which I will develop later with regard to Dali and Lorca. But most significant, Poggioli indicates how surrealism has developed an intricate repertoire of genres and techniques. That is, it has cultivated new artistic forms, transformed themes, and depicted the metamorphoses of objects by means of a radically different idea: the identification of the aesthetic vision with the dream state. For Poggioli, as for virtually everyone else, the poetics of the dream is the most important principle of the surrealist mode. It is the premise of any work, no matter how slight the degree of actual fantasy in that work.

If we accept this account of surrealism as being internationally valid, we can begin to speak more intelligently about a surrealist mode in Spain. As far as this book is concerned, I will employ the word surrealism in the least doctrinaire and most generous way possible. That is, the term will refer to an aesthetic mode which first received its name in France, but which was present throughout Europe in many forms: painting, literature, theater, ballet, music, cinema. Its roots were cultural and artistic, rather than historical and national. In other words, its practices did not come about because certain people issued a proclamation at a given moment in the history of a nation. On the contrary, surrealism grew out of similar irrational tendencies in the aesthetic history of many nations. It was also the product of modern technological culture or, better, the awareness of a technology which was shared by a number of countries either directly or through the medium of internationally circulating ideas. In short, surrealism was a phenomenon greater than literary history, one which involved the intellectual and cultural development of modern Europe. In this light, it is clear that just as the French may look to Baudelaire and Lautréamont as the antecedents of their surrealism, so too might the English claim theirs in Blake and Hogarth, and the Spaniards in Quevedo and Goya. The history of ideas evolves with roughly the same rhythm in most of Western Europe. And to the extent that these ideas find artistic expression, the history of aesthetics will be equally rhythmical in revealing trends across national boundaries.

The term surrealism, therefore, must have two levels of meaning. The first is its general definition, which describes what is characteristic of every surrealist work, regardless of genre or nationality.[6] It is this meaning that makes it possible to explain why a work is surrealistic and not, say, realistic or futuristic. The second level of meaning is more specialized, intended to characterize the surrealism of a particular country or school. My objective in this book is to reach such a definition in terms of surrealist modes in Spain. In the final summation, I will compare this definition with the ones proposed by commentators of the French movement. But for the moment, let us bear in mind Poggioli's view and explore the nature of the broad definition. It was the latter, needless to say, which first caused me to identify the works discussed in this book as being fruitful for determining the nature of the surrealist mode in Spain.

There are several criteria for determining whether a work is surrealistic. Probably the most infallible is the subjective effect it has upon the observer, the feeling that he is in the presence of a strange, disturbing world. This is invariably the impact made by the paintings of De Chirico, Ernst, Dali, Tanguy, and Magritte. The odd sensations of uncanniness, incongruity, and absurdity are all part of the aesthetic experience of surrealism. A more objective criterion, however, is the technique of irrationality involving a new type of illogic based on free association. Here, traditional forms of meaning are replaced by the unrestricted juxtaposition of words, ideas, and images. These haphazard relationships produce a reality that is no longer bound by the laws of logic, causality, or syntax. The result is a work of art filled with unusual encounters, dissimilar planes of reality, and psychological dissociations of many kinds. Whether these results are due to pure psychic automatism, or to a deliberate and rational attempt to create an incongruous or grotesque world, the aesthetic consequences are the same. That is, surrealism projects the forms of distortion and the emotions of alienation. This is often accomplished by the artistic use of dream states and hallucinations, the adaptation of Freudian psychoanalysis to art, and the exploitation of occultism and the supernatural. But more often, the artist uses these elements in conjunction with other, more conscious techniques. Consequently, a work of art may be surrealistic only in part, and yet be just as interesting to us for its contribution to the aesthetics of the surrealist mode.

This is exactly what happens in the Spanish mode of surrealism. Very few works are surrealistic from beginning to end, although, we might add, French surrealism is only slightly better off in this respect. What is important, however, is not the quantitative presence of a technique, but the qualitative presentation of an aesthetic. There should be no undue concern with the purity of a work, or with how successfully it is insulated against the nonsurrealistic world. On the contrary, the degree to which surrealist elements are fused with other elements can be a useful indicator of the relationship between differing aesthetic trends. It can also help us to determine the manner in which surrealism drew away from the old aesthetic norms. Conversely, the special character of surrealism stands out most clearly when it appears to be atypical of the career of an artist who is known for other styles and themes. For this reason, a study of its presence in Spain cannot be limited to "thoroughbred" models of surrealist practice. Its emergent forms must also be examined. There are critical moments in the waning life of an old aesthetic mode that are more important to our understanding of surrealism than the routine patterns of a pure but derivative work that follows established surrealist norms.

By allowing this latitude, it will be possible to observe the genesis as well as the flowering of surrealism. And, most crucially, it will be possible to see what Romantic roots there are in the growing sense of incongruity and alienation that differed so radically from tradition. In short, a clear view of the break that occurred between the old subjectivism and the new emotional dislocation that separates the Spanish surrealist mode from the Romantic era will emerge. This break has not received the attention it deserves, for it reflects the crisis of contemporary art and marks the emergence of a new sensibility which is basically anti-Romantic. Given the fact that virtually everyone emphasizes the Romantic qualities of the Spanish Generation of 1927, I must point out that this book stresses what is different in the modern spirit. This is one of the factors affecting my approach, and it requires a word of explanation.

After the Romantic revolt, an evolution in artistic sensibility took place. In the chapters that follow, I shall discuss the mechanisms involved, but for the moment let it suffice to point out one general syndrome. Post-Romantic literary movements grew progressively more obsessed with the senses and the self, until both became distorted in their representation. By post-Romanticism I mean the entire range of aesthetic positions, prior to cubism, in which this obsession was a characteristic. At one end of the spectrum were the Parnassians, whose narrow preoccupation with sense data isolated the artist from many other forms of reality. Greater hermeticism was found among the symbolists, who developed narcissistic tendencies, deranged the senses, and established an important distinction between subjectivism and irrationalism. In the Hispanic world, the post-symbolist school of Modernism tended to display sensual and sensorial exacerbations which bordered on the neurasthenic, thus preparing the artistic mind for the psychological rift that was to follow.

It was against this background that Spanish writers began to transform the literary techniques that they had either innovated or inherited from the previous generation. However, since they left few theoretical documents, we face the problem of determining which elements in so large a body of literature belong to the surrealist paternity. Indeed, we must also accept the fact that there is a complex diffusion of surrealist techniques among artists of differing age groups and literary backgrounds. In Spain, the surrealist mode was a broad aesthetic category, encompassing at least three generations which, from 1910 to 1935, practiced the irrational in art for profound cultural reasons. Therefore, to understand Spanish surrealism is to comprehend not just one decade of homogeneous techniques and theories, but a longer evolution of intellectual and social attitudes as well. These involved, from 1890 to 1936, the breakdown of fin-de-siècle values, the dispersal of the Generation of 1898 and its cohesive moral force, the establishment of a new cosmopolitan orientation, and the steady replacement of traditional forms of subjectivism by the grotesque, the dehumanized, the violent, and the absurd.

Thus, our definition of surrealism depends on more than the broad specifications outlined earlier. As we shall see, Spanish writers drew inspiration from a variety of revolutionary sources, thus obscuring the surrealist nature of the techniques they were evolving. Their comprehensively active experimentation took the place of narrow theorizing, and often, unlike the situation in France, it was not possible to know their artistic principles until after their works had been produced. This fact will of necessity influence the method of analysis in this book. I will not attempt either to elicit a systematic philosophy of surrealist aesthetics or to cover all the examples of surrealism that exist in Spanish literature. Both tasks seem to me to be fruitless in an introductory book of this kind. Even if it were possible to identify every manifestation of surrealism on the basis of a systematic theory, the result might be historically useful, but not essential to the understanding of aesthetic principles. And, as I have noted, the purpose of this book is to characterize the broad outlines of surrealism in Spain as an aesthetic mode.

Bearing in mind what was said about the breakdown of Romantic values in the post-Romantic sensibility, let us return to the problem of the choices for textual analysis. My criterion for selecting the works to be studied was always that of aesthetic pertinence. All of the texts illuminate what I believe to be the central characteristics in the evolution of Spanish surrealism. They represent the full course of its artistic development, from its link to Spain's tradition of the grotesque, to its emergence from the crisis of Romanticism, and, finally, to its apogee in both poetry and the novel. The organization of this book, consequently, follows the outline of that development, not any chronological determinism in the relationship of one author to another. But the book does recognize that there are four basic problems, if not stages, in the evolution of the surrealist mode.

The first of these problems is the emergence of surrealism: where it began to stand out against its aesthetic background, and how its practices differed from the established ones. In this respect, we have to contend with the wider tradition of Spanish grotesque literature and painting.[7] As examples of these issues, Jiménez, Machado, and Solana seemed best suited to illustrate the post-Romantic crisis, with its themes and images of alienation and distortion. And as a transitional figure between the bad dream of post-Romanticism and the nightmare of surrealism, I felt that the early Aleixandre exemplified the descent into a subconscious world of anguish and mutilation.

The second problem concerns the nature of surreality: its cultural roots, its psychological basis, and how they both help to shape its imagery. Here, what is involved is the artist's urban experience, the way in which the city's violence and squalor triggers reactions of paranoia or nightmare in him. On another level, the impersonality of metropolitan life brings up the question of human and inhuman behavior. The relationship between man and machine is complicated by the relationship between instinct and civilization. Thus, the biological and cultural aspects of existence become dominant concerns in surrealism and are represented by the motifs of metamorphosis, the techniques of dehumanization, and the emotions of a victimized psyche. To illustrate this surreality, I chose several poems from Lorca's *Poet in New York* and Dali's prose works. And, again, as a transitional piece, Lorca's ode to Dali is included to bridge the gap between post-Romanticism, cubism, and surrealism.

The third problem in the development of surrealism is the matter of expressiveness: the language and structural form by which the surrealist mode takes shape as literature. This is an ever-present concern in my study, and in almost every chapter I will have something to say about style. But the role of words and images as symbols of two worlds—external and inner reality, society and psyche —is a problem common to all styles, and is particularly insistent in the representation of surreality. In focusing on this topic, I selected one long poem by Alberti which is particularly revealing because its linguistic crisis recapitulates many of Lorca's and Dali's preoccupations, and, at the same time, points the way to social realism. With regard to composition and structure, certain novels by Gómez de la Serna, Jarnés, and Arderius are indispensable to any discussion of surrealism. Moreover, they provide a more benevolent counterpart to the psychological violence already mentioned, due to the fairy-tale quality of their narratives.

The fourth and last general problem involves social awareness. This, too, is an issue raised indirectly by a number of surrealists. However, its most original and brilliant expression in Spain, and perhaps in all of Europe, are the *esperpentos* of Valle-Inclán, with *Tirano Banderas* preeminent among them. Aside from its contribution to aesthetic theory, this work reaches out in every direction to unify historical and political reality on one hand, and deformation, narcosis, and "black humor" on the other. Thus, while the *esperpento* maintains its link to both surrealism and the theater of the absurd, it makes them relevant to their cultural context as well. In no other author, Lorca excepted, is the social and the aesthetic sense so exquisitely balanced.

This, then, is the rationale behind the selection of authors and works to be examined in this book. Clearly, there is a good deal of overlapping, which is to be expected. There are no clear-cut categories, and if I have spoken of four general areas, it was to clarify the reasons for the textual choices made.[8] My hope is to serve two not unrelated kinds of audiences: the specialist, who will expect to find the sort of detailed internal analysis that can support exegetically the broad statements about Spanish surrealism made in the final chapter, and the general reader interested in aesthetic theory, and particularly in surrealism as a European phenomenon. It is for the general reader that the translations (my own) were made, especially in view of the chronic neglect of Spanish literature by English translators.[9] Background material that is not directly connected with surrealism has been eliminated, although the bibliography will indicate where it can be found.

Chapter One

Surrealism in Spain

Before turning to the characteristics of the surrealist mode as it evolved among individual Spanish writers, it would be useful for us to survey a number of theoretical issues. Generally speaking, literary theory and practice did not go hand in hand during the Spanish vanguard period. The great poets and novelists were not interested in writing about their art, and they hardly practiced literary criticism at all at that particular time. Except for Benjamín Jarnés, and perhaps Pérez de Ayala, Spain lacked the synthetic genius of a Valéry or Gide who could combine creative writing and literary analysis. On the other hand, Spanish journalism had been for many years at a high intellectual level, and this tradition gave rise to a number of essayists who were active in publishing their views on the cross-currents of philosophy and the arts that descended from Paris. A situation developed, therefore, in which two fairly well-defined groups of writers existed side by side, one apparently out of contact with the everyday world because of its aestheticism, and the other constantly in touch with the events and ideas of that world.

Nevertheless, this apparent division of the intelligentsia is deceptive. The fact was that both types of writer shared the same platform for expressing their thoughts, and they could not help but know each other's position even though this was not explicitly declared in their works. That platform, of course, was the "little magazine," a vehicle which not only provided the arena for aesthetic experimentation but also made possible the theoretical background against which the creative artists worked. Thus, there is no reason to doubt that a mutual influence between theory and practice did exist, despite the lack of direct acknowledgment to that effect. Had the poets and novelists desired to be more articulate, they most certainly could have expressed their views on the many new trends of their day, surrealism included. Indeed, painters like Dali and Gasch were not reticent, nor was the novelist Jarnés, and if people like Lorca and Alberti were silent, it cannot be concluded that they had no interest or opinions about what the others were saying. The very proximity of all these writers to one another indicates the contrary, and to think otherwise is to ignore the unifying function of the vanguard journals. This is why a critical approach which denies the existence of Spanish surrealism on the grounds of scanty historical evidence starts from the wrong premise. It would be better to assume that writers were familiar with French surrealism even if they did not say so.[1]

In any event, several important essays of an analytical nature do exist which should be noted here, and by doing so we will be in a better position to judge the surrealist mode itself later. One of the first articles to appear after Breton's manifesto of 1924 was by César Arconada, who sought to describe the relationship between musical composition and surrealism.[2] This should not be surprising, since the main legacy of the preceding generation of modernist poets was musicality. It was, for example, the lyrical aspect of Juan Ramón Jiménez' language, rather than its imagery, that made him the unrivaled idol of young vanguard poets. The phonetic tonality of his verse was often more subtle than its chromatism, and his virtuosity in this area alerted the ears of many to the importance of modern music as a function of poetry. Thus, poets like Lorca were critically aware of Debussy's work in a way that Falla's more accessible compositions did not require.

At first glance, the connection between music and surrealism appears slight, since the two basic media of sound and image are substantially opposite in quality. Nevertheless, Arconada's term "musical surrealism" was justified in both its historical and functional senses. To begin with, he considered surrealism to be an affirmative aesthetic. After the destructive revolutionary period following the war, Breton's call for artistic constructivism was a positive gesture. Since preceding experimental movements had effectively negated traditional values, it seemed pointless to repeat the same gestures in an imitative iconoclasm. The logic of this argument is self-evident, but normally, any artist who might adhere to it in practice would do so with some degree of self-consciousness and intellectualism. Not so the surrealist, however, for his approach was based on a "subscientific discipline." Its reliance on subconscious—not unconscious—mechanisms released the individual from the inhibitions of rationalism, and thus prepared him for a situation conducive to "creative superexcitation"—hence, the special role of music.

Since surrealism requires a technique that depends so completely on irrational modes of expression, the most successful medium must be the one that submits least to the order of mental categories. Music fits this qualification very well, in spite of its own demand for a certain temporal perception. The music listener, like the reader of automatic writing, relies heavily on intuition. And this is the value of psychic automatism, for its effect lies not in the release of words from their linguistic limitations, nor even in the great numerical increase of possible images. Although these are important results of automatism, still more essential is its call for criteria that place meaning beyond the control of intellectual discipline. Similarly, whereas words and images tend to succumb to some kind of order, music is more elusive. Even irrational plastic images are regarded by the eye with a certain perspective, or with an instinctive act of spatial relationship. But in music, the listener can fall so deeply into the emotion of sound that he is unaware of making sense out of the score. This is why the subconscious element of creation is so important. When the walls of mental classification have collapsed, the mind can rest from its active discipline. Its condition becomes passive, and in this state of receptivity or "mental obscurity" its "subterranean and abysmatic thought" is revealed. The distance between listener and composer is narrowed, and both enter into the stream of melody without the aid of reason.

In developing these ideas, Arconada failed to distinguish between the aesthetic experience and the creative act, and assumed that since the categories of reason had broken down, the two processes were interchangeable. In effect, Arconada was more interested in the psychology of poetic creation, and so he quickly pointed out how the latter was affected by the subconscious technique of automatism. He claimed that surrealism destroyed the traditional "divine prestige" of creation. Artists had always exalted the poetic process regardless of their differences in technique, but now that conscious will was no longer a part of creativity, the entire process was reduced to a mechanical articulation of the brain. Not that the brain was functioning rationally, but it did work without the active help of the artist's will. As Arconada phrased it in the style of his period, "the slightest particle of rational light is enough to decompose the acid and obstruct the free flow of the magic surrealist creation. Magnetic forces are the mechanisms of creation." In other words, the subconscious state is of itself spontaneous and creative, needing no additional intellectual stimulus. The kind of art it inspires is totally emotional, and since music is usually defined as an affective art anyway, the short step into surrealism becomes inevitable.

Nevertheless, in the nearly half-century following the first surrealist manifesto, this short step has become a long leap. At the time that Arconada was writing, the movement had not yet established the pattern which we now associate with it: distortion, grotesque humor, absurdity. For Arconada, it was sufficiently defined as the revolt against reason, conceived in terms of psychodynamics. Quoting from Breton, he considered surrealist art to be "dictated by thought, in the absence of all control exercised by reason, outside of any aesthetic or moral preoccupation." When read today, this seems to describe Lorca and De Chirico very well, but at that time it sounded just as accurate when applied to Haydn and Mozart, because the characteristic practices of surrealism had not yet been invented. In fact, these two composers were surrealists at least in "theory," if such a theory took as its criterion the total disaffection by an artist from intellectual and moral commitment. According to Arconada, whereas Händel was concerned with mysticism, Bach with morality, Beethoven with the Ideal, Wagner with Beauty, and Chopin with feeling, "only in Mozart and Haydn does thought function freely, unconcerned with objective finalities." Thus, a surrealist position was considered above all to be a new utilization of human thought, where reason is suppressed in order to avoid intellectual distraction, and where the workings of the mind operate without restriction. Paradoxically, this was a rationalism without reason.

It is clear, then, that in the early stages of the surrealist movement people were confident about the theory of the new art, even though subsequent practice has proven them to be inaccurate. To Arconada, the specific attraction of Breton's manifesto was that the subconscious mechanism succeeded in divorcing all ideologies from the creative act. Eventually, he thought, this would produce a pure artistic distillation free of sentiment. In music, composers were already on the road to achieving just this. Arconada's allusion to Debussy's "chemical laboratory" suggests the trend in this direction, and yet he called for a complete exclusion of feeling from future musical composition in the light of the new surrealist experiment.

So much, therefore, for the elimination of nonfunctional elements from modern art. But the question of the difference between realism and surrealism still remained unsettled, particularly in the already abstract realm of music. Once again we would be wiser to regard Arconada as an early commentator on surrealism instead of a critical analyst with the advantages of historical perspective. His quotation of Schopenhauer to the effect that "music is not only above reality but outside of it," is not very helpful as a rigorous statement. But it does show how strong the pressures of post-Romantic subjectivism still were, just prior to the birth of surrealism. For a literary critic writing in a vanguard "little magazine" to cite a Romantic philosopher at this date, is an indication of the degree of maturation still necessary before the surrealist mode could qualify as the anti-Romantic and often dehumanizing movement that it eventually became.

In any event, Arconada's discussion of realism began with the assumption that reality was a pernicious element in art, and that the use of this element transgressed the law of alienation. This did not mean that the components of the artist's environment were barred from his creations—an obvious impossibility—but it did prohibit "the logical order of the real world from intervening mandatorily in the [work's] construction." The musical counterpart of this injunction would require the elimination of feeling, for reality was to literature what sentiment was to music: the goal of traditional art, and the point of departure for surrealism. The latter principle was best embodied, according to Arconada, by the compositions of Satie and Honegger, because they disguised or "evaded" the real objects and feelings which inspired them. This intentional concealment of reality led to a "superior" reality in the creative work, known as surrealism. The first kind of reality was comprised of the objective, palpable forms that make themselves known to human perception, while the second type included the world of personality, the subconscious, and subjectively created forms. Consequently, the modern composer who wished to liberate his work from tradition must attempt to dislocate the creative act from reality and devise a musical parallel to the "imagistic spontaneity" proposed by Breton.

In the final analysis, however, Arconada could not imagine the kinds of sounds that would later be classified as surrealistic. He praised "Les Six" for their advanced aesthetic, singling out Satie, also, as the best of those who rebelled against Debussy's landscaping. The clouds, mists, and fragrances that Cocteau admonished "Les Six" to abandon, had to be replaced, said Arconada, by "the accelerated vibration, the overflowing sonority, and the broken, mad rhythm of the modern age." Surrealism is reached via the expressway to the city, presumably because its fast pace and rapid turnovers in style impede any realistic evaluation of life. But beyond these

ideas, Arconada was unable to indicate what was specifically surrealistic about the compositions already in existence because the
practices of this movement had only just begun, thus making the
search for antecedents premature.

When the historical perspective lacking here was supplied by
Guillermo de Torre, it created other problems.[3] Torre wondered
whether surrealism was not merely the evolving realization of Dadaism's dreams. His discussion of the relationship between these two
movements recognized that the waning Dadaist energies of the 1920's
were being properly channeled into a new stream of pure fantasy.
Nevertheless, it could not be truthfully said that surrealism in 1924
offered anything newer than what Apollinaire had already proposed
in 1917 or even in 1912. The surrealist groundswell was simply
drawing its strength from the established landmarks of contemporary
art, and was at times supported by "ignorant and senseless men" who
had tried to "grotesquely monopolize" the creative scene. The best
proof of this charge was Tzara's manifestos, and especially his "Dadaist Spontaneity," with its concept of artistic noncontrol. Nevertheless, to extinguish the light of reason did not mean to abandon the
lower recesses of the mind to the instinctual workings of man's
psyche. As Torre implied, the surrealist movement may have been
post-Freudian in its discovery of the subconscious, but it was anti-
Freudian in its attitude toward the latter's function. In other words,
an artist's penetration into the irrational subsoil was done not for
analysis, but for synthesis: in order "to localize in the subconscious
the wellspring of pure poetry." Even though Breton had proclaimed
the "omnipotency of the dream," Torre was suggesting that its content was only of interest for its metaphorical value. Conversely,
absurd imagery in art did not represent a symbolic code for the
analytical deciphering of man's psychological structure. Such an attitude would signify a dualism of reality and symbol that the surrealist was not prepared to concede. Quite the contrary, the dream
was one element which combined with everyday reality to create
an absolute reality that superseded all else. Instead of being functional, the dream was constructionist, for its purpose was not to
represent another reality, but to create its own surreality by means
of synthetic transcendence.

Thus, it is accurate to make a surface analogy between man's
dream-making apparatus and the free-associating imagery of surrealism. As Torre argued, psychic automatism relies on the random
arrangement of words and the "linking caprice of subconscious impulses." These evidently are irrational checks comparable to the repressive role of the censor. But in truth there is no valid parallel,

for the technique of association produces an independent creation which, although engendered by the mind, is neither symbolic of it nor representative of its psychic condition. The human dream process is governed by fixed laws—which even Torre admitted to be regulated by the Preconscious—that operate for comprehensible reasons in spite of the dream's apparent absurdity. Thus, even though the surrealist has, according to the author, a "spiritually somnambulistic disposition toward reality," the fact is that the only similarity between the oneiric and the artistic processes consists of the irrationality of their product. Otherwise, a rather delicate system controls the dreamwork, in comparison with the anarchy of artistic free association.

The detachment with which Torre regarded Breton's theory is remarkable for such a period of extreme partisanship. Not only did he have historical reservations about surrealism with regard to its earlier forms but he expressed misgivings about possible corruptions of the new technique. For example, he feared that the simulation of dreams might be perverted into spiritualism and the use of mediums, or that false beliefs in the occult powers of the poet might arise. Moreover, surrealism implied "the poet's absolute abandon to a state of near-religious inspiration," and this heightened the danger that his work would be unintelligible to the reader. Furthermore, there was the objection that to cultivate the subconscious impulse was one thing, but to convert it into a methodical, solitary rule of procedure was another matter. Although poetry was engendered by subconscious forces, the process had to be kept involuntary in order to prevent affectation. Beyond this, it was self-contradictory to advocate a spontaneous creative act and at the same time convert it into a dogma and ritual formula. But in spite of these reservations, Guillermo de Torre declined to be hostile toward the movement, calling his position a "marginal dissent." As a committed member of the Spanish vanguard, he approved of the gratuitous nature of surrealism, of its unmotivated recreativity. But at the same time, he thought he had discovered its basic sterility in its refusal to perpetuate itself or to find alternatives for its dehumanization process.

A similar position of skepticism was adopted by Dali, whose article on "reality and surreality" grasped and advocated many genuine surrealist principles without being duped by the subjectivist fallacy.[4] I will discuss his ideas at length in a separate chapter, but it is worth noting at this point that Dali's acceptance of the "cruel and jovial revision" made by the new aesthetic also extended to the "brutally" narrowed horizons of creative possibility. That is, he interpreted the movement as causing a reduction, not an increase, in the number of opportunities for artistic expression, as well as eliminating the beautiful and the ugly as intrinsic values. On the other hand, he found that the surrealist mode rejected "intellectual impressionism," "elegant self-irony," and "hybrid approximative poetry," which were all part of post-Romantic aesthetic subjectivism. For Dali, reality was less a structure than a mode of perception, and while the latter may very well have been subjective too, he refused to admit it. As will be seen, Lorca also regarded Dali's perspective as basically objective. In this respect, the future surrealist painter came close to the "surrealist nominalism" of José Bergamín, who also sought to determine the configuration of reality by "poetically pure thought," which is to say, by simply naming it in the "illogical intimacy" of one's mind.[5]

Another Catalonian painter of that period, Sebastiá Gasch, wrote an article surveying the concepts of reality from cubism to surrealism.[6] He argued that disfiguration was an established practice even among the first cubists, and that artists often deformed reality without minimizing the need to maintain a realistic connection with the natural world. The subsequent "fall into abstraction," as Gasch termed it, came with the recognition that everyday reality had always been a pretext for pictorial reality. Painters asked themselves why they should not, in view of this unintentional deceit, create pure painting, where the pictorial elements would appear untrammeled by their vehicle—reality—and where forms and colors would be abstracted from the natural world. This was the implication of cubism, and without this stage in modern painting, surrealism would have been impossible. According to Gasch, cubist abstraction eventually became so formalized and emotionally empty that a "neo-Romantic" countermovement began to stir which culminated in the last "delirious convulsion," which was surrealism. The new Romantics, as Gasch labeled them, were not satisfied in having the plastic qualities of their work act independently. It was more important to make them represent the painter's emotional state. This was the beginning of an interaction between artist and medium which then led to automatism. The latter, in turn, blurred the boundary between the thinking process and the thought produced. By virtue of this analysis, Gasch became the only vanguard critic who openly and without reservation disapproved of surrealism. His reasons, however, were moral rather than aesthetic, for he judged Freudian symbolism to be excessive and in bad taste. He felt that without the discipline of a moral preoccupation, the surrealists would become slaves to instinct, and although their techniques were interesting—like the "subterranean platforms of the foredream" of the Catalonian Foix—their school was not fundamentally original. Gasch called it "puerile," and found their absolute reliance on fantasy a traditional concept.

This, then, is the extent of the commentaries on surrealism in article form. Although few in number, their scope is quite broad, encompassing the significant problems of the movement succinctly and with a variety of positions. Most important, discussion began early in 1925 and was assured a wide dissemination. We must remember that the vanguard magazines were the media for publicizing new currents in art and cultural progress, and that their size, ephemeral character, and dedication to creative rather than speculative work were all factors in determining the kind and extent of critical statements on surrealism that did appear. In succeeding chapters we will see that in practice a great variety of surrealist techniques were originated by Spanish writers, and that the absence of a visible school was perhaps fortunate for surrealism as an aesthetic, considering how deeply it penetrated the literary world of several generations.

Two Forms of the Grotesque
(Machado and Solana)

In the last chapter, I mentioned that the theoretical essays on surrealism created a background, rather than a school, for several generations of Spanish writers. This was one reason why surrealist practice could exist without the impetus of an official movement. Another reason was that certain grotesque characteristics in this surrealist practice were already deeply ingrained in Spain's aesthetic tradition. Not that the Spanish surrealists deliberately drew upon the grotesque tradition for their inspiration. But it was one of the natural idiomatic alternatives which were culturally available to them, and it was another factor which made a surrealist mode possible in the absence of a formal school. At the very least, this tradition is a reminder of the aesthetic continuity of the modern grotesque, and at best, it can account for the grotesque in Spanish surrealism—partially, to be sure—in a more organic way. Any other approach would be forced to explain these grotesque elements by means of spontaneous generation, linked neither to France nor to the history of Spanish aesthetics.

The grotesque mode has always been popular among Spanish artists and writers.[1] Works by Cervantes, Quevedo, Goya, and Lorca testify to the variety of forms the grotesque can take, from the comic and pathetic to the pathological. Yet the exact nature of this aesthetic category still eludes us, and we permit genres and media of diverse psychological and philosophical tendencies to be included under the grotesque. This is unavoidable as long as a theoretical treatise is not written, although the works of Kayser and Clayborough are giant steps in that direction. But even without such a treatise, it is clear that in the twentieth century, the grotesque has tended toward a certain homogeneity. Whether we consider the Freudian aspects of literature, Dadaist humor, the Pirandello-Gênet theater, or surrealist distortions, whatever is grotesque is also self-conscious, anti-Romantic, and absurd. An ulterior purpose seems to motivate the modern grotesque, whereas in earlier periods it enjoyed a certain abandon and purity of expression.

What we must bear in mind is the fact that the grotesque is a larger category than either surrealism or Romanticism, one which embraces the latter much in the same way that tragedy or comedy embraces or informs classicism, the baroque, and Romanticism. It is important for us, therefore, to find the relationship between the grotesque as it exists traditionally, and the surrealist mode, with its own revision of the grotesque. Toward this end, I have selected the poet Antonio Machado and the painter José Gutiérrez Solana as representative of a transition between the aesthetic heritage of the Spanish grotesque and the contemporary adaptation of the grotesque by surrealism. With regard to Machado, Hispanists will immediately recognize that my discussion departs from the general scholarly assessment of this poet, although several other studies have also focused on the eccentric or the aberrant threads in the large fabric of his work. My purpose in calling attention to Machado's poetry and prose in this way, as well as to Solana's literary works, is to explore the differences—or similarities—between the Romantic position and the surrealist mode, at least with regard to grotesque elements. I also hope to determine what the convergence of painting and literature means in terms of irrational imagery. Finally, we will be able to find the historical location of surrealism in the evolution of absurd, distorted, and psychologically disquieting aesthetic practices.

The poetry of Antonio Machado provides us with a rare opportunity to examine an important concept in the history of aesthetic ideas, namely, that the grotesque in our age emerges from the disintegration of Romanticism. There are a number of critical moments in his work when the mirror reflecting the poet and his environment abruptly cracks, causing certain distortions in image to appear. Lest the general reader be misled, let me say that from the standpoint of Machado's poetry as a whole, these moments are relatively infrequent. However, they do occur in twenty poems, as well as in his prose writings, and their implications extend to the aesthetic crisis which led to surrealism.[2] Basically, Machado developed this problem in two phases: externally, in the image of Castile, and internally, within his own consciousness.

The austere and noble vision of Spain that appears in the *Campos de Castilla* is occasionally disfigured by glimpses of *la España negra,* the bleak and stunted subculture that symbolizes the nation's socio-moral failure. Machado's representation of this dark reality could not have been possible without the influence of Goya's black paintings. In order to understand the poet's position vis-à-vis Goya and Romanticism, it would be useful to recall the role of the grotesque among the French poets, especially Hugo and Baudelaire. As the preface to *Cromwell* reveals, the grotesque genre was not alien to Romantic ideology. Hugo categorized it with the beautiful, arguing that it eliminated monotony from drama and that it could inject horror or laughter into tragedy. This "reverse side of the sublime" reflected part of Nature's infinite beauty, where darkness and light, evil and good, the unshapely and the graceful existed side by side. From the fruitful union of the grotesque and the sublime issued modern genius. Nevertheless, this idea suffered the limitation of making the grotesque a technique that served some other effect. It was only after Baudelaire and Goya released the grotesque from this aesthetic instrumentalism that it came to be valued for itself.

Goya's principles of art revealed to both Baudelaire and Machado an aesthetic of violence, of the uncanny, and of the fantastic that was self-sufficient and yet which painted an ethical portrait of man in society. Goya raised the purely formal and the purely ethical to their highest power, keeping them independent and yet linking each to the other cryptogenically. Although Machado replaces much of the fantastic with the ugly, he keeps the basic rule unchanged. For example, he refers to a convent's "cloistered piety, erected on a refuse heap," or he describes a moribund Castilian village thus: "Yonder the heroic castle. In the square, beggars and boys: an orgy of rags."[3] The poet effectively controls his sentiments while allowing the external incongruities to represent themselves. This is essentially a Goyesque approach: the eye selects from reality details which are intensified, enlarged, and carried to their logical extreme. Deformation, then, is a selective magnification.

This technique is used sparingly by Machado, but with a range that covers the supernatural, the fantastic, insane and criminal types, and impressionistic landscapes.[4] What results is an un-Romantic national portrait, whose moral image is in good measure penciled in with naturalistic distortion; a wounded Spain "dressed in dirty carnival tinsel," "poor, squalid, and besotted" with blood, a nation whose citizens once were young and "tried to ride a bareback chimera pregnant with gloomy presagings" (CXLIV). The carnival, a frequent scene in the surrealist mode, is used in other contexts by Machado to introduce the mask motif, as will be seen. In the quotation cited, the scene is carried away from complete objectivity by a strong undertow of sentiment—Machado's love for Spain. In this he differs from Goya, for his discreet emotional presence in his verse heightens the effect of the technique by dignifying the grotesque with pathos. Goya, in contrast, often appears to have had no interest or feeling for his deformed subjects, and this lack of sympathy explains Goya's style and the fact that his human beings are often interchangeable with dolls, and have masks for faces.[5]

The grimness of Machado's Goyesque humor in these cases is tempered by the irony of his attitude. However, comic elements in any form are much less common in his poetry than they were to become in surrealism's droll or whimsical fantasies. Although Machado is noted for his humoristic attitudes in the philosophical writings and verse aphorisms, the Spain that he casts in the shadow of Cain is unrelieved by laughter. In this he differs substantially from Romantic theorists. Nietzsche, for example, described two possible forms by which the artist represents the true nature of things: the sublime and the comic. Once the artist penetrates the core of reality —which is the terror and absurdity of existence—he transforms his reflections either by the sublime, which is the artistic conquest of the awful, or by the comic. The comic, according to Nietzsche, is the artistic release from the nausea of the absurd. In Machado, however, whatever is grotesque in the image of Castile is represented by the horrific rather than the humorous. It is true that with respect to his own existence, as I will show, Machado reacts with mockery to the dilemma of personality. But his laughter is real, not artistic, and does not release him from the absurd, but is rather the product of it. In this respect, surrealist humor is closer to Machado than to Nietzsche, for it emanates from the depths of absurdity and never escapes from it. As for Baudelaire's post-Romantic theory, which defines the grotesque as the "absolute comic," the genesis of laughter is Satanic, and while this concept may apply to Goya, it does not to Machado.

For the most part, however, Machado's foreshadowing of surrealism resulted from his critique of Romantic psychology. He found lyric poetry to be suspect on one of two counts: either it was insincere or it expressed emotions that no one really felt anyway. Carrying this notion to a devastating conclusion, Machado invented a character with a "troubador machine," a piano-phonograph apparatus that manufactured poetry. Since the individual sentiment of Romanticism was suspect, the inspirational force behind this machine had to be a collective muse. The reason for this seemed clear enough. First, the Romantic poet had bared his soul with what Machado termed the ostentation of a bourgeois boasting of his coaches and his mistresses. Thus, the distance between his Romantic feelings and those of ordinary people had grown wider, and his singing had acquired the sound of a falsetto. As a result, the mainstream called the Romantic lyricist insincere, although it was not so much that the poet was singing of unfelt emotions, but rather that the people could not feel these emotions in the same way. Hence the troubador machine, which would compose songs for the masses about generic feelings. Its poems would be about the group, not the individual, and whereas the Romantic might have written a poem like "The Hangman's Song," this modern invention would produce a "Song for Partisans of Capital Punishment." And as a consolatory note, Machado added that the machine has only an interim purpose until a new poetic sensibility arises (AM, 52ff).[6]

Such new aesthetic sensibilities had followed in the wake of Romanticism's demise, but Machado found them all to be tending toward subjectivism. Nevertheless, this subjective quality gradually became transformed, and Machado noted its deterioration in the modern period. Indeed, he traced the self-awareness of modern art to the artist's own doubts about his emotive values. Since it was not possible to sing about the self, he argued, attention was directed to a world without feeling. Artists compensated for their loss of self-esteem by engaging in what Machado called a "fetichism of objects."[7] This was first attempted by the Parnassians, who retained some quality of subjective lyricism, and then later by the cubists, who made no pretense of integrating their inner feelings with the objects they were painting. But Machado realized that even this objectivism failed, and that external things had themselves lost their value because they depended upon the very sentiments that were no longer prized. Thus, contemporary art was unable to take itself seriously. Objects "free themselves from the affective bond that formerly controlled them and now seem to attack and corner the poet, lose respect for him, laugh in his face. Amid the imagery of a bazaar, the poet feels his intimate failure, laughs at himself, and, consequently, gives no other value to his creations than that of mechanical toys" (C, 36-37). This statement represents more than just the description of the breakdown in Romantic values. It also foreshadows many of the elements of surrealist practice: the cultivation of critical paranoia, the obsession with mannequins and puppets, the cold efficiency of the artistic instrument operating upon its materials.[8]

Moreover, Machado went on to reveal a sophisticated understanding of several psychological distortions. He distinguished between the irrationalism of the Romantics and the collapse of meta-physical idealism in the post-Romantic era. The irrational Romantic artist adhered to an idealism and faith in the universality of language which, paradoxically, affirmed his belief in reason. In contrast, the post-symbolist poet confined his world to the boundaries of his private psychological awareness, and "explored the more or less subterranean city of his dreams" (C, 114-15).[9] Thus, Machado credited the symbolists, and especially Verlaine's exaltation of music, with the defeat of Cartesianism.[10] Thenceforth, artists aspired to the pure expression of the subconscious, calling upon obscure faculties rooted in the subliminal areas of their being (AM, 98). Surprisingly, Machado made no mention of Freud, although he knew his work, and he remained skeptical of psychoanalysis throughout his life (JM-II, 38). Yet elsewhere Machado declares that he himself was a dedicated self-analyst, and he interprets a dream about a professor (Machado) who is accused of corrupting students by training their minds instead of their bodies (JM-II, 145ff).

This dream is given a political explanation by Machado, but several details, including its sexual overtones, make it pertinent to the surrealist aesthetic. In the dream, the professor is accused by a strange, stentorian-voiced little man dressed in an ecclesiastical cassock and the three-cornered hat of the civil guard. This figure represents the authority of aesthetic orthodoxy, who is prosecuting the artist for his deviations. A similar motif appears in Lorca's ode to Dali, where the government's rules must be obeyed by the poet. At the same time, this strange little man is also a representation of ambiguous masculinity, and in this respect has bearing on Machado's constant self-doubt as a poet. The tininess of the man, coupled with the strength symbolized by the civil guard's hat, show an ambivalent attitude toward the nature of creative activity. The fact that Machado had avoided physical training in the dream supports this idea, since the poet was unsure of how to regard his own artistic powers, not to mention the norms dictated by the precepts of traditional art.

As for the civil guard, he is the tough embodiment of authority in real life, and a frequent symbol of potency and brutality in Spanish art. The motif reappears in a nightmare where Machado is led away to be hanged for an unspecified crime. This second example of accusation and guilt is ample proof of his insecurity in the role of a creator. Here, the tricorn symbol becomes a hatter's block set upon a slowly rising scaffold mast. It is on this that the poet will be executed. Thus, Machado's lack of confidence causes him to succumb to forces stronger than his own. In fact, the hangman is intentionally represented as a barber, and what is more, he looks like the accuser of the previous dream. The link between the erotic and the aesthetic is strengthened still further by a number of other details. There is some discussion in the nightmare, and in a subsequent verse fantasy similar to it, as to whether Machado should be decapitated instead of hanged. The barber image also occurs in an early poem where Machado curses an artificially trimmed garden and the ineffectiveness of his poetic office (LI). In all cases, Machado is uncertain of himself and the power of poetry. This insecurity extends to a verse fantasy, where he hears a chaotic fanfare of drums and trumpet blasts that contrast with his own weak-winded horn (AM, 67ff). Machado's dream symbolism combines the mechanism of displacement with surrealist details like wax figures and disquieting street settings. What is significant in these examples is their objective extension of the Goyesque and the pathological, so that the latter embrace contemporary forms of expression. Moreover, their link to the erosion of Romantic values and to the artist's own inner conflict is essential to understanding surrealism.

In order to appreciate what the breakdown of post-Romanticism means, we must realize that the focus directed at the natural world had shifted its perspective many times. From the point of view of subsequent hermetic poetry, it is not unfair to say that the Romantics suffered from an overexposure to nature. The familiar apostrophes which poets addressed to their natural surroundings would have sounded insincere on the lips of Machado, whose generation found the intimacy between man and nature already broken. Whereas the Romantics enjoyed an informal relationship with their environment, the moderns were acquiring the formalities of scientism. The familiarity of one was analogous to a dialog between independent personalities, while the detachment of the other resembled the confrontation of a knower and an object. This estrangement had two aesthetic expressions: the emotional distance of an Hérédia or a late Cézanne, and the masquerade of a Verlaine. Machado converted this second form into the grotesque by muting a morbid note with a burlesque one, as in one poem where a premonition of death in a damp garden is greeted by a hidden bird's mocking whistle (XXVIII).[11] Both styles represent the same idea: that the physical intimacy between man and nature is incompatible with the affective distance between them. Yet, Machado's grotesque is the later and more acute representation, since the intellectual structure of the discord is reinforced aesthetically by an incongruity. Even when the poet is absent from his environs, these environs respond in the same key, as in one poem describing the backdrop for a village scaffold: "the canvas of the East bled tragedies daubed with grotesque clouds" (XLVII).

When Machado viewed this problem of nature's independence

in the light of the symbolists' rhetoric, it awakened his sense of the grotesque. He even had moments of protest against himself for having employed the modernists' diction, and he exclaimed, "The devil take your garden! . . . It seems today a coiffeur's handiwork" (LI), and once he ridiculed the style as a cosmetic (XCVII). The question of the independence of nature had not troubled either the Romantics, who were too occupied with their experience of reality, or the symbolists, who were busy analyzing their psychological states before nature. But Machado was incapable of such analysis without feeling the absurdity of half a landscape submitting to the shadows and silences of a mood, while the other half swaggered out of reach (XLV). He regarded Amiel's observation that "a landscape is a state of the soul" to be true only to the extent that poets were committed to an introspective consciousness of landscapes. But as soon as a poet tried to know it independently of his spirit, he introduced a disruptive attitude that differentiated between subjective and objective reality. This attitude, which is intellectually expressed by antithesis, is formulated poetically by the grotesque. A good example of the progressive dislocation of the poet's awareness is the treatment given to the moon during these periods. Conventional Romantic depictions, like those of Leopardi, for example, make the moon autonomous, with attributes that coincide with the poet's ideals. On the other hand, the symbolists imprison the moon within their own subjectivity, as in the case of Baudelaire.

However, when Machado saw the moon being manipulated by the symbolists' egotistical sensibility, his rational impulse was to restore the objective balance. But he could not do it without also pointing out the absurdity of the symbolists' delusion. Thus, he set, on the one hand, a familiar nocturnal scene—the clock striking a melancholy one A.M.—while, on the other hand, the moon appears as a gleaming skull against the lowered horizon. Meanwhile, the ill-played music of a mazurka floats by half-innocently and half-mockingly (LVI). Thus, Machado accomplished what Marinetti would propose several years later in his futurist manifesto *Tuons le clair de lune*. Elsewhere, the poet satirizes a "tin-foil moon" (CLVII), a tambourine-playing moon (AM, 70), and, in a general travesty of Romantic sentimentalism, a "candid April moon" (LII, LXXI). The importance of this transition to surrealism can be seen when we recall Lorca's tin-breasted moon and the nightmarish violence attached to his lunar imagery in general. Thus, we find successive modifications of the ego-phenomenon relationship. In the first period, the poet's sentiments are genuine and he is content to find a correspondence in the objects he contemplates. In the second period, these genuine sentiments transfigure the object and make it part of the poet's "soul-state." In Machado, the object is made to contradict his feelings in a mocking reassertion of independence which casts doubt on both the legitimacy of his emotions and the adequacy of their poetic setting. That Machado's dissolution of the symbolist pathos is a grotesque achievement becomes still more obvious when we examine Verlaine's *Clair de lune,* where nearly sad bergamasks dance fantastically among ecstatic fountains without becoming incongruous, because all of the poem's elements are covered with the same emotional aura.

Machado's grotesque was more than just the fruit of a mismated rationalism and symbolism. His own mind seems to have been bored with the emotions that his heart took seriously. In terms of contemporary philosophy, this means that the grotesque results from the broken image of an existentialist's self-contemplation. The source of this image is derivative—the tradition of Mallarmé's *Brise Marine* —but its special deformative character depends upon Machado's ironic observation of his own irony. This is developed in several stages. In the earliest, we find the genuine feelings of Machado the man: the "pure flame" of Romantic love and a *mala tristeza* that attenuates it. These two real emotions had to be dealt with by Machado the poet, who, finding listless love to be an unworthy hybrid, responded with a "yawn." This is the second stage: the poet's emotional response to the man is tinged with irony. But Machado the man was also aware of Machado the poet. Hence the final stage, the poem itself, which contains not only the poet's yawn but the man's ironic judgment that his poetic attitude is a histrionic declamation. The poet yawns at the man, concealing his irony with an actor's rhetoric, while the man is ironic toward the poet for his fraudulence. The written poem incorporates both ironies, and is grotesque because it gives an overlapping image of Machado, whom we view with the double focus of two ironies (XVIII, XLIX, LVI).

This psychological analysis is new in poetry because it shows the serious man contemplating himself in the act of self-mockery. It is comparable to the case of a man grimacing at himself in a mirror, a theme currently popular among existentialists. The grimaces are not important in themselves; what is significant is that the man wants to see himself making them. This desire to see is quite serious. Thus, the contemplator converts the grimacing man in the mirror into a clown who bears no resemblance to himself. Meanwhile, the object of the grimaces is the original man, previous to his wish to see and prior to his facial distortions. This original man becomes the mirror image, and although he will appear physically to be grimacing, the contemplator knows that it is "someone else" who is staring back at him grotesquely from the mirror. Thus, the image, like the poem, remains a serious reflection, and because it is serious but appears to be mocking, it is also grotesque.[12]

We should also take notice of the distance between Machado and traditional Romantic irony. The Byronic pose, for example, is not self-analytical, but is directed outward to deal with a social conflict.[13] Byron's self-consciousness and self-ridicule were defense mechanisms designed to make others think that there was another Byron. In reality, there was only one, a Byron of indivisible seriousness whose sensitivity was protected by a burlesque veneer. In contrast to Machado, Byron cultivated his pose seriously. He was aided by an artist's faith in the effectiveness of his medium, for only an unruffled confidence in his poetic office can account for Byron's assiduous masking of his real emotions. Machado, however, concealed neither his true feelings, nor his ridicule of them, nor his impatience with the verbal form they both took. He wrote, referring to the poet and his audience, "His singing voice wavers. They no longer jeer his verses, they jeer his heart" (CLXI: liv). No one, not even Machado, can be interested in the poet's heart, for its readiness to confess makes it suspect. Nor could he esteem poetry in itself, as did Byron, because it had become a disguise or an evasion. Machado's sense of the grotesque awakened to what appeared to be a self-torture but was really the laceration of lifeless poetic tissue.

There was, however, one form of Romantic irony that approached Machado's transcendence of his own ego. This was the self-parody which Irving Babbitt describes as the Romantic ironist's striving for the Infinite.[14] The poet must stand aloof, then aloof from this aloofness, in an infinite transcending process. But once again, such a poet is not concerned with the psychology of his awareness, and he is serious about his irony because it is a way of affirming the self. Machado's grotesque, on the other hand, depended upon the duplicities of his own consciousness.

The consequences of these new mechanisms lead us directly to the disquieting aspects of surrealism.[15] Although Machado was not a surrealist, we find in him the first elements of the modern nightmare. In one poem, for example, the ego is represented by a shadow on a deserted steppe under a fiery sun, with no one knowing whether its tears are its own or those of a *histrión grotesco*. The ego then becomes a spectre wandering in a nebulous labyrinth of mirrors, while moans echo from deep grottoes (XXXVII). Here the themes of alienation, loss of identity, and dehumanized reality are treated more coherently than in their fully disfigured surrealist forms. Machado appears to be disturbed by the symptoms of personality disintegration which have been hastened by his solitude.[16] He thinks of his memory as a network of galleries that store recollections in pictorial guise. But the further he explores, the more intricate the maze becomes. Not only do the galleries descend to ever-darkening levels of awareness, but the depiction of some past remembrances seems more vivid than present reality. When faced with portraits of himself, Machado is confounded by the spectacle of his personality objectified. He becomes a spectator to his own drama, seeing it through temporal mirrors whose sharp images alternate with blurred reflections. When Machado writes his poem, he is like the man who, having awakened from a nightmare, scarcely recognizes who it was in it that wept.

These intuitions, which prior to their artistic expression are a matter of human psychology, are in poetry exorcised, so to speak, and manipulated at will like pliable shapes. Their total effect is grotesque because as erstwhile serious elements they are now arranged in vaguely distorted, sometimes absurd, attitudes. The poet commandeers his memories, visions, and fears like a puppeteer mounting his show with complicated figurines, a theme which later becomes one of surrealism's most grotesque features (XXX). Or, he summons up past hopes on a marionette stage in the form of smiling little figures that are an old man's melancholy toys (XXII). Or, again, he merges a reverie of rose-tinted chimeras and flowered walks with a dream of twisted paths through a bitter land, shifting scenes from sunken crypts to ladders above the stars (XXII). The entire structure of the grotesque, from the symbols of depth psychology and escapism to the poet's voluntary self-transfiguration, is based on Machado's ambivalent feelings toward his own performance. We must bear in mind, of course, that he is about to enter a new phase of social realism. And it is also true that this latter phase is more typical of Machado's poetry than the phenomenon described here. Nevertheless, it is difficult to find comparable examples in literature of this grotesque limbo between the comic innocence of earlier puppets and harlequins, whose artificiality was never in doubt, and the subsequent eerie absurdity of surrealist mannequins. Machado's aesthetic crisis occurs where the planes of reality and emotional abstraction intersect.

The problem of death also lurked beneath Machado's distorted surfaces, and this is a theme which persisted throughout his literary activity. In the majority of the poems, death is treated with utter gravity or with an unmistakable stoic irony. But occasionally it also erupts as a bizarre protest against temporality: "most of all I want to get drunk, you know . . . Grotesque! A pure faith in dying, pitiful joy and macabre dancing before the hour" (LXXV). This last gesture of gladness, born of desperation and perhaps defiance, is made at the edge of nothingness, but instead of a sober existentialist affirmation—which Machado finds empty—he chooses the most perfect kind of absurdity: one where the very method of mocking death —drunkenness—is inadequate, pathetic, and grotesque. Elsewhere, the poet refers to himself as a visionary, a melancholy drunkard, and a lunatic guitarist (LXXVII), and this Dionysian strain recalls more conventional grotesque patterns where morbidness is counteracted by frenzied affirmations through song and excess. Inebriation has always played an important role in saturnalian distortions, but missing was this new element of time's assassination. The importance of this aspect for the surrealist mode will become clear in later chapters, where the problem of time is virtually nonexistent.

Machado, having analyzed the relationships of personal experience, mortality, and the aesthetic expression of both, had no choice but to denounce his artistic posture as inauthentic. He saw his poetic sentiments as a facade which concealed a circus performer who was Machado in disguise. Reflecting upon his own death, he observed: "A new Hamlet will say, after looking at my skull, What a fine fossil, this carnival mask!" (CXXXVI; xlviii). And with these words, we are told an awful truth: Machado could not overcome his self-awareness even when contemplating his own death. As Sartre said of Baudelaire, his fundamental attitude was that of a man bending over himself, watching himself see. By transcending the self that is to die (the skull-mask in another man's hand), Machado transcended the horror of death's inevitability, something that neither the drunkard nor the visionary could accomplish. At this point he understood that his death would be nothing more than a carnivalesque image of his life and, indeed, that his *life* was in fact an emotional pastiche. Machado spares himself nothing as he portrays a buffoon laughing at his tragedy. The buffoon is ruthlessly deformed, a hump-backed little dervish, big-bellied, jovial, and picaresque, engaged in a twisted dance (CXXXVIII). The distinction is still finer elsewhere, as the buffoon himself is derided by a malformed wall-shadow (CLVII). The poem, then, disparages the artist's psychological conflict while making of it and its philosophical consequences the very subject matter of poetic deformation. And by this route Machado leads us to a fundamental aesthetic principle of our time, that no aspect of existence is absolved from the absurd, or from the artistic derision which absurdity encourages.

We may conclude, therefore, that Machado's contribution to

the grotesque is best understood in terms of the shift from a moral-aesthetic preoccupation to an existentialist one. The deterioration of Romantic values was but temporarily checked by the symbolists. Once Machado ceased to be distracted by the problems of style and image, he developed a self-awareness that placed the entire post-Modernist aesthetic in doubt. His grotesque usage, consequently, expresses the poet's transcendence of his ego and the ambiguous nature of his feelings. Whereas its more objective, Goyesque form is linked to the distortions of external reality, its subjective form foreshadows the psychological practices of surrealism. In all cases, Machado reveals in the grotesque the loss of Romanticism's absolute frame of reference. It is from the incompatibility of emotional and expressive planes that the sense of absurdity and the grotesque emerges.

As we have seen, Machado's external form of distortion was based on Goya's socio-moral portrait of *la España negra*. This tradition of a deformed Spain was carried still further in this century by a painter whom Machado once called a "necromaniac Goya." This was José Gutiérrez Solana, whose work prompted Machado to record some significant observations. The poet found three key elements in Solana's aesthetic: the unhealthy voluptuosity of painting what is dead as if it were alive and vice versa; the nightmarish reality of animating mannequins and paralyzing human faces; and the fever-ishness of an ingenuous naturalism (C, 19). What is of most interest from the standpoint of evaluating the surrealist mode is that Solana confirmed Machado's notion that "every poet has two muses: the ethical and the pathological." Although this statement was made with Solana's paintings in mind, it is also true of his prose writings.[17] These sketches of Madrid low life, as well as certain impressions of episodic and scenic value in the Castilian rural and city areas, are of the same psychological cast. Since they make up a considerable body of prose, and since they also approximate Solana's plastic conception of existence, I will deal with them here.[18]

Most of Solana's literary and graphic representations depict what he called a "disquieting reality."[19] This was a vision which he arrived at by two related methods. The first produced a confusion of realities in which an incongruity was established by the coexist-ence of a recognizable reality and its partial deformation. The second method involved a paranoiac reaction in the perception of sem-blances of reality, as, for example, in the quasi-real world of dolls and automatons. Solana conjured up his "disquieting reality" by focusing upon the horrific aspects of a subject to the exclusion of all others. The result was such a concentration of these unsettling features that it led to an aberrant view of the whole. For example, an intense description of old women on a pilgrimage relates that some of them "carry sick and crippled infants in their arms, with faces of wax and eyes that seem like glass."[20] The realism is unmistakable but so inordinate that it causes discomfort in the absence of counterbalancing elements. This is the beginning of a progressively overfocused lens, whose picture is too real because it isolates one plane of reality from the total frame of reference.

This technique of distortion by omission does not in itself create a grotesque aesthetic. But when the element of dehumanization is added, that is the effect. In one such scene, we find a "one-eyed woman, with a blinder on her eye like the horses in bullfights, her mouth toothless and as black as a grave ditch; a maimed, knock-kneed woman who plays the castanets with the movements of a doll, her sandaled feet going up and down as if she were dancing" (I, 107-8). The crippling of human vitality, which occurs in the first example too, is here reduced to an animal level. Furthermore, the image of a woman moving not as a human being, but with the awkwardness of a puppet introduces an uncanny distinction between the live and the animated, a problem to which we will return. In other words, human activity is given in terms of doll animation. It thus becomes clear that previous references to "faces of wax" and "eyes that seem like glass" were neither conventional nor accidental. Solana's fusion—or confusion—of human and doll figures is the principal force in his grotesque prose.

The mannequin, puppet, wax statue, and mechanical figure elicited many prose descriptions from the painter. For Solana, the two-dimensional canvas was an impossible medium for conveying the conditions of a four-dimensional man. Spatially, of course, dolls are as close to human reality as artifice can come, and they acquire temporality through motion. But while such representations surmount the limitations of painting, in literature they endanger the distinction between imitative semblances and reality. This is the psychological foundation of Solana's prose. Our imagination has the function of establishing unconscious rules of propriety by which it judges the extent to which a work of art has transformed reality. Imagination adjusts the mind to the margin of deviation between verisimilitude and reality. Since dolls are often too real, they confuse the mind as to what is real and what is imitative. For a moment, their artificiality is forgotten, and when it is remembered, it conflicts with the original impression of reality. From this arises the grotesque sense of art.

In his descriptions of elaborate doll scenes, Solana was absorbed by a confrontation with a plastic medium that, unlike painting, bordered ambiguously on the real. He described these miniature tableaux with literary embellishments which realist authors reserved for human scenarios. In one case, this human touch is stated with simple factualness:

> By the warmth of the fire sits a village woman with a blue tammy cloth bodice and a yellow skirt of baize; on her head is one kerchief and another covers her hair [made] from a real person. In her hand she holds some cotton yarn: she is spinning. From time to time she straightens up with the movements of a doll and rocks the cradle of a baby who is crying in its diapers. In another compartment we see two dolls representing two elegantly dressed Negro children, their bodies made of rag cloth. One is hanging from gymnastic rings, the other from a trapeze, and they twist about and do pirouettes. Their parents, old Negroes sitting on chairs, watch them with cardboard heads (I, 158).

The first scene is as subtly human as the other is obviously mechanical, but their deliberate juxtaposition in this way is momentarily disconcerting. At the beginning, the duplicity is aided by the human clothes, sound, and activity, but the subsequent allusions to rags, cardboard, and the trapeze are unequivocal. The phrase "movement of a doll" once again increases the ambiguity of Solana's technique because here it is gratuitous, whereas in the previous case it was necessary in order to describe the real woman. Once the threshold of feigned reality is crossed, there is no doubt about where human and animated borderlines meet, but it is the first, fleeting hesitation which makes the scene grotesque.

Solana's vision of life is that of a pathetic tragedy, and he extends this concept to include automatons. This is done by adding an emotional facet to their behavior, which in turn dislocates our affective orientation. The resulting incongruity is the product of an obvious artificiality which is conceived with sentimental values usually reserved for human situations. In one passage, for example, an "old man straightens up with the squeaking of springs that move all of these mechanical figures, and he sits down on the bed suddenly as if asking for water and feeling himself die of fever, his face frightened and anguished because no one comes to help him" (I, 159). Here Solana shifts from mechanical action to the sphere of pathos, and enters into an emotional rapport with automatons, appealing to the reader's feelings in the process. The entertainment of such sentiments is, of course, absurd, because mutually exclusive areas are merged in a call for compassion. Yet, Solana's aesthetic is based on a need to portray his somber conception of the world. Thus, he supplies the link between the real and the pretended, and suggests a relationship between meaningless mechanism and tragic vitality.

Elsewhere, when visiting a wax exhibit of medical operations, Solana remarks that "at this moment, it seems that we too are figures of wax that can come apart or break" (MC, 33). And in reverse situations he infuses mortality into a group of wooden dancers whose inner wheels break down, causing them to stop brusquely (I, 160). By such connections between the real and the doll worlds, the notion of death becomes grotesque. The humanization of the mechanism parallels the dehumanizing depiction of live people, with the same disquieting effect. Nevertheless, Solana was cognizant of a ridiculous disharmony in the proximity of dolls to people, and he juxtaposed the "tragic" pose of one mannequin with the "ridiculous" postures of others which had chipped noses and ears (EN, 46). Thus he was quick to expose his own ambiguities, and yet, could perceive tragic or deformed aspects in the game of animation.

We find, therefore, that one cause of the grotesque is the tenuous boundary between pretense and reality. Solana tends to overstep the border and portray one by the other, or to imply that the distinction is difficult to see in any four-dimensional realm. The use of mannequins is a form of plastic representation that is not as far removed from life as painting or sculpture can be. That is, mannequins do not have the kind of dimensional restrictions that normally reassure a doubtful observer. As the barrier between reality and its representation grows fuzzier, the more uncanny the experience of each becomes. Both worlds can become grotesque if each one contains an element of the other. For example, a carnival suddenly appears unreal when the imagination fixes upon details that do not appear natural to the setting. And conversely, the failure of a plastic work to maintain its independence of the reality it represents leads to an incongruity.

This last idea was important to Solana, who understood how easily human and modeled figures can exchange characteristics. In one scene, for example, he notes the consternation caused by a pair of lovers in a wax museum who make believe that they are statues. At a distance, other visitors contemplate the immobile couple seriously, until they draw closer and realize their error.[21] The questions raised by such incidents are disturbing, to say the least. Do we know what the real difference is between man and these figures? And if we do, to what extent are we like automatons in our movements and bearing anyway? Solana undermines our confidence in what is human by reversing the usual technique. Instead of describing dolls in terms of men, he describes men in terms of dolls: "a jovial man, who speaks with the immobility of an automaton, rigidly and without moving a crease on his clothes, begins to remove his frock coat and vest before the crowd's stupefaction, and remains in his shirt sleeves. Then he takes off his pants, remaining in his knitted union suit, and sits down on a chair. One can then see that he has straps along his chest. He stands up and separates a leg, holding it in his hand and showing it to the crowd" (II, 28). This vendor of artificial limbs then declares that once he is dressed, no one will be able to tell which of his legs is artificial. Hence, the technique of "disquieting reality" promotes doubt as to where the limits of artificiality are defined: in dolls, it is acceptable; in men, it is unfortunately frequent; but to describe one by the other is unnerving.

The most perfect example of the confusion of realities occurs in a puppet show where the main character goes berserk. He trips the heroine, knifes his rival, and chases the ventriloquist, who flees in terror. As the curtain falls, "the people don't know whether he was a doll or a man dressed as an automaton. Perhaps he was the old man that we saw taking tickets at the door with great immobility. He seemed like a wax figure, with his black suit, white beach shoes tipped with patent leather, grey hair, and two canines in his toothless mouth which glistened even more than his eyeglasses in the light" (II, 133). The opposite situation occurs elsewhere, when Solana himself realizes with great irritation that he has mistaken a wax statue for a sleeping doorman. The latter's "disquieting immobility, as if he were sleeping the sleep of centuries and time had stopped," is enough to narrow the distance between the statuesque and the human (Solana, 252). Just as the naive audience was deceived by the puppet show, now Solana begins to wonder about the nature of automatism. The implication is that animation is not necessarily a human activity, nor immobility a sign that life is absent.

In all of these examples, we must remember that Solana's mind is functioning as would a painter's. That is, it acts in a dual capacity, separating the human mode of perception from the aesthetic mode. In the former, he perceives visible objects, which, if alive and human, are recognized in their normal condition. In the latter, these same objects are apprehended in terms of their plastic qualities. A figure is no longer real and alive, but is reduced to a set of textural, chromatic, and dimensional properties, without consideration for its human element. Both are valid realities, but the second mental process usually goes unnoticed in painting because the work itself is there to represent it. However, in Solana's prose, the description contains both the human experience and a literary representation. Thus, we come across unexpected reminders of Solana's mind as a painter, his "dehumanizing mind." Since such intrusions are uncommon, a strong sense of the incongruous occurs.

So much, then, for the way in which semblances of reality are treated. Let us now turn to Solana's paranoiac reaction to these semblances. To begin with, the painter's preoccupation with masks is well known, as is his penchant for describing the physiognomies of mannequins. What is interesting about this is the fact that at times he attributes human attitudes to mannequins whose postures are generally transfixed in innocuous passivity. In one prose evocation, Solana is attracted by some store-window models, but when he pauses to look, a transformation occurs in his relationship to them. He ceases to be an observer of unresponsive objects and begins to imagine that the models possess live faculties which enable them to enter into a human association with him (EN, 34). The mannequins watch him, engage his attention, and invite him to tarry. Solana is no longer the only actor in the situation, for he endows the models with motor and even volitional responses. As such, they assume in his mind active—which is to say aggressive—intentions: they take the initiative and behave with motivation. This imagined aggressiveness indicates Solana's susceptibility in noticing attitudes directed toward him, whether they are genuine or fancied. Thus, for example, the same passage refers to some clothes hanging in the wind, which, when they fill with air, seem to acquire human form and threaten the writer with their waving arms.

These rather mild instances take on severe overtones when viewed in the psychological context of Solana's projective tendencies. His fancy inclines him to suppose attitudes in neutral situations that actually reflect his own state of mind. He admits, for example, that he will never be able "to dissimulate the impression of mystery produced by these glass-case figures who seem dead, and yet, will continue to use the same clothes worn while alive, and who contemplate us with their cruel, impassive, and fixed eyes" (EN, 47). Solana is ready here to superimpose a private interpretation with paranoiac suggestiveness on the entire scene. First he refers to a sense of mystery, and begins to engage personally with the wax figures, whom he believes to be watching him. Then, he perceives an attitude of cruelty in their eyes, but returns to a more judicious appraisal when he recognizes an impassive expression. Nevertheless, the element of morbid speculation is visible as the writer produces a weird admixture of realistic and irrational details.

The most outstanding example of the paranoiac vision is a bisectional dream that occurs in the "bellicose" city of Oropesa. In the first half of the dream, the town attacks Solana as he is lying in his hotel room. He sees a shadowy form slipping away between the walls of the narrow room, and then the town's "iron-like silhouette was approaching me; its pinnacles looked like they were going to crush me. The town was as if glued to the sheet, without air or distance; it seemed painted and was coming closer and closer, resting completely on my chest" (EN, 153). The dream incorporates some details of Solana's actual physical setting, but proceeds to distort them. Since his tiny room is oppressive, he imagines the escaping outline of a vague shape. And since the room is lacking in space, he dreams of a two-dimensional representation—the town glued to his sheet. This sense of enclosure becomes even more stifling when the threatening village is finally stationed on Solana's own chest.

What happens in this account of the dream is that part of Solana's reality has been projected into the dream content. The real sheet is fused with the one dreamed about, as Solana senses the cloth weight upon his chest. To what extent his narrative recalls an actual dream, rather than being just a literary fabrication, is a question of little importance here. The technique employs a psychological confusion of realities, and this is what surrealism is all about. The narrator's mind is aware only of his sensations, and even though the reader knows the origin of the dream materials, he does not miss the scene's psychic value. Still more pronounced are the formal aspects of the dream, which reduce its general emotional tone. Thus, while there is spatial contraction in the dream, there is no immediate reaction in feeling, nor does the motif of flight add much emotion. On the other hand, the plastic elements seem to dominate the awareness.

Solana's passive attitude, and the fact that he is helplessly victimized, is indicative of his paranoid aesthetic. Sensorially, he is very active, but his emotional rapport with the reality around him is unaggressive. This attitude is translated into a fantasy of persecution, which first takes the form of a real dream and then is presented in a literary account. An examination of Solana's paintings and biography would show the validity of this point, but since we are only interested in aesthetics, it is sufficient to point out how events in the dream appear to be happening to him, without regard to their biographical role. Turning, then, to the second section of the dream, we find a Goyesque procession that turns into a nightmare:

> . . . I saw enormous boots walking along the floor, and as if by magic, out came some belts of a harsh and murderous yellow color, and the disagreeable patent leather tricorns of two civil guards, their long beards stuck to their livid faces. These figures pieced themselves together part by part. The ears appeared, but they had no eyes; then their noses sprang forth, loose fingers ran along the wall, and so on until those ridiculous and fearful phantoms were completed. I saw their fierce hard eyes nailed on me, and the shininess of their gunbarrels. They took aim at me to shoot and not let me escape, as if I were a terrible criminal (EN, 154).

The dream ends with Solana awakening with shouts of terror, and this conclusion is a sobering one despite the ambivalent phrase "ridiculous and fearful phantoms." The nightmare must not be taken lightly, especially in view of the horrific motifs already cited elsewhere. Moreover, its similarity to Machado's dream of the civil guard is no coincidence. Regardless of the personal relevance of these visions, they are clearly part of an aesthetic that uses victimization and terror in grotesque situations. What makes them grotesque is the element of irony or humor that suddenly enters, plus the fact that no direct emotional involvement colors the mood of the scene. For example, if we compare these episodes with the intimacy of the Kafkaesque nightmare, we realize how relatively detached the perspectives of Machado and Solana are.

The sense of incongruity in this second section of the dream is due to the fact that a real man is imprisoned by imagined phantoms. The motifs of liberty and escapism, which in the first section are projections of Solana's own sense of oppression, are here inverted. The moving shoes and the disembodied members do represent freedom, but they belong to the very civil guards who are menacing the dreamer. The symbols of authority and potency are also prominent, and Solana appears in helpless passivity, as he did when he imagined the wind-inflated clothes threatening him earlier. Eyes are again prominent in the paranoiac reaction, and their counterparts here are the round gunbarrels that stare pointing down at him, shining metallically like "fierce hard eyes." And finally, the violence and potential brutality that charge the scene suggest the authentic quality of Solana's art. He is able to objectify his fantasy, and even add a ludicrous detail to it, but the result has a deep emotional origin in human experience.[22]

In summation, the dream plays an important, if not central, role in certain trends leading up to the surrealist mode in Spain. It is mostly used to resolve the problem of reality, and tends to avoid subliminal explorations for the sake of individual case studies. Freudian psychology has never taken root in Spanish literature, and although it is impossible to avoid unconscious symbolism, the dream-work of Solana and Machado seems to be cultivated in literary form, without undue reference to depth psychology. It is true that in their work we can find symbolic expression, but their main concern is with the cleavage between reality and subjective experience. Hence the use of mannequins and dolls, since these represent the unhinging of objective, plastic reality from human emotion. The nightmare arises from the humanizing effort of the dehumanizing artist to reunite his affective world with the objective reality about him. What is grotesque, however, is the absurdity of this juxtaposition, as well as that of his intention, which was bound to be futile.

Chapter Three

Descent and Castration
(Aleixandre)

In the last chapter, the two types of grotesque found in Machado and Solana were seen to begin with a psychic disturbance within the artist which later became externalized in literary form. The question now is to determine to what degree this is relevant to the emergence of surrealism from its Romantic background. In other words, in what way does this disturbed psychological state proceed from a previous Romantic disposition, and how does it develop into an even more disturbed "surreality"? The poetry of Vicente Aleixandre provides the best opportunity for analyzing this problem since his early works are a mixture of both aesthetic modes. Although Aleixandre did not cultivate the grotesque, his distortions follow the same spiritual pattern set by Machado. That is, the end result is a self alienated from nature, with implications that lead directly to a surrealistic atmosphere.

Aleixandre's poetic world has a murkiness which allows only the vaguest of physical and emotional contours to be seen. There are several reasons for this gloom, notwithstanding the poet's description of his work as an aspiration toward light. First, concrete objects—vegetation, fauna, meteorological and mineral states—are never depicted for their intrinsic value. Instead, they are made to induce the shapeless obscurities of feeling that are the real subjects of his poems. Furthermore, these tangible phenomena of nature serve an elusive, nonmaterial frame of reference. That is, they refract everything, sunlight included, through the turgid twilight of the poet's sentiment. And finally, there is neither chromatic

40

variation nor lineal precision, so that Aleixandre's vocabulary fails to create any visual appeal. His words have a substantive richness only, making them a perfect medium for the grey and groping masses that haunt his early verse.

Nevertheless, the poet's frequent claim to be aspiring toward light confirms the basic tenebrosity of his surrealist verse.[1] The two extremes of his perceptual experience are brittle sunlight and lymphatic darkness, and each poem dated before 1934 aches with yearning to escape the second in order to reach the first. Aleixandre writes from the damp pits of the imagination, straining for the "tremulous celestial light" which is also the "fervid hope of an unquenchable breast."[2] And yet, his condition is one of submergence, like a creature of the sea with "feet enmired in muck," who knows the "impossibility of ripping loose from the abyss" (312). The imagery of eyeless birds, hidden jungle life, unlit stars, and triumphant sea is not just conceived imaginatively, but seeps forth from the irrational crevices of Aleixandre's mind. His search for understanding, symbolized by a parallel imagery of wings, angels, and heavenly bodies, is caused by his original hermetic state, which in turn produces not only a deeply private literature but one whose conflictive titles *(Espadas como labios, La destrucción o el amor)* suggest the difficulty of our gaining access.[3]

However, Aleixandre is essentially a Romantic, and through this sentimental crack in his linguistic armour, we can penetrate to the artistic nerve endings of his inner life. There is an unashamed lyricism in his expression, but it is covered over by a vaguely ominous rhetoric. And yet it is just this rhetoric which we must learn to decipher, for it conceals a human suffering that is almost unrecognizable as being human. Nature, for example, fluctuates between peace and violence, prefiguring a tension between herself and man. Then too, there are word polarities *(harmonious, wounding, gentle, crushing, flower stems, teeth)* which set the poems' intelligibility slightly off balance. Finally, as the natural setting intensifies its divisive state, Aleixandre invests it with references drawn from the human realm. This has the effect of abstracting what is human in the poet's world and transferring it to an inanimate sphere. A good instance is the image of time. In the hot one o'clock light, a "sheaf of sharp-edged lances"—the sun's arrows—is tied by a "band of transparent time" (129). Generally speaking, the sense of time is curiously abstract in Aleixandre, especially for a poet so obsessed with organic destruction. He merely witnesses time's visible mark on the concrete world, even though its meaningful impact is felt on his own troubled spirit.[4] As a result, there is an ever-widening gulf between man and nature as the qualities of each tend to separate and become denaturalized.

This process is interesting to watch. First, Aleixandre withdraws from the physical landscape into his memory, the "clear valley of absences," where the "humid" solitude suspends him over the full river of time (138). This physical removal, however, is compensated by a strong mental plasticity, in this case the texture of loneliness felt moistly above a temporal expanse of water. Thus, we find the poet and his inner reality on one side, and the concrete world of matter on the other.

The second step in the process of detachment is to affirm the supremacy of subjective states. Aleixandre discovers "subtle waves of memory" that flow over a "subterranean riverbed" (90). These blur the edges of reality, causing time to dominate space and matter. The mental evasion here is aided by linguistic confusion in the form of a Gongoristic syntax, which acts as a veil over the description. Also undermined is the fidelity to verbal logic ("parentheses oppress words"), and metaphors reflect reality in terms of the dislocation between substance and psyche. For example, a landscape is real, but a river carries "forgotten, submerged ideas," and "at the bottom of it, your body seems like earth." Thus, we find a mind that is abandoning its rational categories and inserting reality into the abstract framework of memory. At the same time, the mind's metaphorical categories have taken the process of decay and turned it into an abstraction. These interchanges have little to do with the traditional subjectivism of Romantic metaphors; rather, the image has been stirred up from the subconscious dregs of mind and time. As a result, the boundary between the two realities disappears, and we discover that the antithesis of body and earth produces strange syntheses: "flesh: horizon"; "arms of copper"; "torsoed lights"; "the marble's frozen skin wounds the light" (90–91).[5]

The poet's alienation from nature is mirrored by nature's own state of frequent conflict. This dissociation is used by surrealists to create an objectified representation of reality that reflects neither man nor nature. Aleixandre, however, is just on the brink of this surreality. He withdraws first into himself and then, more abstractly, into memory. In his private awareness, he is anguished. Thus, when he relies on the world of objects for images to express his inner experience, those objects are only useful in their violent phases, or to the extent that they can be twisted into unnatural states. In themselves, they have no value, and are of little interest for the clues they might furnish to the meaning of reality.

Aleixandre, then, is concerned only with his own reality, which consists of the way he articulates his feelings with the raw material of the outer world. Hence, he occupies a position midway between the post-Romanticists—whose crisis we observed in Machado—and surrealists like Lorca. That is, he is no longer disturbed by the fallacies of subjectivism, but he is not detached enough to abandon it altogether. Remaining basically Romantic, therefore, he is of interest to us because he turns the phenomenal world into a lexicon for self-expression. To Aleixandre, objects are only important for the nominalistic conversion to which he submits them, and they are evoked not for their qualities or effects, but in order to become verbal images. In theory, things have an outer dimension; but in fact, the poet experiences the word, not the thing. Consequently, the image is more than a symbol. It no longer represents the object, but controls an association of meanings that have nothing to do with the outer world. There is only one reality now, surreality, in which words create their own logic and emotion without reference to objective phenomena.

This is especially true of *Pasión de la tierra,* which is incomprehensible if we attempt to infer meaning from the normal logic of things. In fact, the book is not only metaphorically difficult but it is pictorially deficient as well. Aleixandre's surrealism is peculiarly nonrepresentational, and his word symbols are so hermetic that the ordinary visual connotations of his imagery have no bearing. There is much plasticity, of course, but this is a different matter, as will be seen. Aside from the barest of graphic outlines, the images offer none of the sensorial qualities that are implied in the term "imagery." Everything is conceptualized, even the mood. The poet's feeling has no real dimension, and the sensation of inner violence is confined to the linguistic realm.

As Aleixandre enters his surrealistic period, the separation of language from experience grows more complex. For one thing, the motif of submergence continues to herald the poet's spiritual condition. For example, references to caverns and the sea allude to emotional states rather than to nature. Then too, the poet's subjectivity comes to be less important in itself and more a part of the technique used to describe it. Style becomes all-consuming, and there is no longer any subject matter left to be stylized. Since the poetic allusions are ambiguous, they create mood more than meaning. And since private experience is divorced from reality, it too loses its interest as a subject. All we are left with is a subjective *mode*—a style and a technique which function at the heart of the poem. There are no ideas, feelings, or perceptions as such. There is, however, an emotional subjectivism based on the ambiguity of style and references. For example, in *Espadas como labios* we find sentiments described without the support of any logical or empirical structure. The feeling of sadness is "a hole in the earth, gently dug out by words"; it is "like a well in water, a dry well that probes the breadth of sand"; and, finally, "sadness does not always become a flower that grows until it reaches air, springing forth" (257–58). The effectiveness of this imagery cannot be denied. What is important is that its vividness has no reality. The phenomenal world is not mentioned here, nor is the poet's perception of that world. What does appear is a paradox of graphic abstraction, an earthen well and a sandy beach that exist in a limbo between private emotion and objective reality.

Thus, what began as an alienation of self from nature, ends as a dissociation of language from reality. Whether we define reality as a personal or a phenomenal world is irrelevant; in either case it is difficult to relate expression to experience of any sort. Where no distinction is made between "a well in water" and "a dry well," we have gone beyond even the tenuous logic of metaphor. And when no effort is made to separate objects from concepts, then the referential system of poetry has become confused. Take, for example, the phrase, "Mother, mother, this wound, this hand touching at a well or errancy open in my breast." To identify "wound" with "hand" may stretch the imagination, but we can admit that some vague emotional connection might justify the equation. Moreover, both nouns are qualitatively equal: they are human, made of flesh, and part of the same person. On the other hand, the identification of "well or errancy open in my breast" abandons all semantic sense. The reader is disconcerted until he realizes that the physical emptiness of the well corresponds to the conceptual emptiness of errancy. But by this time the mood has already been established, and the disorientation is carried into effect.

In the same poem, the use of metaphor intensifies the lyricism while sustaining the absurd break with reality. In one case, the description deals with some light seacraft floating on the waves: "As light as nubile birds, as loving as ciphers, like that last desire to kiss the shore or a lonely man's afflicted bearing, or a stray foot." These comparisons are comprehensible only through an act of vague intuition, but the poet's psychological state is clearly perceived. Still sharper is the declaration: "It is I, holding my loving heart outside like a wire." This jarring metaphor is right in the spirit of surrealism, even up to the wire material and its echoes of mechanical springs. Nevertheless, the poem fails to create a total subjectivity because it has no central theme or event linking metaphorical expression to the self. Instead, it erects a psychological screen which allows one emotion to pass through a mesh of equally conditioned allusions. The emotional conditioner is the concept of sadness, which is attached to neutral objects, such as a hole in the earth or a well. The latter are transformed into symbols of the poet's spirit, disturbing symbols due to the fact that they give no indication of why they have been selected. In other words, the screen of associations makes us breathe the filtered air of the poem's emotions without letting us see the substantial cause of these feelings. It produces further unease by excluding both logical and metaphorical meaning. Of course, it does not enter completely into the absurd, for we can, after all, understand the poem. But no logic or metaphor is possible in a context where ciphers are loving or where words dig holes in the ground.

From what has been said, we may conclude that Aleixandre's technique is an arbitrary emotionalism of neutralities. He communicates feelings by placing neutral nouns in disconcerting contexts in order to tip the balance of emotional uniformity slightly off center. The results vary from pathos to terror, but they are always without an imagistic or intellectual core. Consequently, each poem is, in itself, often incomprehensible. But as a group, they reveal certain obsessive motifs that recur in fixed emotional patterns. For example, the sea symbolizes the poet's entire psychological world, and ships are the rational and irrational activities that occur in it. The notion of hollowness or cavity is a form of inwardly falling subjectivity. And the various types of personal affliction—breast wound, heart of wire, stray foot—project an image of the poet's vulnerability and spiritual inadequacy. Apart from these symbols, meaning is also determined by the technique of making unlike terms synonymous. Relationships such as "sadness or a hole," and "a well or errancy" establish a semantic identity between disparate concepts. This use of *or* is frequent in Aleixandre, with the result that certain poems can serve as glossaries of synonyms that help to deduce the meaning of other obscure poems.

Once these patterns are recognized, the task of providing an exegesis of the poetry is less formidable. But beyond the specific themes, there exists a general attitude toward poetic activity that is relevant to the surrealistic mode. Aleixandre has a poet's "afflicted bearing." He often wanders or errs, misleading himself and his readers in both feeling and idea. Full of pain, his self-exploration hurts as might a clumsy hand on an open wound. At certain moments, he sees himself submerged in an ocean of intimacy. For example, he describes a motionless swordfish that cannot bore through the shadows under the sea. The fish "feels on its flesh the chill of the sea depths where blackness gives no love" (311). This image is a marine version of the poet's own striving for sunlight. The fish, filled with a "moaning sadness," rolls a tear into the water and filters with its gills the "deceptive fantasy of a dream." The poet's Romantic sensibility is submerged to a depth where his only faculties are the dark processes of the dream. Unlike the upper waters, his level has no "fresh yellow algae for the sun to gild." Nevertheless, the sea floor provides the foundation for a mountain whose crests agitate in a "dark dream." Thus, the sea impedes the fish's conscious effort to penetrate its shadows, but allows the unconscious dream mechanism to operate.

Aleixandre's wish is to be liberated from the darker half of his existence. Although he has his "feet enmired in muck," he longs "to rise, green-winged, above the dry abyss, and lightly flee unfrightened into the burning sun." This duality, of course, cannot be overcome, since it represents the poet's inherent capacity for both rational and spontaneous creative activity. His yearning is for freedom and light, the Romantic quest for a pure expression of love. But Aleixandre cannot be a Romantic poet, for he is too aware of his roots in the irrational. His poetry is immersed in dark water that "crushes the wing of a drowned nightingale, the beak that sang of love's evasion" (311-12). This symbolism transcends Aleixandre's stated desire for escape, telling us why he must follow the road to surrealism. His power of flight has been crippled, his song drowned in the subterranean waters of his mind. Even his swordfish fails to penetrate the watery shadows. Moreover, Aleixandre is aware of his own impotence, and reflects this fact in his images of bodily injury. Self-exploration extends to experimentation with metaphorical distortion. What is a problem of poetic creation for the man becomes a projection of multileveled allusions: fish, metal, sea, wing, insects, earth. These imagistic patterns of obsession reach their climax in the collection of prose poems *Pasión de la tierra,* which will occupy us for the remainder of this chapter.

Aleixandre's surrealism results from his failure to reach the starting point of Romantic aspiration. Like Machado, he is skeptical of poetry's value as an accurate expression of sentiment: "I am dying because I don't know whether form can perceive the sunlight, or if the depths of the sea can be found in a ring." Recognizing the limitations of technique, he doubts whether any formal vehicle is strong enough to support feelings of such magnitude. And again like Machado, he has private fears about his own ability to perform poetic functions. The fact that he is dying as an artist is explained by his excessive study of his soul's anatomy. The incisions into his emotional matrix have been cut too deeply, and "in my hand I have a breathing lung and a broken head which has given birth to two live serpents" (159). Aleixandre now looks at himself objectively, with the vital organs of his existence alive but dismembered in his hands, producing monsters. What he sees is largely an image of self-mutilation, but one which began with his sense of inner failure.[6] It is only natural that he express this inadequacy by sexual symbolism, as did Machado before him. Finding himself locked up within himself, he seeks creative release. The repression is designated by symbols of immersion ("I am lost in the ocean"), while the outlet takes a violent form ("to break this crystal of a world that creates us" [201]). Aleixandre needs to free "this wild song which I carry in a ring inside me," his inner circle of feelings. But the usual art forms are insufficient for expressing beauty or for breaking through his emotional wall "because I don't like cages for canaries, because I detest gold-filled teeth and tears that don't open other doors" (201).

The need to overcome the polarity of internal and external realms, and to penetrate the latter, creates a great conflict for Aleixandre. His art form does not open the hearts of others, and his broken spirit has given birth to two monsters. He has waited so long in this condition that his "beard of time has woven two faces, a windmill of scissors with which I may interrupt my life of silence" (211). Thus, his voiceless passion rages in repression. He feels the impotence of the situation and, not being able to break out of his cell, he strikes out at himself. He cuts off his life with a pair of scissors, finding this to be the only relief from his silence. We have already seen Aleixandre compare silence to a dry well, defective teeth, and a crushed wing that contrasted to the green wings of song. But these themes of sterility and castration are more than mere representations of artistic failure; they are willful acts against the self. The poet must procreate, but in order to do so, he needs a "muscular wing made of firmness, whose edge is not afraid to wound the sky-prison, the dark storm clouds in the whitened heights above" (211). He yearns to shatter the very heaven with his song, aspiring to reach the horizon of the sky-receptacle, "that instantaneous zenith which at its highest makes pendulum and blood beat as one."

The convergence of these themes at the dense core of Aleixandre's problems results in a tangle of emotions. The marriage of poet and universe, the procreative act, the appearance of blood, and the upsurge of hope are all involved in *Pasión de la tierra*. In a moment of depression and self-doubt, the same motifs of blood and breakage appear: "Trying to come into existence was a dense growth of palpitating nothingness, and the blood's rhythm beat against the window, asking the sky's blueness for a shattering of hope" (176). The wish for happiness is now a desire for poetic potency. Conversely, hopelessness and nothingness are devoid of color and sensation. Thus, in the midst of bold and troubling imagery, graphic, sensorial elements fade into abstraction. Meanwhile, the poet's struggle with his self-destructive symbolism leads him back to his own reality ("I am a windmill of roads that leads me to myself" [198]).

Given the erotic overtones of the imagery, it is not surprising that a biologically oriented vocabulary should be used. This kind of rhetoric is deeply ingrained in the surrealist tradition, as we shall see in Dali's primitive metamorphoses. What is strange, however, is that the physiological effect has no reality of its own. Aleixandre's uncertainty about his .poetic prowess is projected beyond his subjective self, and yet not quite into exterior reality. The imagery hangs in a nether world of abstract carnality. For example, he asks, "Where is my brightness, my fund of truth, my polished surge that moans almost harp-like to the Aeolian sob of flesh?" (198). This combination of idealistic faith in his artistic qualities and insecurity about his actual performance shows up in the vocabulary. Both beautiful and ugly elements are used, in conceptual and concrete allusions. And yet the texture as a whole belongs nowhere, except in a realm that can only be called surreality.

This principle of physiological abstraction makes possible a title such as "The Sea is Not a Sheet of Paper." In this poem we may caress a melody ("what a lovely thigh!"), and note the antithetical relationship of musicality to physiology. Yet, the beauty of a lyric can be so sensual that it approaches the erotic. Thus, "the sky emits its protest like ectoplasm. Shut your eyes, ugliness, and lament your misfortune. I am he who invents the affirmation of shoulders, who accuses the subsoil of its open guilt" (183). The constant ambivalence of poetic sensibility permeates the imagery. Self-affirmation, poetic yearning, idealism (sky, shoulders) fight against self-doubt, inner failure, and loathing of the lower depths. Meanwhile, the poet searches underground anyway, ferreting out hidden and sometimes shameful things. Here are the subliminal impediments to his artistic flight, the sediment that mires his feet. He cautions us, "Don't fall asleep on the water, for the harps will lower you into the abyss" (182). It is a mistake to be lulled by the depths of the self, because this is not the way to lyrical expression. Subterranean life is treacherous to a sensitive temperament, arousing destructive tendencies in spite of the vitality found therein. As Aleixandre says, "the eyes of fish are deaf and they beat opaquely against your heart." Whether beneath the soil, under the sea, or within the human heart, it is not always possible to utilize the elements that lie there teeming with poetic viability. Emotions change as one probes deeper, and "beneath the waters, the green of one's eyes is mourning." Still further down, the horror at the roots of the soul paralyzes the creative impulse: "rotten fish are not a still life" (182-83).

Paradoxically, Aleixandre warns against using material which becomes, in spite of him, the substance of his surrealist verse. He is a surrealist without knowing it, because his poetry contains the very allusions which his Romantic temperament opposes. In other words, Aleixandre strives romantically for heaven and beauty, and so urges against subsoil and decay. But these references to fish and foulness, ectoplasm and evil, all help to compose the special sensibility of his surrealism. He imagines himself to be like a songbird, and promises a "final chastity" wherein the "cross of memory" will be burned, and he will be forgiven for unspeakable sins "that throb beneath the earth" (195). And yet, his manner of describing the bird is surrealistic: its music comes from a guitar held by snowy fingertips. So too is the underground throbbing more appropriate to surrealist than to Romantic imagery. The traditional nightingale "no longer has parlance with the moon, but seeks waters, not mirrors, withdrawn shadows in which to hide his trembling wing." Thus we find that solitude and dark meditation are no longer possible. That Aleixandre considers this lamentable is a fact which confirms his romantic nature. But the symbols of submersion (water) and anti-narcissism ("not mirrors") belong to the rhetoric of surrealism.

By dwelling on the inability to achieve Romantic flight, Aleixandre brings inevitably to his poetry an obsessional imagery. Since the central issue is his own talent, many of his poems can be read as surrealist analyses of poetic selfhood. The nightingale that avoids the moon and withdraws from its own reflection is the poet who cannot face his own failure. He does not fulfill his aspirations, and so his verse reflects self-hatred and death. The desire to hide his trembling wing in water, where it will not be seen is a type of self-effacement in which he denies his own image. He becomes more destructive by describing the bird's death amid indifference and unfulfilled desire. And finally, in an act of punishment, he envisions a castrated metamorphosis of himself as the nightingale: "a mutilated trunk where your thought fails, decapitated by the ax of that

tenuous sigh which grazed you without your knowing it" (196).
Aleixandre has been effectively rendered impotent by his own Romanticism.

This deep-seated concern for artistic virility is manifest everywhere. The "hunger for loquacity and force" links physical action
with verbal prowess. The poet fears losing his power of thought,
but knows that it is already lost in the limbo between the banal
sentimentality of Romanticism and the deaf eyes of surrealism..
With slightly deranged vehemence, he exclaims, "I am fed up with
deafness and with lights, with sad, second-rate accordions and with
the raptures of wood that put an end to governesses." And, gravest
of all, he says "I am afraid of being left with my head hanging
like a drop [of water] on my chest, and of the sky decapitating me
for good" (177-78). Here, then, is the psychosymbolic expression of
the poet's identity and the definition of his activity. The fantasy
of being beheaded focuses attention on the basic mechanism of self-
affirmation. The head is the source of the poet's strength, and the
locus of action and ego fulfillment as well. What began as a blunt-
ing of sensibility in the area of perception and poetic expression,
now threatens to become a total extirpation of power. Moreover,
the irony is that the poet is robbed of his energy by the sky, an element of nature for which he has striven and has attempted to
describe artistically.

Elsewhere, the castration theme appears along side of mutilated
natural phenomena. When this occurs, the entire complex of symbols representing poetic theory comes into view. In one case, Aleixandre writes:

> I remember that one day a siren, who was colored green like
> the Moon, took out her wounded breast—parted in two like a
> mouth—and tried to kiss me upon the dead shadow, upon the
> still, trailing waters. Her other breast was missing. No abysses
> were flying. No. An eloquent rose, a petal of flesh, hung from
> her neck and was drowned in the purple water, while her fore-
> head above, shadowed by throbbing wings, was laden with
> sleep . . . (149).

We find here a transference of the motifs that were previously identified with the poet himself. Nature has acquired the characteristics
of humanity. A rose is now flesh, the poet's wings are associated with
the siren, the siren herself has suffered an amputation. There is also
a repetition of the self-mutilation image. The breast that is split
in half corresponds to the poet's broken head that gave birth to two
serpents. The artist's inner failure is here projected upon an in-

dependent figure, but the horror of truncating a life-giving organ is again imprinted upon Aleixandre as the breast kisses him.

Thus, it is clear that the problem of creativity grows progressively more irrational. The poet's spiritual agony can only be characterized by the violence of a visceral terminology. He depicts the external world in terms of physiological abnormality in order to reflect the torture of his own mind. However, he realizes that he has twisted his very real feelings into unreality by creating a deformed natural world, whose beauty he had originally aspired to represent. Hence, his self-confidence is undermined, and his anxieties concerning his powers of articulation take the form of castration fantasies. But even fear can be put to good artistic use. If the poet's rational processes have become disjoined, he may proclaim an aesthetic of unhinged visions instead. As Aleixandre advises: "Seek not that story which chronicles the madness of the Moon, the color of its brightness when it has earned its rest. Consistency of spirit consists solely of forgetting limits and seeking the form of nubile girls when the time is unripe, seeking the birth of light at nightfall" (171). In other words, the traditional quest for Romantic sensibility should be abandoned in favor of still more irrational situations. This provides the justification for writing surrealist verse, since the precept suggested is to ignore normal limits, which is to say, not to prescribe rational limitations for poetry. Hence the reference to looking for light when evening falls, indicating that other forms of meaning should be elucidated in the darkness of irrationalism.

Aleixandre's credo is stated with explicit symbolism later in the same poem. He tells of his subterranean creativity, which developed after he had done violence to himself and his ineffective Romanticism: "My arm is an expedition in silence. My arm is an outstretched heart dragging its lamentation like a vice. Because it doesn't have the knife, the sharp wing which sunk beneath the ground after parting my forehead in two. Therefore, I'll drag myself like a nard, like a flower growing in search of the earth's bowels because it has forgotten that the day is up above" (172). This negative-sounding passage is actually strong in affirmation. What claims attention are the working conditions of a surrealist poet who has forgotten what daylight is like, but who can exist as an underground flower anyway. He laments his affliction, calling it a vice, but this judgment is made in reference to his private emotion. On the aesthetic level, the flower is engaged in a search of its own, in the earth's bowels, symbolizing an active poetic life. The wing represents, as always, the strength by which Aleixandre can soar above his condition into the light. Its capacity for a masculine role is made clear by the knife comparison, although here the wing is sunk beneath the ground. The knife-wing can turn upon its master and mutilate him, but the cleaved forehead is still a source of poetic inspiration. The surrealist nard will still flourish, even though it grows in the crevice of a self-inflicted wound.

A final aspect of the castration theme is the association of love with the writing of poetry. They are both acts of pleasure-seeking and the imposition of the self. Love and poetry also have in common the creative impulse, but Aleixandre deforms this kinship by introducing the element of destruction. In a poem called "Soul Under Water," the affirmative side of the eros-poiesis relationship is revealed. The poet is in the middle of the sea, liberated from the accidents of reality. He recognizes the dark descents of his soul, but delights in the joy of being free under water. He admires the sky and the stiff, high shipmasts. The only danger comes from the beams of light that are capable of beheading him, but he is unafraid, and listens to the water music and says that love will save him (207). The mild eroticism of this fantasy is countered by a highly sexual scene elsewhere, in which the fear of injury is elaborately detailed: "I love you, I love you, I don't love you. On your lips earth and fire taste like a lost death. A rain of petals crushes my spinal column. I'll drag myself like a serpent. The dry tongue of a well dug from empty space raises its fury and beats my brow. I break my skull and fall down. I open my eyes against the moist sky. The world rains down its hollow reeds. I have loved you, I. Where are you, for my solitude is no dwelling place. Cut me into perfect sections, and my viviparous halves will drag themselves along the purple earth" (152).

In view of the symbolic background already discussed, this passage requires little exegesis. My point is that Aleixandre's image of himself is usually destructive. Moreover, his fantasies with regard to lovemaking and poetry cast him in the role of a victim and a violated poet. Instead of his operating upon the world, the world crushes him with its component parts. The very ethereal elements that should go into his verse (petals) attack him rather than submit to his poetic rule. Aleixandre is spiritually isolated, and his imagination invents ambiguous references to insulate him against his fears: wells, enclosures, physiological parts. The descriptive violence that ensues in these scenes of despair is an expression of rage at his frustration, and at the same time an evaluation of himself as helpless and disabled.

The obscurity and frequent senselessness of *Pasión de la tierra* must be explained in terms of these dualities. Actor-victim, love-poetry, creativity-destruction are three axes that spin simultaneously.

Furthermore, their motion is interior, taking place in the submerged mental state of the poet. There is, consequently, little need for orienting his material toward reality: "there are so many inner brightnesses that I want to ignore the number of stars" that exist (210). The surrealist foundation of this subjectivity rests on the poet's psychological need to create deformed images to represent his attitudes.

In most cases, Aleixandre's imagery is sober and disturbing. But at times he exhibits the lighter half of surrealism's harlequinesque mask. One of the book's prominent motifs is the deck of playing cards. The time to take out the deck is also the "hour for observing the oily sheen of the moon on the round, swollen-cheeked face of a bundled king. Upon the old velvet cloth, a crown of lyricism would have the effect of a delayed melancholy . . ." (190). The king on the playing card represents the slick emotionalism of a superficially convincing yet identifiably artificial type. Kings and aces are on the verge of bursting into laughter, their sterile mascarade being of sporting value, but otherwise unsuitable for genuine lyrical expression. Sometimes Aleixandre himself feels that he too is inauthentic, riding a horse on a joker card, and yet, trying to escape his falsehood while on this same horse (177).

There is a tragic sense underneath this lightness, of course, but it does not prevent the depiction of people as cardboard figures or mask-bearing phantoms. Some are made of sticks and poles, others have nickel-plated heads or are simply mannequins (176). Existence itself is as fragile as an empty eggshell (181), and the poet's sense of the grotesque begins to form when his private state of sensitivity clashes with the circus-like chaos of the natural world (168). Aleixandre is always capable of hope, one day crying but laughing the next (209, 211), and insisting on the importance of reason in a world without logic. He affirms the purity of light in a world of eyeless people (184), although the value of his poetry consists of its murkiness. Referring to himself as "dead reason," he suggests the ambiguity of the role played by rational thought. Thus, reason must be amplified by a call to the irrational heart to search for eyes, in order that the forces of life ("the fountains of daylight") might reaffirm the meaning of existence by allowing the name of life to resound in the hollow of darkness (185).

Now that we have reconstructed the main obsessive patterns from an undifferentiated mass of associations, we must remind ourselves that Aleixandre did not intend to state a poetic credo in *Pasión de la tierra*. The fact that we have found some coherence amid the obscurity does not mean that he had been working from a carefully formulated set of precepts. His poetry represents an essentially emotional universe, one whose subjectivity does not admit rational access. Each poem is a kind of Romantic "soul-state" whose cluster of feelings is more important than any conceptual value that might be deduced. But neither feeling nor concept is significant in comparison to the presence of word associations and their psychological effect. The atmosphere created by symbols and motifs are of greater import than either the poems' rational meaning or their possible relevance to the poet's private world. Thus, no matter how clever we are in detecting the artistic foundation of the poetry, the latter is intended to stand or fall on the evocative power of its psychological impact. Similarly, the poet's emotions are secondary to the motifs themselves, whose purpose is to create a mood rather than to convey meaning.

Fish

We may conclude by noting several other motifs that seem to function extrasymbolically, with no apparent significance other than to induce an atmosphere. One of these is the fish, which in part follows the larger analogy of sea and mind. The fish operates as a supplement to images of motion and unpleasant textures. In most cases it assumes an aggressive role, or else retains an ominous quality that falls somewhere between vagueness and undesirable immediacy. Where it is palpably viscous, its mass is suited to the poet's nonvisual condition of groping and listening to the flow of water. And where it has no sensorial role, it imparts adverse moral traits and destructive tendencies. The poet introduces similarly ominous threads that have no relevance to each other, but which enable him to draw a tight web of chilling events and objects. In one passage where "there are fish that do not breathe," he refers to "an asphyxiation coming out of my mouth" (151). Another passage tells of a similar disaster: "A river of blood, a sea of blood is this kiss dashed against your lips" (151). Two lovers wait in a room whose "bloodless walls were not of cold marble," and where "a curtain of smoke became all blood" (153). Every example suggests the idea of a barrier or repression, and when the poet describes disillusion, he likens it to clear lagoons that turn into "torn breasts, wretched coagulated blood that breaks open into cracks" (197).

Eye

The obsessive nature of the poems is in part due to the eye motif. Eyes are either sightless, or they follow people, or they become the antithesis of beauty. Sometimes they fade from the scene (154) and lapse into a detrimental condition for the sake of a better artistic expression. For example, since eyesight is the instrument of rational analysis, surrealist verse is best served by the absence of both light and the faculty of sight (182, 205). In one passage, the motifs of eyes, blood, and love are fused into a multileveled mosaic of associations: "Upon your breast some letters in fresh blood say that the time for kisses has not come. . . . One autumn afternoon a nubile heart, gushing light in the absence of eyes, goes asking for darkness without contact, souls that know no sensation" (184). Love and blood are linked, and, elsewhere in the passage, both are related to artistic activity. The poet refers to himself as "dead reason," and he covers his eyes while urging his heart to remember colors. Thus, he advocates aesthetic perception by memory or by some other non-visual form of experience. The young heart gushes light even when blind, and the poet himself wants to be loved by a beautiful but blind body. He feels reassured by the fact that "forms remain in spite of this sun which dries out throats" (185). This echo of the parched blood motif, mentioned earlier, is also part of the castra-tion theme, as is the idea of blindness in general. Thus, the thirst for creativity goes unrelieved by love and sensation, just as love goes unsatisfied for lack of kisses and spiritual contact.

At this complex point, the card game motif is associated with the poet's shut eyes, and new thematic relationships are opened. There is a chaotic interplay of serious intentions ("false appearance of youth, showing its swollen fingertips in a masked sterility"), and the awareness of pastiche ("I now have my solitaire. Here is the final figure . . . that can be stuck into the white earth like a sick rose-bush, where its eyes will never open" [191]). This passage is, how-ever, one of the less complicated examples, in spite of the abundance and confusion of its motifs. Its meaning is not as important as the fact that it demonstrates the book's structure. Each motif proliferates minor ones, many of which can be traced to other contexts. The point is not so much that we can infer patterns of meaning and function, but rather, that Aleixandre is offering a structural form which suggests a coherent psychological meaning.

It is easy to dismiss *Pasión de la tierra* as a senseless and amor-phous welter of words.[7] Often it does appear to be this, and it is true that the work is Aleixandre's least admired effort. Yet, this is not because it is without surrealist value, but because its symbols spill over with great wastefulness. There is neither control nor direction among its metaphors, and without this the possibility of meaning disappears. That the symbols are intelligible is, I hope, clear from the passages that we have examined. But for the most part, each sentence speaks on several levels at the same time without further elaboration within a given poem. When we trace a motif through several poems, we may get an inkling as to the meaning of the motif, but this does not usually help to explain the poems individually.

For this reason, it is tempting to reject *Pasión de la tierra* as an aberration, especially since Aleixandre has provided similar themes in more accessible books of verse. Yet this very similarity is what confirms the validity of his surrealistic collection. If some motifs can be examined analytically, the majority of them may be experienced intuitively. The text should be confronted as if it were an unreal world of words, a jungle of references that have no application outside the range of the reader's mind. Thus, any sensitive reading cannot help but arouse the uneasy conviction that everything is all vaguely familiar, but that just as we are on the verge of understanding, it slips out of reach again. *Pasión de la tierra* constitutes the triumph of the irrational over the impenetrable. Since there are some aspects of the book that yield to analysis, we may not dismiss it as incomprehensible. Rather, it leads us to the frontier of reality, where we must stop and contemplate the zone of non-reason by means of intuition.

Chapter Four

The Aseptic Garden
(Lorca)

The road to surrealism can be traveled by cutting through the emotional morass of post-Romanticism, as Aleixandre did, or by following an alternate course, and passing through the realms of abstract art and cubism. Such was the route followed by Federico García Lorca, a poet who was relatively untroubled by the problems of expressing a personal lyricism. A glance at Lorca's early poetry shows at once that its sophisticated interest in children's songs, metrical games, and popular ballads was matched by a mastery of the most advanced techniques of European art. In most of these poems, the subjective element is considerably subdued. In 1929, however, a sudden explosion occurred, and the first compositions for *Poet in New York* took form. These poems were, of course, different from the earlier pieces in language and theme. But if we were to state a more fundamental difference, it would be that they lacked aesthetic distance and emotional control. When we enter Lorca's surrealistic world, the order and restraint of his first poetic garden is exchanged for the emotional density of an urban jungle.

This does not mean that Lorca did not foreshadow his own surrealism. On the contrary, the best guide to his surrealist poetry can be found by examining the transitional works between his popular ballads and his New York poems.[1] Of these, the most revealing in its form and content is the *Ode to Salvador Dali,* a poem that leads us straight to the edge of the surrealist jungle. It is important not only for its artistic theory, which is the most explicit statement made by any poem at the time. It is equally important because it represents an attitude toward post-Romanticism

57

and cubism that reflects the social milieu portrayed in the surrealist poems. That is, the ode offers a special approach to modern technology which shows the latter's role in both surrealism and in the post-Romantic (and, later, cubist) sensibility. Thus, by selecting this poem of 1926, we have the opportunity to watch an aesthetic in transition between the civilized restraint of the early Lorca and the baffling urban primitivism of *Poet in New York*. Later, in the next two chapters, we will enter Lorca's fully surrealist period.

The ode to Dali is a fairly clear piece in its rhetoric, with several bold metaphors but without any really undecipherable passages. It contains a critique of cubism, not surrealism, even though Dali seems to occupy a position of prominence in the poem. We must remember that in 1926 Dali was not yet known internationally, and that Lorca did not write the poem to comment on the style of painting for which his friend later became famous. There are, of course, several private allusions that could only apply to Dali, but the overall intent and effect of the ode pertains to modern painting in general, and to certain problems that led inevitably to surrealism, although Lorca did not know this at the time.[2]

The ode itself is the most direct aesthetic statement ever made by Lorca in verse form, and it moves through several dimensions at the same time: poetry and painting, sense data and emotion, reality and fantasy. It maintains two levels of discussion, both of which are firmly built into the structure of the poem and alternate with each other. The first is a theoretical analysis of art, and of the industrialized cultural background which produces it. The second account, less detailed but quite realistic, describes the Spanish environment and embellishes it with an occasional fantastic note. This alternation of planes is significant because it reflects Lorca's view that the artist's search begins with reality and ends with a deliberate displacement of it. Such an evasion of the concrete world is the essence of Lorca's subsequent surrealism, although here it is only prefigured. Essentially, it consists of a very specific, almost naturalistic, groundwork of associations which seem dislocated from reality because of the illogical images they evoke. The technique is crucial for surrealist practice, as we will see in other chapters, because it makes the image a center of imbalance between fact and fancy.

In this ode, the distinction between reality and imagination is not a question of substance, but of image. A single metaphor of the rose can suggest both proximity and inaccessibility. The "rose in the high garden of your desire" expresses Dali's quest for artistic fulfillment, a flower beyond human conception and as unreal as the most impossible of dreams. But there is also:

> The rose of the garden you live in. Ever and always the rose, our north and south! Tranquil and concentrated like a blind statue, ignorant of the subterranean efforts it provokes.

This other flower is more familiar, and the artist living with it every day uses it as his compass for aesthetic direction ("our north and south"). Nevertheless, both roses are insubstantial, belonging to an imagery more appropriate to symbolism than to Romanticism. Yet the second rose, despite its closer connection to the artist's life, does not remain locked in its symbolic framework, but reaches down into the roots of a hidden psychological reality. This is why it has surrealistic value, whereas the rose of the high garden never descends from its metaphorical symbolism. To do so would establish some link to reality, material or otherwise, and to proceed from there to a surrealism beyond.

The difference between the two flowers also points out two separate aspects of beauty, one idealistic and the other tangible. The aspirations of art place beauty beyond human reach, whereas in the garden of life the concrete counterpart of the ideal rose lies within the emotional or sensorial grasp of the artist. And yet, in this case there is still another aesthetic dimension, created by the metaphor of the blind statue. The rose is "tranquil and concentrated" like a statue, being self-sufficient and contained within itself. Its calm presence contrasts with the poet's agitation, and its imperviousness dramatizes the energy of his senses. As a lifeless object of beauty, it remains impassive to the vitality of human sensibility. By emphasizing this, Lorca indicates his debt to the sensuality of modernism, which explored both the qualities of inert objects and the way they stimulate man's senses. The rose is statuesque, shapely and appealing to sight and smell, but also blind, as meaningless as a piece of stone, which needs to be perceived by human consciousness in order to have validity.

The implications of this metaphor for the surrealist mode in Spain are profound. A new concept of the autonomy of matter is hinted at, where human activity is superfluous except as the means by which the beauty of matter becomes known. Whereas the modernist took delight in the pleasures of substance and senses alike, the surrealist will insist on the primacy of substance alone. As a result, the entire notion of meaning must be revised. While it is true that the rose is meaningless without man's intelligence, the latter has only a cognitive force and does not comprise the totality of aesthetic value. Hence the importance of the blind statue. Lorca's purpose is to stress the dissociation of the aesthetic situation by equating the rose with a statue, that is, an unfading thing of beauty regardless of whether the poet is there to recognize it or not. Human meaning is irrelevant in any form—awareness, perception, intelligence, or desire. What is important is the sightless statue, an object lacking in the insight and feeling by which the poet appreciates it. The redundancy of "blind statue" is an essential subtlety. Lorca makes it emphatically sightless precisely because *he* can and does see, for this is his function. Thus, we have the concept of dissociation. Even with the poet absent, substance has value.

The dissociative process carries the duality of the subject-object relationship to a point of disconnection. This can be seen in at least three stages. In the Romantic tradition, the poet projected his subjective attitudes upon the object that he was contemplating, whereas in modernism the sensorial values of the object were cultivated for their own sake, a practice which assumed the independence of the poet's senses. Nevertheless, both movements kept the affective link between subject and object intact. In contrast, Lorca divorces the two worlds completely, placing the rose in one of them, concentrated within itself, and the poet in the other, in an emotional incommunicado. The object is "ignorant of the subterranean efforts it provokes," namely, the unconscious feelings and ideas of the poet. In turn, the latter suffers the isolation of not having his feelings articulated, of striving for an artistic activity which thus far has not risen to the surface. The poet's efforts are underground in the psychological sense and, still being subliminal vis-à-vis his awareness, have only the remotest of connections with the object that is stimulating them. Thus, the subject is cut off from the aesthetic object because his feelings remain unconscious, and the substantiality of the object is given independent validity because it need not provoke a visible affective reaction in the subject.

It is clear, therefore, that the tendency of Lorca's objectivism to turn into a mode of surrealism does not involve the perception of objects as much as it does the disjunctive feelings toward them. The atmosphere of his surrealist ballads, for example, is strange due to the fact that they sound subjective and irrational when they are really written in an impersonal and objective manner. Their sentiment may often be Lorca's own, but it grows discordant as he removes it from context and puts it behind a psychological glass window. The effect is then like a dream in which the dreamer sees himself at a distance and experiences no more than a muffled form of his emotions. We are not often interested in the sensorial information of a dream, but the fact that its sentiments seem to be out of joint is of enormous importance. The beginnings of this disjunctive process are suggested in the ode to Dali, where Lorca is concerned with the divorce between subject and object, and nothing else. The rose stands for the material of artistic creation, and it is this half of the creative relationship which is analyzed behind glass. Since the poet's "subterranean efforts" are still unarticulated, he talks about the condition and structure of the rose as an object instead. There is no mention of the artist's psychological makeup, or even of his technical problems, except to the extent that they are products of the subject material behind the glass. And this inevitably leads to questions of form.

Let us take, for example, the stanza about the

> pure rose which cleans away artifice and sketch, and opens for us the tenuous wings of smile. (Pinned butterfly meditating upon its flight.) Rose whose equilibrium is without sought-after sorrow.

Every aspect of the creative process is dealt with here from the point of view of the object. The painter's perspective is not considered, and he stands in a passive role, moved to pleasure in the rose's presence. Nor is this reaction quite spontaneous, for the smile comes hesitantly, with the gradual delicacy of "tenuous wings." As the smile turns into a butterfly, the subordination of the contemplator's feelings to the object is dramatically exposed. The viewer's mental state is metaphorically pinned down, "meditating upon its flight" and thus potentially artificial. As the observer's mind deliberates, and the painter's eye hesitates, another kind of dissociation takes place. The world of contemplation grows strained with inhibition, while the phenomenal world remains free and natural. The aesthetic counterpart of this situation separates the art object from its creator. The latter remains in a state of arrested emotion ("pinned butterfly"), and if he bestirs himself, it is for a greater confinement. The "sought-after sorrow" which is avoided by the rose is cultivated by the artist, who follows the pattern of contrived, reflective dependency upon his material. Such behavior was normal for the various forms of post-Romanticism, but in the early stages of surrealism, it is rejected. Given the disaffection in the subject-object relationship, the naturalness of phenomena is preferable to the artifice of spirit. This is why the rose is said to have equilibrium, in contrast to the unstable quality of the human temperament.

What we have, then, is a repudiation of the artist's unbalanced passion in favor of the well-balanced rose. In aesthetic terms, this means that stylistic complexity is superseded by the purity of objectivism. Respect for the object ("pure rose") free of the poet's mood is as great as the abhorrence of mannered technique. The rose "cleans away artifice and sketch," thus preparing the way for a contemporary revaluation of art. It becomes the secular arm of the symbolist priesthood, which, at the end of the century, exalted art with religious fervor. At that time, however, the purpose was to sanctify poetic techniques, whereas now the problem is how to liberate the sacred articles from these sacramental vestments. Hence the new reverence for the "pure" rose, whose cleansing effect ventilates the garden air, allows genuine artistic expression, and sharpens the visibility of the rose's composition.

In Lorca's hierarchy, consequently, the object which is treated by art is ranked above technique, and emotional content is ranked third. But this does not mean that the rose is submitted to so minute an analysis that it suffers from denaturation. Although this is the case in cubism, it is not true for surrealism, and looking at other motifs in the *Ode to Salvador Dali,* the reason can be understood. The purification theme found in the rose is continued in another stanza by the "aseptic flower of the square root," which has been cut from the garden of modern painting. The difference between the two flowers lies in the technique with which they are gathered, and it is clear that the degree of dehumanization in the second case does not apply to the rose. Similarly, in the motif of the "pinned butterfly meditating upon its flight," there is the implication that free impulse is better than vacillation. This motif later becomes a scene where butterfly collectors flee from the same sterile painters who cut the aseptic rose. The meaning here is again that of spontaneity and freedom taking precedence over artifice and analysis. Both motifs extend Lorca's idea of restoring integrity back to matter, and not submitting it to the artist's mental processes.[3]

It is difficult to determine what Lorca's personal beliefs were with respect to rational and irrational transformations of the object. The ode is a strong censure of the exclusively technical zeal found in contemporary artists, and yet, Lorca's own poetry has a formal brilliance that tends to minimize its content. There is no contradiction here, since Lorca is really after a dislocation of feeling which would give priority to the subject matter of art. Both sentiment and technique corrupt the purity of the art object, and the latter's independence in this sense can be called formalism. But is it a revolt of the surrealist imagination, or just the end product of realism, where even cubist abstraction might be considered the ultimate in dehumanized objectivity? The answer is that Lorca is on the road to surrealism.[4] In contrast to his friends, painting in "white studios," Lorca does not clutter his poetic chambers with the yardsticks, antiseptics, and other devices of the modern age. He does use them, but only to expand the dimensions of his art beyond the norms of reality. What Lorca is interested in is freeing the objects of his perception from their sensorial and logical substance in order to create a new world of forms and hallucinations. This goal is not made explicit in Lorca's ode to Dali, but it is one reason behind his criticism of certain approaches to reality.

The trouble with this poem is that it is more than just an aesthetic credo. Lorca censures some ideas while accepting others, and he rejects in theory certain techniques which he employs in practice. But this difficulty is less perplexing than the configuration of fantasy and reality that takes shape when Lorca illustrates his ideas with metaphor. We have seen, for example, that Dali's garden meant three things at the same time: it was part of his real home, it was a metaphor for his creativity, and it demonstrated graphically one of Lorca's poetic concepts. But there is still more. The garden is part of a larger social setting in which the ode was written, and beyond this, the poem itself incorporates the imaginative worlds of other artists. We may count, therefore, several "realities." One is the pragmatic reality of life: the garden at Cadaqués, the environment of Paris and Madrid, the phenomenal world that supplies the artist with his subject matter. Another reality lies within the framework of Lorca's own fancy, and consists of the images he invents and objectifies. And finally, there is the reality of other creative visions, borrowed from different artists to illustrate Lorca's critique. All of these distinctions will be treated in the section that follows.

The *Ode to Salvador Dali* has a setting whose concrete references provide less lyricism than they do matter-of-fact information:

> The man steps firmly on the flagstoned streets. The crystal glass shuns the magic of reflection. The Government has closed the perfume shops. The machine eternalizes its binary rhythms.

This stanza appears at the beginning of the poem, just after an allusion to the river Seine, and it prepares us for a literal, almost journalistic reading of the scene. The first verse seems realistic, the second makes a reportorial observation, and the fourth comments on industrial culture. However, the third verse narrates a rather strange event which causes us to reevaluate the other lines, thus disrupting the apparent unity of the stanza. On the surface, the sequence of associations makes sense, because we move with some logic from street to glass windows to shops to machines inside those shops. And yet the link between Government and perfume shop has a suggestion of absurdity that causes the four-line assemblage to collapse. This breakdown is one of Lorca's fundamental techniques. What occurs is the subversion of realistic sequences by means of associative dislocation. Since all of the poem's elements are drawn from everyday reality, with each sentence communicating a reasonably factual message, we cannot find a trace of fantasy or subjectivism anywhere, except for the word "magic." But during one moment in the rhythm of these associations a syncopation occurs, the sequence misses a half-beat in logic, and the entire structure falls.

In this case, the technique barely reaches the embryonic stage of surrealism. Even though the stanza relinquishes its realistic meaning, it avoids irrationalism by creating a higher significance which is no longer symbolic and yet is not quite surrealistic. This new meaning is germane to Lorca's analytical purpose of theorizing on art. Nevertheless, the aesthetic concepts that emerge are expressed by symbols whose penumbra foreshadows the transition between post-Romanticism and surrealism. For example, the most traditional symbol is the perfume shop, originating in the modernist lexicon and representing the sensorial qualities of art. More appropriate to modern psychology is the symbolic role of the Government, a figure of authority established by the founding fathers of an aesthetic movement. Most contemporary of all is the machine, which stands for the indestructable power and poetry of dehumanized activity.

Together, the perfume shop and the machine polarize the old and the new techniques of aestheticism. In the past, the creative act was based on human sensibility; today, the means of production are impersonal and sometimes even automated. The fault of the perfume dealer, however, was that he dispensed beauty in artificially adorned packages instead of in its natural state. In contrast, the machine pursues the eternal ideals of art, not by the old-fashioned "magic of reflection," but with its "binary rhythms." These rhythms are as essential to modern art forms as the senses were to the texture of post-Romanticism. Nor does the machine lack the ritual skills of creation, and it can replace traditional art because it too "eternalizes." Moreover, despite the ambiguous word "binary," the artist's scientific vocabulary projects an image of sleek precision and durability, quite appropriate to the futuristic goals of an industrialized era. The truth of this is not diminished by the social reality of Spain in the 1920's, which was not very advanced industrially. Artists everywhere in Europe were conscious of the new technology, regardless of where their particular country stood with regard to its practical development. In this respect, Spain was no different from Italy,

Russia, and other poor countries which produced an intellectual elite.

Generally speaking, then, the machine is a splendid monument to the superior performance of contemporary art. It meets the formal requirements of composition by supplying rhythm, and it is progressively oriented, shaking off the preceptualism of the preceding generation. Unlike the perfume shop, the machine operates in total freedom, not subjected to the regulations of an authority empowered to shut it down. There is no artist-legislator to invent and enforce rules of law and order, for such control would eventually become restrictive and perverse. Whereas in the past, aesthetic orthodoxy had stifled the expression of beauty, now, the self-replenishing machine can produce endless, measured flights of fancy. New creative vistas are opened at the same time that the machine is grounded realistically in what is tangible. All of this contrasts with the perfume shops that once exuded the heavy fragrance of the imagination. Even the four-line stanza shows the difference with its item-by-item narration, each verse written with the same syntax, and each example marking the limits of reality. Thus, the man who "steps firmly on the flagstoned streets" maintains unshakable contact with the practical world. He may have once delighted in the confusions of sensorial play and the enchantment of their unreal refractions, but now "the crystal glass shuns the magic of reflection." And worst of all, the aromatic essence of art has been bottled up by the seal of the "Government's" aesthetic theory.

What we have seen up to now is the interpenetration of several realities, each varying in its degree of pragmatic value according to what it consists of: descriptive detail, metaphor, or intellectual concept. If we pay closer attention to the imagery itself, we will find an intimate connection between metaphor and concept. The techniques of Lorca's poetic world are rooted in the ideological themes of the poem, and these themes are illustrated by technique and metaphor. It is a reciprocal situation, one in which the aesthetic principle can be inferred from the technique, and where the technique seems to be a logical consequence of the theory. In all of this, the real world is used as a stepping stone to these other levels of reality. Take, for example, the following metaphors:

> Wandering along the rooftops of old houses is an absence of forests, screens, and frowns. The air polishes its prism above the sea, and the horizon rises like a great aqueduct.

Despite the realistic detail, the total effect is to make the scene more abstract, due to Lorca's dissociative technique. An absence of forests cannot go wandering. That is, it is impossible to engage the concept of absence with a physical activity. It is equally difficult to imagine that "air polishes its prism," especially when the geometrical connotation raises the level of abstraction. The "absence" that goes wandering is made up of "forests, screens, and frowns." This trio of allusions helps to expand the scene beyond the city streets and machines, from the housetops to the sea, and finally to the mariners who will appear in the next stanza. The absence also conveys a sense of loss which parallels the loss mentioned before, that of spontaneous beauty now gone.

The images of the prism and aqueduct are related to the machine because they all fulfill the same ideological function. Linking them is their tendency to insulate the poetic world against human sensibility. With the perfume shops closed, we can no longer smell their fragrance directly, but must reinvent it in abstraction. Hence the machine is constructed, with its binary rhythms based on principles of mechanical and geometrical law. But this new design contravenes the pragmatic logic of reality and introduces a mathematical logic which is dissociated from the affective sense of life. Although the metaphor of the air polishing its prism is still comprehensible, it turns away from the sensorial experiences of reality. Its logic is of a higher order, and by making a different demand on the nature of meaning, it sets poetry on the road to surrealism.

In this respect, it is useful to distinguish between the imagery of the ode to Dali (or even the *Gypsy Ballads*) and the surrealism of *Poet in New York*. In the ode, there is a cerebral quality to the metaphor which induces certain minor feelings or moods without really appealing to the reader directly. These psychological by-products have nothing to do with the rational purpose of the metaphor, which is to cause a new aesthetic experience that is isolated from feeling. In contrast, Lorca's surrealist poetry shows a marked rehumanization, despite the chaotic images and deformations involved. As we will see in the chapters that follow, surrealism is clearly related to real emotion and scenic mood. It does not remain independent, or, like the aseptic flower cut by modern painters, appear wiped clean of feeling. On the other hand, the two metaphors discussed have a dynamic quality that is found in the tensile character of a mathematical line. Their conceptual energy offers the same visual appeal that a cubist painting does, although with little plastic effect. That is, the metaphors' plasticity is minute, and except for the surface smoothness that might be inferred from the stanza, there is no textural or chromatic evidence present. In practice, therefore, Lorca's technique closely resembles the artistic theory that the ode is describing and admonishing.

The two stanzas just discussed represent reality with increasingly less reliance on the phenomena of the outside world, and with a more marked turning inward to fantasy or abstraction. In the third stanza of this sequence, the inversion deepens in both of these latter categories. However, the difference between fantasy and abstraction is like the difference found in the two types of secondary reality mentioned earlier. In the latter, the hierarchy of poetic realities depended upon their degree of pragmatic value: descriptive detail, metaphor, intellectual concept. So too in the relationship of fantasy to abstraction. Lorca's frame of reference for his poem is conceived through his own imagination. But his metaphorical reality tends toward abstraction, as we have seen. Where, then, is the fantasy? It is found in the imaginative frames of reference which Lorca borrows from other artistic traditions. He uses images, symbols, and allusions that are foreign to the modern aesthetic developed in the ode, adapting them to his illustrative purposes. Consequently, both fantasy and abstraction are present, as for example in this stanza:

> Sailors unaware of wine and shadow decapitate sirens in the leaden seas. The Night, a black statue of prudence, holds the round mirror of the moon in her hand.

All of the elements here are Lorca's creation, of course, but we cannot help noticing that what is peculiarly his are the act of decapitation and the metaphor of the Night, which tends toward the abstract. On the other hand, certain symbolic conventions of traditional art—wine, shadow, sirens, moon—do not belong to the aesthetic that we have been describing, since they add a fantastic note.

We have, then, a good instance of how Lorca fuses his own creativity to past tradition. The result is that the stanza has formal unity, and from the latter we can deduce an implicit statement of aesthetic belief. Lorca is saying that the old ways of expressing beauty by intoxicated states of mind (wine) are no longer valid. The rapture, melancholy, and nocturnal communion of the past (shadow) have no force for the modern artist. Instead, he is aware of an unfeeling, harsh detachment from everything. Like the man stepping firmly on the flagstones, the sailors navigate coldly, untouched by the flights of fancy that once envisioned beautiful sirens in the water. In fact, the mariners, being ignorant of the powers of wine and shadow, are the executioners of these mythical inhabitants of their medium. The sirens represent exoticism and fantastic art, both to be suppressed in a destructive, but obviously passionless, manner. Not unsimilar to the siren in Aleixandre's poem, these mythical beings lure dreamers to their death, and this also argues for their demise. Lorca is hinting that the modern artist should be wary of being led astray by a harmful aesthetic creed.

The last two lines of the stanza present one of the most significant metaphors in modern Spanish poetry. The Night is characterized as a statue of prudence, thus changing from a natural phenomenon into a conceptualization. With this moral quality, she becomes an accomplice in the overthrow of traditional aesthetic sensibility. Unlike the sailors who are ignorant of the old values, the Night knows them, but prudently refrains from making them visible. Her complicity lies in the fact that she shelters the homicidal mariners in her darkness, concealing the death of traditional art. Ordinarily, the moon in her hand would have been a luminary, throwing light on the murderous act. Instead, it is a mirror which reflects the black statue of Night, revealing nothing but darkness. Thus, Night has a static role which is the reverse of the sailors' active one. So too, her round mirror, made of moon, contrasts with the shapeless seas of lead, just as her metaphorical abstraction ("statue of prudence") is the opposite of the mythical symbolism of the fantasy.

The entire image, therefore, turns about the single axis of the mirror. Each element finds an inverted reflection, or a parallel. The leaden sea has a texture and color that contrasts with the statuesque Night and her sensorial qualities. There is a similar opposition between the moon and the sirens. Traditionally, both were objects of beauty, but Lorca defaces them, slaying the sirens and turning the moon into a useless looking glass. The latter fails to mirror the beauty of Night because darkness cannot be reflected, and this is the enormous irony of the image. The Night, even if she did desire to contemplate herself as a beautiful black statue, would not be able to see anything in the glass. Moreover, the same aesthetic atrophy has befallen the moon. It too has changed, from a transmitter of beauty to a functionless ornament. If the moon had once been, at the least, an aesthetic artifact, it is now an abstraction of itself. By the same token, the sirens bear a more tragic fate, for their mythical decorativeness is mutilated in the most horrible fashion. Thus, the sailors participate in an artistic conspiracy which Lorca exposes but does not totally repudiate. He has withdrawn from the fanciful conventions of the past, and to some extent is intrigued by the emotionless course charted by the modern navigators of art. But at the same time, he is preparing to break loose from this cold and measured formalism.

Lorca's ambiguous position toward the new aesthetic is the result of his own uncertainty. He finds, in the same reality that Dali submitted to reductive analysis, fantastic evocations that are artistically sound. Lorca can no longer accept the post-symbolist sensibility, but he cannot renounce myth and fantasy either. Unwilling to systematically dehumanize, he is incapable as yet of the surrealist alternative. He stands hesitant, oblivious of the schizoid descent he is soon to make into a nightmare reality of his own creation. In this ode, Lorca observes the simple phenomenal world, while his mind idly invokes some of the mythological associations of the past. The result is a charming diction, but along side the bold imagery of other stanzas, it is unimpressive ("Cadaqués, balanced between water and hill, raises its stone stairs and hides its conches. Wooden flutes becalm the air. An old sylvan god gives fruit to the children").

In this setting, where Lorca and Dali actually did vacation, the poet also speaks of the "fishermen [who] sleep without reverie upon the sand." Their spiritual kinship with the sailors before them is obvious, since they all refrain from imaginative activity. The atmosphere is realistic, with no place for dreams or fancy, and rest is to be found on the hard sand, not in the soft darkness of sea and night. When these same fishermen are "on the high sea they use a nautical compass," thus making adventure impossible. The essential identity of these mariners and the sailors is also confirmed by the reappearance of the siren motif:

> A hard crown of white bergantines encircles bitter brows and sandy hair. The sirens convince, but have no influence, and emerge when we show them a glass of sweet water.

The prolonged attention paid earlier to horizontal and vertical planes now reaches its logical conclusion here in the beach-level perspective of this stanza. The loose chain of boats against the horizon seems, from this angle, to form a semicircle above the heads of the fishermen. The latter are seen lying flat on the beach, their hair full of sand, with the crown of ships foreshortened above their brows. Why these should be "bitter brows" is uncertain, although one clue may be seen in the slight futility implicit in the new aesthetic practices. The men lay prone on a hard bed, fatigued by the romantic storm and involved in a lower-keyed artistic experiment. The sirens, as symbols of beauty in the arts, now play a smaller role. They are still appealing or convincing, but the force of their destructive magnetism has been dispelled. Far from exercising a persuasive hold on the seamen, they themselves are enticed by the latter's bait, for they come out when shown a glass of sweet water in place of the brine to which they are accustomed. Indeed, this fresh water, like the new art for which it stands, is more palatable than the salt water of the past, just as the glass that holds it is superior in form to the shapeless sea.

The new aesthetic tenets that we have been discussing are made vividly clear by the ode's graphic language. Less obvious are Lorca's own feelings about these innovations. At the outset of the poem, his tone is dry, detached, and clinical. But this does not mean that he remained emotionally cut off from his ideas, for later in the ode he introduces a personal, impassioned note.[5] And since he adhered to well-defined aesthetic practices of his own, he could not have been indifferent to a theory of art that was the subject of his own poem. Lorca's tactic, therefore, was circumspection as he accommodated himself to the accents of his artistic theme. The clinical tone of the ode proves to be an appropriate response to the hygienic purposes of the new aesthetic, and to the surgical effectiveness of its practitioners. There is a prevalence of words denoting neatness, cleanliness, trimming, and other meticulous tasks of a well-kept hospital. The air "polished" its prism, sailors "decapitated" sirens, the pure rose "cleansed" away artifice, and "modern painters, in their white studios, cut the aseptic flower of the square root." More than simple housekeeping, this is a sanitation process which coldly attempts to deal with reality as a germicide does with undesirable living things: elimination by neutralization. Instead of removing unwanted elements from the scene, the technique abstracts or arrests them, and renders them harmless to the new aesthetic.

At the same time, the artists neutralize their own lives by surrounding themselves with articles once-removed from life. But this does not reflect the old problem of art versus reality, where art is judged to be less vital or more inert than life. The issue now is whether art can parallel or represent the vitality of real life. It is a question of dehumanization. When we think of the rose in Romanticism and later movements, we know that it corresponds to a real rose in spite of its artifice. Now, however, it is not even an artificial rose, but a mathematical abstraction of one, its square root, so to speak, whose nourishment comes neither from the real earth nor poetic sensibility, but from the groundwork of a metaphysic. Thus, the "white studio" is less a descriptive reference than it is the depiction of a value. "Aseptic" is more of a judgment than a qualifying adjective, in view of the many alternatives that exist for the same idea. And the artist becomes an anesthetist in the delivery of his creation.

As modern art practices sterilization more often, the concepts underlying its techniques become more sterile themselves. Artistic reproduction is no longer an organic process, but an artificial formula for germinating numbers in a series or for duplicating square roots like rows of icecubes in a rectangle. The lifelessness of this method is expressed metaphorically by images of coldness: "In the waters of the Seine a marble iceberg chills the windows and dispels the ivy." The sense of destruction to life is perceptible here, a will to freeze desire rather than to inflame it. But even the image of ice is insufficient to convey the stillborn quality of this creation. The iceberg is once removed from reality, made of marble even though the original substance was just as capable of benumbing the senses. Thus, the petrification of life is complete: the ivy is dead, real ice turns into art material, and painters sit by their windows, risking frostbite as they watch the city. Nor does it matter whether they are frozen, anesthetized, or disinfected, for Lorca links them all as he tells Dali: "Hygienic soul, you dwell upon new marble." In every case, the artists' sensitivity to primary sensation is enervated. Moreover, the consequences of this condition affect the psychology of art. The painter who "dwells in new marble" is inhabiting a realm of sensorial barrenness, where color is absent, and where the reduced temperature dulls the emotions. By narrowing the scope of his experience in this way, the artist limits his creation regardless of how high he aspires:

> A rose in the high garden of your desire. A wheel in the pure syntax of steel. The mountain stripped of impressionist mist. The greys surveying their last balustrades.

Here are all the precepts of the new formalism, which we will proceed to analyze according to motif.

The machine, as I noted earlier, is the most perfect and eternal guarantor of formal beauty. Something in its metallic substance intimidates the modern artist into the belief that the natural instruments of his personal domain are too frail for transcendent creation. Language is one such frailty, for it is constantly submitted to a tempering process of revaluation. So too are other immediate media of artistic expression like materials and paints. But modern machinery, with its size, performance, and impersonality, is situated just beyond the artist's immediate human scope. With its technocratic symbolism of steel, it embodies the essence of the modern age and many goals of the artists. The "pure syntax of steel," therefore, is an advanced form of experimentation, with successful techniques of artistic expression. Every aspect of the new aesthetic is represented here: that art must reflect some kind of communication or articulation ("syntax"); that modernity transcends human intimacy ("steel"); and that art is defined in terms of its own self-refinement ("pure"). The "wheel" in this pure steel syntax emphasizes this perfection by its circular form. But beyond this, it symbolizes the functionalism—formalism—of modern art. The quatrain cited above states this principle as an equation: the rose is to the wheel as the desired garden is to pure syntax. In other words, the artistic goal of reaching beauty and form (garden, syntax) is realized through specific creations that embody these ideals (rose, wheel).

As for the concept of transcendence, this is best understood in the light of human frailty. Lorca's generation exalted the machine as the emblem of perfectibility and indestructible beauty. Machines seemed to surpass the most valiant efforts of men even while they remained in the latter's power. Moreover, their transcendency left sense perception and objectivism behind them. Why not, then, also create a work of art that would be free of sensorial limitations as well as structural imperfections?[6] The reproduction of sense data merely duplicates man's subjectivity, instead of attending to the qualities of the object. There appears to be no point in allowing human sensibility to place a curtain between the creator and the object as it actually is. It is better to go beyond the intimacy of the artist, and strip the object of its lyrical decoration in order to give it a clarity of appearance. This is why Lorca's mountain is naked, sharply outlined after the mist of impressionism has evaporated.

Nevertheless, the absence of human feeling is a disadvantage for other artistic reasons. The work will be less vital in tone, and its energy more impersonal. Unlike the objective realism which keeps its emotional ties with the artist, the perspective here will be alienated as well as detached. And the work will be colorless, a body drained of its life blood without having lost the power of its unfeeling frame. As Lorca says metaphorically, "the greys surveying their last balustrades" offer a viewpoint which is already transcendent, and which cannot go any further. We are not shown the artist's perspective, but that of the object itself. If a man were looking, he would find some color gradation. From the object's point of view, there can be no impressionism, only greys. Hence, at the edge of the balcony, the vista is colorless, and beyond this there is nothing.

Lorca's analysis is perhaps too generalized. Not all painters of his epoch dismissed color value, but there is no doubt that most of them subordinated it to other formal elements. This is, at any rate, Lorca's position, and the fact is that his own ode lacks chromatism too. In many stanzas we can find good examples of how line and volume effectively control the artist's attention. On the other hand,

Lorca regards the warmth of colors to be as emotional as sentimentality, a nonobjective entity in the world of forms:

> A desire for limits and forms overtakes us. Arriving is the man who watches with a yellow yardstick. Venus is a white still life, and the butterfly collectors flee.

No longer do we find a high garden of idealistic desire. The artist has ceased to yearn for the unlimited depths of psychological experience in both the sensorial and the emotional realms. He realizes that the purpose of creative activity is to reduce the perceptual faculties to a finite scope. As for feelings, since they cannot be measured with a yardstick, they are useless in the world of forms. Even the more sensual aspects of perception are removed, and the act of seeing is accomplished achromatically by an eyeless ruler—ironically, yellow—that is sensitive only to line and mass. In other words, the artist who watches the world with a tape measure is a man with no concept of infinity. He holds securely to the world of dimensions, and cannot fall into the pit of his subjectivity. From the standpoint of surrealism, this is a disadvantage, and as we will see in other chapters, it is corrected by providing approximate measurements as the price for greater subjectivism. In this case, however, beauty is depicted as a still-life goddess, without character or animation. Art thus parallels life, for where the artist permits a reduction in his organic functions—the senses—his creation acquires a comparable degree of dehumanization. The fate of Venus, consequently, is the same as that of her siren half-sisters. Slain by the metallic arm of the machine age, she is afterward subjected to decoloration, drained white in a continuation of the blood motif. Both acts horrify the butterfly collectors, who run away.

The reason that color and light now have secondary functions is that their greatest asset, sensuality, is no longer wanted. Like many painters of that period, Lorca turned away from tangible pleasure and affirmed instead the beauty of linear value. This does not mean that color plays no part in Lorca's later poetry, or that surrealism will be found lacking in sensuality. But the role of color frequently serves a more abstract purpose, creating mood or conveying an emotion. For example, the psychological overtones of green in the *Sleepwalking Ballad* have little to do with sensual effect. So too, the vision of a bloodless, alabaster Venus startled the butterfly collectors into fleeing, since its effect was to produce the same kind of unearthly experience that occurs when a technicolor film abruptly changes into a black and white sequence. In Dali's generation, as in this kind of film, color continues to be important for painting, but in its aspect of light. Its use and variety helps to set off volumes from each other, accenting silhouettes and boundaries between forms and masses. When Lorca addresses his friend by saying, "Oh Salvador Dali, with olive-green voice! I don't praise your imperfect, adolescent brush or your color which approaches the color of your time, but I commend your longing for the eternal limited," the poet is contrasting precisely these two functions of color and line. Dali is praiseworthy less for his brushwork than for his desire to achieve formal limits.

This yearning for the eternal has a more subjective counterpart among the post-Romantics, who also longed for infinity. In other words, no one has a monopoly on either longing or infinity, but there are varying degrees of sensorial and spatial commitment involved. The moderns are concerned with the "eternal limited," that is, the mathematical limits of space, and many have abandoned the impressionists' obsession with color. Lorca and Dali consider linear and volumetric relationships to be eternal insofar as they continually recur and pervade every aspect of concrete reality. Lorca himself is ambivalent on this idea of reduced chromatism, as his allusion to the "olive-green voice" shows. On one hand, the olive color grows more abstract with its use as a modifier of sound, since it is applied to a phenomenon without plastic quality. On the other hand, the element of sensuality is still present in the connotations of a voice with a thick, liquid consistency. What remains clear is that color as an emotional force plays a subdued role.

Later in the ode, Lorca returns to the distinction between color and light by treating them in terms of rationalism. Light is the symbol of reason, and hence an ancillary of mathematical discipline. The artist who is interested primarily in geometrical expression will use light as a function of measurement. In painting, this means the judicious employment of color on behalf of strengthening the linear configuration. Color is used rationally in support of what is largely a message of formal planes. This idea is not restricted to cubism, but to all experimental movements that choose precision of line over impressionism. Thus, light is to color what reason is to feeling—a force for distinguishing clearly among the phenomena of reality. From the standpoint of the history of aesthetic ideas, this position is a retreat from the mass of emotions and sensations that characterized the nineteenth century. Lorca finds in Dali's work a return to classical moderation, a careful indifference to the Romantic unknown, along with a rational charting of the creative venture.

Lorca emphasizes this classicism by the use of mythology, which is made to describe the color-light relationship: "On grasping the palette, with a bullet-hole in one wing, you ask for the light which stirs the olive-tree tip. The broad light of Minerva, who constructs scaffolds, where neither dream nor imprecise flowers may fit." Although the diction is somewhat mannered, the artist's principles are plainly stated. He is less interested in the variety of paints on his palette than in light. It is the moderating quality of light which attracts him, for his own desire is to achieve tranquility in painting, an equilibrium of spirit and brush. This is further symbolized by the reference to the olive tree, which is associated with the light. By contrast, the palette, with one of its ends bored through, is likened to a bird whose liveliness is comparable to the range of colors. Light, therefore, represents peace, and the deity ruling it is the goddess of reason, the woman who gave man his most valuable prize: the olive. Minerva's own creations are themselves models of restraint, for her scaffold, like the mythical looms upon which she weaved, left no room for irrational or Bacchic constructs. Thus, the poet himself builds a tight symmetry of opposing symbolic themes: reason-dream, tree-bird, palette-light.

In general, the ode reveals that the *furor poeticus* is anathema to the inheritors of post-cubism. Lorca insists on the absence of irrationalism in Dali because he regards the new aesthetic as a departure from the various forms of subjectivism that followed the Romantic movement. From this historical vantage point, it can be seen that most twentieth-century art is in an advanced stage of Romanticism, but Lorca was unwilling to recognize any intellectual ties between Romantics and moderns. His basic premise was that geometrical form is the standard and norm of rational art. Since he characterized the new art as detached and precise, Lorca quite naturally stressed form over feeling. However, it is not always possible to find confirmation of this notion in Lorca's own poetry because of its strange mixture of visual exactness and dislocated subjectivism. In the *Ode to Salvador Dali,* his position seems ambivalent, although he identifies himself with his friend as a modern artist. But a few years later, in Lorca's surrealist period, his poetry contains a great deal of irrational expression. His subjectivity is, of course, controlled, and often deranged to the point of appearing objective, but his images are hardly a product of rational vision. Here, then, is the difference. Lorca distinguishes between reason as a technique of self-control, and the product of this technique, which may be irrational. His reference to Minerva describes the rational method—altogether different from the subjective metaphor that may be its result. It should be noted that this distinction has relevance to surrealism, even though Lorca is referring to cubist painters. In the case of Dali, both the method and the product are rational. In Lorca's poetry, the method is rational and the product irrational. In French surrealism, especially in automatic writing, irrationalism prevails in both method and product.

Beyond Lorca's critique of methodology lies the question of the artist's psychological disposition. Here too, Lorca makes symbolic use of classical myths in order to sharpen the historical contrast between techniques: "You asked for the ancient light that remains upon the brow, without descending to man's mouth or heart. The light feared by Bacchus' intimate vines and the unchanneled force borne by curved water." The conflict is explicitly stated: Minerva against Bacchus, reason (light) against both sensation (mouth) and emotion (heart). By listing these faculties of human temperament, Lorca sets off a string of ideological antitheses. The request for an "ancient" light proclaims the return to the moderate aesthetic of antiquity. But this is not a matter of chronology. What is important is not to "descend" from the mind to the emotion. The poet must shun the elemental regions of experience, which were, until recently, the domain of Romantics. The implication, however, is that the power of wine is greater than reason, even though the vine trembles in the light of Minerva. In other words, emotional energy is an "unchanneled force" which represents abundance and creativity. It is not wholly effective because it can be diverted and dissipated before being used, and this is one argument against it.[7]

A second image is also used by Lorca as a counterpart of Bacchus: "the dark jungle of unbelievable shapes" from which Dali tries to escape. Both images reflect the state of creative intoxication wherein the senses are freely indulged. The dark jungle represents a world removed from understanding, and it is one more motif in the surrealist descent into the irrational. The primitivism inherent in this realm stems from two sources. The shapes found there baffle the mind: they are "unbelievable" to an artist whose world is governed by rules. Furthermore, there is a submergence into the senses in order to achieve uninhibited freedom of association. As has been shown, Dali is incapable of this state, preferring the regularity of the sonnet to the unmapped regions of chaos ("you enjoy the sea's sonnet in your window"). But Lorca indicates thereby that a surrealist can choose differently. The latter regards imagination as something akin to a jungle, a dark wilderness lighted by flashes of intuition. He knows that his submerged potential reaches deep into the imagination, beyond his reason and sense perception. Indeed, the creative imagination uses the senses for larger purposes, and is never bound to them. To limit creativity to the sensorial realm, as Dali does, is to impose an unwarranted inhibition upon the self.[8] Although it is possible to achieve artistic success with this handicap, the result is likely to be calm, subdued, and unexciting.

The element of excitement is least likely to be found in Dali's repressive sonnet form. His work, as Lorca describes it, is a symmetry of sensualism. Its modern restraint is a product of the cubist contempt for the Romantic exacerbation of the senses. It recognizes that impulse and disorder lead to the unknown, whereas coherence is the child of self-control. This is why Dali can be seen fleeing from the jungle, and why he disciplines his emotional reactions. Moreover, this apparent insensitivity to pain seals off another route into the dark regions of his subjectivity. The artist may well be perceptive in his creative sensibility, but he must not be hurt by personal feelings to the point where this is manifested in his work. Thus, for Dali, the modern artist shields himself behind his intellect.

This self-enforced emotional distance is in great measure an aesthetic principle consciously chosen by the artist. Nevertheless, we can also consider it to be an evasion of reality, an unwillingness to engage the emotions in the complexities of life. In cultural terms, this has come to be known as dehumanization, an attempt to correct life's random structure by eliminating the spontaneous. Its aesthetic counterpart is the psychological conflict between the desire for form and the fear of emotion. This dislocation is reflected in the way the artist sees reality, as divided into perfect order and total chaos. Retreating from the real world into a sphere of systematic action, the artist uses for his subject only those aspects of life which he can control.

None of this is to argue conclusively that Lorca was either attacking or defending Dali's practice.[9] It is clear that there are discrepancies between Lorca's own techniques and those of Dali which are described in the ode. I shall also show in the next chapters that Lorca could be supremely rational while producing the impression of a nightmare. This is, of course, the essence of surrealism. But there is nothing in this poem to suppose that Lorca took a categorical position toward Dali's art. The latter was for the most part an occasion for analyzing the evolution of aesthetics from the end of Romanticism to the first stirring of surrealism. Take, for example, the themes of time and death: "Time's current dams up and arranges itself in the numerical forms of one century and another. And vanquished Death takes trembling refuge in the narrow circle of the present moment." This idea takes an optimistic view of time, when compared with post-Romantic art movements. The victory over time and death is one and the same. It is achieved externally by escaping from the temporal flux created by sensory experience. The perception of time is confused by indulgence in the senses, so much so that the artist's consciousness becomes intoxicated and his temporal awareness grows distorted. There is also an internal conquest of time which comes from avoiding memory and halting the stream of consciousness. This rejection of subjectivity, along with its morbid self-contemplation, banishes thoughts of past time and future death. Thus, Dali's method enables the artist to gain control of his temporal circumstances and to exploit it by means of a mathematical system.

The difference between Dali's method and the ones used by the heirs of Romanticism can be seen by a few examples. In the past, artists depicted time—and its mistress, death—as a nonstatic quality. They either indicated the erosion of life by depicting architectural ruins, or they paralyzed the moment of perception by fusing volumes and planes, or they used flurries of sensory impressions to suspend the concept of chronological time for the sake of expanding the present moment. All of these techniques tended to weaken the objectivity of time's role. There was no attempt to devise a single standard of measurement, and, indeed, no standard was possible as long as sense perception was the primary instrument. In contrast, Dali's procedure denied the importance of the senses. He abandoned his personal notion of time in order to discover the ordered sequence of time's current. That is, he imagined time to be a dam instead of a flowing river, with each wave lined up one behind the other, like the chronology of the centuries. This meant, in pictorial terms, that he was relying upon linear perspective rather than sensualism; as Lorca's image shows, there are a series of planes backed up into infinity. In addition to this, Dali scores a triumph over death. The "trembling refuge" of death in the "narrow circle of the present moment" is a negation of death's eternal character, for its existence is confined to the now, to a limited minute and nothing more. This geometrical limitation of a heretofore unknown entity is, because of its rationalism, directly opposed to the surrealist vision. If we think of Dali's "Persistence of Memory," painted subsequently, the contrast becomes evident.

Thus we find that the principal defect of the new methodology is also its main virtue, namely, the rigidity of its system. Within the strict patterns of geometrical form there can be no bland sensual perception of the kind found in the melting watches—in Lorca's words to Dali: "As a painter you don't want the form to soften in the changing cotton of an unforeseen cloud." The most undesirable element in an aesthetic of hard form is the surprise factor, born of idiosyncrasy and introspection. Cotton and cloud have implications that must be avoided: the mutation of time, the emotional mist of impressionism, the liquidation of linear distinctions. On the other hand, Dali is careful "to post warning flags in the dark limit that shines at night." This alludes to the paradoxical nature of the artistic checks imposed upon subjectivism. The unlimited night is dangerous, and warning signals are needed. One such sign can be the invisible horizon itself, "the dark limit" which reminds us that the night does have limitations. Since this acknowledgment constitutes a ray of understanding for the artist, it can be called a "dark limit that shines at night."

A final virtue of the new aesthetic is that it fuses the abstractions of geometrical conception with the concrete durability of the machine. The result is a flexible amalgam of images that can implement old techniques by first recasting them in a modern foundry. Dali studied the consistencies of his materials, the direction and scope of his measuring instruments, and the artistic validity of his inventions. And he found them all without defect:

> The steel compass recites its short elastic verse. . . . The straight line recites its vertical effort and the wise crystals sing of their geometries.

This optimism, however, proved to be short-lived, and within a few years both Lorca and Dali abandoned their machines for the calculus of madness.[10]

ode to Walt Whitman.

Chapter Five

The Georgics of Technology
(Lorca)

In the preceding chapter, we were able to discuss some pre-surrealist aesthetic problems which would have appeared obscure were it not for Lorca's didactic style. In the *Ode to Walt Whitman,* a similar argumentativeness is present, this time to expound a cultural vision in metaphorical form.[1] The poem's moralizing tone is pithy and contentious, and sometimes it nearly breaks down into a catalog of apostrophes. But in spite of this, the imagery surrounding the city and its mismated values creates a nightmarish atmosphere, which is part of the surrealist shadow cast over the entire *Poet in New York*. The mood develops out of the incongruity of two conflicting themes. On one hand there is the New York of "wire and death," and on the other, the flawless and semidivine Whitman, the heroic bard of the filthy city. Thus, the ode fluctuates between stark realism and the idealistic fantasies of Lorca. The environment provokes certain mental states that begin with social awareness and end in terror. And Lorca's imagination sponsors the myth of the American poet in order to cope with a culture "submerged in machines and grief." The result is a ceremonial poem in which Lorca officiates at the strange marriage of industrial and pastoral entities.

At every moment we are reminded that the metropolitan experience is an impure emotion. The individual's native tranquility is jarred by the rawness of modern industrialism, and his rational attitudes are adulterated by the emotions inflicted upon him by the environment. This violation of personality dramatizes the existence of a conflict that most men have long since accepted and forgotten. That is, the special turmoil which emanates from the city is derived from the corruption of innocence by the evils of technology. To most of us, this fact is, more than a truth, a way of life, but when seen through the eyes of the ingenuous Lorca, it regains its primeval force. Hence the traumatic quality of the poems in *Poet in New York*. Lorca cannot overcome the defect of bifocalism, and so he isolates the two poles of urban life—innocence and vice—instead of fusing them into the viable synthesis which in reality it is.

This schism shows up in the imagery, which polarizes primitive and industrial modes by identifying similar traits in both, and separating them. The simple idealist and the city worker have basic activities in common. They partake of one elemental condition which is identical, even though its cultural manifestation is different. Thus, the naked conflict of man and machine is described in archetypal terms, rather than with the precise vocabulary of the age. Young workingmen sing as they labor, "baring their waists, with wheel, oil, leather, and hammer." These are not the specific instruments of a technical society, but the primary materials from which complex artifacts are made. So too with the activity itself, the labor whose rhythmic patterns hold the rudimentary forms of art. They are found in both innocent and decadent cultures, but in the latter they are hidden by a heavy crust of corruption. None of the city workers is capable of displaying the innocent man's simplicity: "No one wanted to be a cloud, no one sought the fern or the drum's yellow wheel." The worker's hammerblows are only remotely related to the drum and its beats; yet, their rhythm builds the music of the machine age. Just as the drum makes primitive music, so do the basic tools of labor represent creativity. The wheel is circular, like the drum's wheel, although its color is not the same. They differ in function, but their essential character is identical, and their activity is reducible to one common denominator. However, contemporary man has lost his idealism, and he does not wish to become a cloud. His work has no aesthetic consequences, and regardless of its generic similarity to the drum, it belongs to an ugly social reality.

Lorca laments this cultural gap. He finds that all primary elements are worthy of song, whether they belong to an idealized past or to current society. Oil and leather are, in industry, the counterparts of cloud and fern in nature. The young men who sing as they work are making poetry out of their tools' performance, and their naked torsos awaken a nostalgia for the idyllic innocence of the past. But this is not the reality of New York, and Lorca's yearning for the ideal reveals his wish to evade the present, to transform it to suit his fantasies. Little by little, his repugnance toward the ugliness of working-class life is overshadowed by more troubling emotions. He uses poetic evasion as a defense mechanism to shield his pastoral sensibilities. Finding labor and leisure to be incompatible, he complains that present reality has eliminated the sensual pleasures of idleness: "But no one fell asleep, no one wished to be the river, no one loved the large leaves, or the beach's blue tongue." In this daydream, color and grace compensate for the flat greyness of reality. The river of reverie is the dream counterpart of the commercial East River and Queensborough Bridge. It also furnishes a solitary setting for other forms of gratification which offset the blows of the real world.

In contrast to the blue seashore is the colorless scene where "ninety thousand miners drew silver from the rocks, and boys sketched ladders and perspectives." The bleakness of their work is magnified by the abstract nature of the allusions to linear design. Moreover, the symbols of sterility—rocks, dryness, miners instead of farmers—suggest how fruitless their labors are. The men are far from water, and even the ladder symbolism, which might ordinarily indicate that escape is possible, here leads downward to the work pits instead. This barren life fades from Lorca's consciousness as he takes refuge in the pastoral dream. He evokes the memory of Whitman to gratify his own wish for respite from the city's social reality. Witnessing the metallic configuration of New York, he needs a countervision: "What perfect voice will recount the truths of wheat?" This voice belongs to the idealistic shepherd, ostensibly Whitman but subconsciously Lorca himself. Here the hope for fertility can be realized, and what is more, it can be done in supreme innocence ("What angel do you carry, concealed in your cheek?").

However, Lorca's bucolic fantasy recalls other classical scenes where the element of fertility is more ambiguous. The self-love of Narcissus and the ideal love between two shepherds reflect situations of chaste beauty, but they also conceal an underlying sterility. Although pastoral flight furnishes a substitute for the ugliness of real life, it brings with it an erotic factor that complicates the entire range of dream experience. We begin to sense that the darker feelings within Lorca are stirred by specific details in the corrupt city. These are the sexual aspects, having their idealized counterpart in the poet's fantasy. At the same time, his erotic awareness influences various levels of dream fabrication. For example, when he contemplates sexual perversion in reality, the result is a psychological nightmare. Lorca's defense is to imagine the reverse situation, and so he creates a rustic daydream characterized by pure love. But the result is that these two planes conflict and produce a disjointed confusion in the atmosphere of the poem as a whole. Reality and

reverie are intensified beyond the limits of congruity, and we discover Lorca careening mentally from one extreme to the other.
Hence, the symbolism of sterility becomes more than a sociological
judgment: it stands for the inability to deal with reality in any way
except through the empty buffer of fantasy.

The degrees of realism, therefore, are calibrated according to
the gauges of emotion. Lorca's disgust for the naked city produces a
stylistic equivalent in the exaggerated selection of degenerate details. To compensate for reality, he takes gratification in the idealized landscape of dream. But since he knows how fruitless it is to try
to overcome the discrepancy between these two worlds, he lapses
into a nightmarish seesaw balance of both. Lorca's admiration for
Whitman comes from the latter's attempt to create poetry out of
the corrupt chronicle of city events.[2] But when Lorca himself faces
New York, he wonders if he will be able to recount "the terrible
dream of [its] stained anecdotes." He does, of course, although
his own perception is stained with the horror and futility of his
confrontation.

In this light, we can see that Lorca's nightmare has two separate
identities. It is the apprehension of reality, and also the aesthetic
product of the latter. On the other hand, the dream is a means by
which the idealist may escape from this same reality. These differences are illustrated by the theme of love, whose extremes best
represent idealism and decadence. The dreamer rests in nature's
bosom, whereas brazen homosexuals are "sleepless enemies of Love."
Whitman, for example, "dreamed of being a river and sleeping like
a river," thus furnishing a substitute for the ugliness of real life. In
contrast to the nest of degenerates in New York, his dream encour-
aged pure love among refined men. Whitman "sought a nude who
would be like a river, a bull and a dream who would join wheel
and seaweed." That is, the ideal lover will be of tranquil character
in his naked splendor, and the vigor of his masculinity will be tempered by the dream-like quality of Platonic idealism. These attributes of perfect male beauty are, of course, part of the escapist's
insulation against the city's moral deformity.[3] And yet, the fantasy
retains an element of reality in its allusion to the wheel. As an
instrument of society, the wheel will be "joined" to the seaweed,
that is, reconciled to one of nature's manifestations. Thus, the dream
is justified, since it unifies the best of reality with the ideal. Rooted
in real life, the dream is a function of existence, a therapeutic for
its pain. As Lorca explains, agony is the way of the world, but fer-
ment and dream are among life's processes.

The references to the dream of becoming a river may seem

ingenuous, but they are part of a larger water imagery that serves as an escape from the social morass. What is interesting is that water is only mentioned in combined form: as a seashore, riverbank, or pool. In these contexts, water symbolizes the attempt to overcome the cultural and sexual horror of New York. For example, Whitman's search is for a nude who will be as pure as a river. His dream is echoed by the statement that "the sky has beaches in which to avoid life." And when Whitman is accused of homosexuality by perverts, Lorca says, "tainted fingers point to the shores of your dream." The poet's wish, therefore, is that Whitman "sleep on the shores of the Hudson," unmolested by his persecutors. A pastoral nuance is supplied by the allusion to sea algae, at least to the extent that it belongs to nature's verdure.

Standing in contrast to the purity of water is the social contamination of New York. City squalor and tainted sex encroach upon the private mechanisms of evasion. A divine poet is accosted, ideal dreams are soiled, grubby fingers bring sexual disgust to pure love. Gradually, moral repugnance changes into an obsession with filth. Escapism from real corruption begins to take on a sense of persecution. Thus, a number of negative attitudes and interlocking motifs contribute to a slow buildup of terror which will soon be released. Underlying all of this is the fact that the physical and ethical rejection of New York conceals a more instinctive rejection of sexuality. Wherever the poem is sensual, it leaves an ugly taste. Even when Whitman dreams of his love, the latter eats an apple that has "a faint savor of gasoline." I will discuss these physiological experiences later, but the point is that dirt and immorality are linked to sexual horror, just as the motifs of escape (sky, shore, breeze, sleep, cloud) are associated with the water imagery.

We find, therefore, opposite poles of erotic interest arising from the common ground of fantasy-fear. At one end is "old handsome Walt Whitman," a "masculine Adam of blood, a man alone at sea." At the other end are the degenerates, "coming out of the sewers in clusters." These conduits drain into the sea, maintaining in this way an antithetical relationship of impurity-purity similar to the one existing between pervert and poet. Whitman himself is portrayed with idealized traits. His manliness is defined by solitude, and also by the fact that he has no contact with women. This is why he is called Adam, who was infused with life's blood before the creation of Eve, and who lived alone without a woman's love. Whitman's other identity, as a mariner-poet, still keeps him cloaked in the loneliness which protects his male chastity. Another important factor is his tranquil condition. Whitman always appears as a motionless figure, and stands in contrast to the pullulating hordes of homosexuals. The stillness of this physical stance is matched by the quiet dignity of his character, and this calm is so complete that it literally never enters the spatial realm. However, pure motion and space outline every feature of the swarming "crowds shouting with gestures, like cats and serpents," sometimes "grouped in bars," or otherwise "trembling," "whirling," or pouring out of the sewers in clusters.

As we noted, Whitman is isolated by the sea, which acts as an antierotic agent to preserve his innocence. Similarly, the previous dream by the river was also antisexual, because it constituted a solitary, almost narcissistic activity. In other words, sex requires company, and this is why it is depicted by the image of men grouped together near bars and sewers. Even their corruptions take place near water, in "the very dark marsh where they sink young boys." The children's natural instincts are stifled in this scene of still water and eventual stagnation. The participants' comradeship is emphasized by the elements of liquid, darkness, submergence, and enclosure, which all suggest a kind of nutritive security for the group. The atmosphere becomes fetid and tumescent, unhealthy but teeming with life, like a bacterial culture. For a moment we are again with Aleixandre, glimpsing rapidly into a magnified amoebic world. But in this case, the degradation is much more pronounced.

Curiously, the scene gives no indication of barrenness. Its eroticism is festering and alive. The pervasiveness of moisture is clearly meant to imply a certain semifertility or capacity for growth. Elsewhere, the perverts are described as having "swollen flesh," and they are referred to as "mothers of mud." These glandular and maternal characteristics in the homosexuals' physiology differ sharply from the Whitmanesque type of love. Let us compare the image of the submerged boys to its idealized counterpart. Although the setting is again near water, everything else changes: "the sun sings along the navels of the lads who play beneath the bridges." The sterility in these lines is complete. There is no penetration or descent to insure any sense of security or enclosure. Instead, we witness the sun's failure to perform its fecundating role. The sunshine is dry, and it glances along the exterior parts of the body. Regardless of these symbols, the boys' navels are unproductive, and make a mockery of the sun's rays.

Young people of this sort are seen everywhere by Lorca. Sometimes they are innocent boys who might have been victimized and seduced. And sometimes they are the potentially normal lovers of the future, like "the boy who writes a girl's name on his pillow."

Otherwise, they are young workers struggling against industrialism, or youths playing ball under bridges, or the uninitiated, furtively experimenting with the mysteries of sex ("the lad who dresses as a bride in the darkness of the wardrobe"). Although Lorca seems to favor innocent youth and nature over corruption and civilization, both sides align themselves under the same emblem. There is no symbolic or metaphorical difference between them, and they are unconsciously placed under a single perspective. For example, Lorca approves of the scene where "the sun sings along the navels" of young men, but he puts his social disapproval on another scene with the same elements. In the latter, some working youths sing while stripped to the waist, and their class hopelessness is no worse than the sun's futility. Thus, the same ambiguity that we found earlier in connection with sterility recurs here, regardless of whether Lorca favors the situation.

Another example of this unconscious single perspective takes place in the context of water and sexuality. The same admired youths are playing under a bridge, and this spatial inferiority duplicates the scene in the marsh where the boys were submerged. In both cases, the young men enjoy Lorca's conscious sympathy, and therefore they are swept into the same spatial arrangement. On the other hand, this very perspective underlines their weakness and subservience. They appear to be dominated by height and by some force towering over them. This unconscious point of view is exactly like another scene which is strongly condemned by Lorca. Here, groups of homosexuals are "trembling between the legs of motorists." When we remember the previous low-angle view of the men crawling out of sewers, the common element becomes obvious. The spatial disadvantage in all instances is commensurate with their social or moral degradation. Thus, every aspect of Lorca's imagery, from idealized fantasy to ugly reality, is tainted with the suspicion of inner weakness.

When we look for evidence of surrealist technique in the ode to Whitman, we find it in the metaphors that comprise the mythology of eroticism. The same bifocalism which we discovered in the polarity of innocence and vice, in fantasy and reality, and in ambiguous perspectives, operates here too. Images move to opposite extremes, twisting the standard typology into a new shape. For example, even though pastoral classicism is impossible on the banks of the East River, pastoral imagery is used to describe the locale. Yet the sense of underlying failure is unavoidable. The ineffectiveness of Lorca's idealism is faintly perceptible, and contributes to the unhinged feeling of the poem as a whole. This inner weakness shows up in the alternating themes of castration and ambiguous potency, which appear in several instances.

In the allusion to homosexuals "trembling between the legs of motorists," this ambiguity is very clear. The perverts are the only representatives of sexuality and semifertility; they are the only spatially active figures; and yet, in this scene they are reduced to a state of sexual inferiority before the powerful motorists. Their presence also contributes to the psychological imbalance of the poem. The loathesomeness of their physiological fulfillment is the cause of Lorca's spiritual nausea. He experiences a moral revulsion comparable to the potency of the homosexual impact. Therefore, he displaces part of this masculine vigor to an area where it does not belong: the idealized sector. As a result, the beauty of ideal male love is asserted by means of a transformed kind of strength. The blatant violence of perversion is changed into a diaphanous potency in which bulls are made of dreams and buffalo of clouds. Along the East River "the sky emptied out along bridges and rooftops its herd of buffalo, pushed on by the wind." In addition to the dislocation of this image, it is also the opposite of the city's energy. The metaphorical buffalo show neither virility nor forward motion, and the sky appears in a feminine post, its nebulous issue weakly flowing out.

This diminution of sexual force leads to the theme of castration. Lorca uses metaphor to express his cultural and economic censure of urban life. The rawness of this reality is depicted metaphorically as a new form of paganism: immoderate, animalistic, and prone to erotic ritual. Since Lorca is hostile to the city's degeneracy, he deforms its sexuality by means of a symbolic retribution against the modern pagans of civilization. These are the industrial and commercial segments of the population, whose exploitation blights the city and plunges the masses into corruption. Thus we find that "young men struggle with industry, and Jews sell to the river-faun the rose of circumcision." The stereotype of the Jew as a trader and traitor calls attention to the idea of betrayal in the city, that is, the sale of erotic beauty (rose) to the pagan (faun). Industrial society has bred male perverts whose emblem is promiscuity without progeny. In this sense, they are as libidinous as the faun and as symbolically sterile as the castrating circumcision makes them. Nevertheless, the ritual itself has been perverted, for the image of circumcision has its sociology of sex as well as its psychology. In this sense, it means a voluntary self-infliction to curtail sexual activity, the withdrawal of the male from heterosexual communication. As I will show, Whitman himself has been so afflicted. The purpose of

this act is to take the initial step toward ideal love between com-
rades. In other words, circumcision properly means love and beauty,
and not mutilation, although the rite has been betrayed by the
ruin of the social environment. Consequently, the purity of abstinence and ideal love is polluted when heterosexual withdrawal
changes into homosexuality.

Thus, Lorca twists the mythology of the faun into a contemporary metaphor. But he finds one more facet of this erotic myth
to transform—the orgy. Traditionally, the orgiastic potion, whether
wine or aphrodisiac, released the organism from the coils of reality.
Body and mind were liberated from their inhibitions, and with this
freedom came gratification and forgetfulness. But these are the ways
of Dionysius, not Whitman, who, we are reminded, is an "enemy
of the vine." Not only is he always found near water but he is guided
by a disciplined asceticism. He has the "thighs of virginal Apollo,"
whose mythical chastity we have already seen to be paralleled by
the sun's sterility. Nor does his voice have the sensuality or richness
of texture that we found in Dali's "olive-hued" voice. Whitman's is
"like a pillar of ash," whose aridity, greyness of color, and perpen-
dicular strictness all testify to its fruitlessness. And finally, Whitman's "corduroyed shoulders worn thin by the moon" bear the
weight of nocturnal solitude, as well as the weary chastity of Diana's
pale light. Here, then, is the adversary of the vineyard, one who
rarely partakes of the garden's fruit, but when he or his companion
does, it is only to taste an "apple with a faint savor of gasoline."

Nevertheless, in Lorca's modern myth, abstinence is wiser than
dissipation. The excesses of the metropolis have transformed vine-
yards into bars, while in place of the fauns sprawled under trees,
there are perverts "whirling on the platforms of absinthe." Intoxication has become narcosis, just as classical moderation (Apollo) has
turned into barren austerity. While New York's debauchery begins
to cloy, Whitman alone remains apparently untouched, his "luminous and chaste" beard reflecting the virginal moon. Lorca's disgust
with the orgiastic elements of the scene is conveyed by references to
orality. Some men "drink with loathing the waters of prostitution,"
while others "love a man, yet burn their lips in silence." Whereas
the idealist denies the senses, the people he condemns bring forth
"icy saliva." Their libations consist of "drops of filthy death with
bitter venom," and they keep "the gates of the bacchanale" open
despite Lorca's attack. The entire mixture of mouth sensations and
drink is distilled by a surrealist alchemy into an unpalatable acerbic
solution. And this too is a kind of rejection of sexuality. In fact, the
modern orgy is simply a negative oral eroticism. Each sip is an

attempt at oral gratification, and in every case the experience fails. Hence, orality, the most primitive form of sexual activity, ends in impotence, the "icy saliva" that deadens sensation and fluidity.

As I have suggested, Whitman is unconsciously identified with the degenerates, and in this case too, his concealed inadequacy can be glimpsed. Although he is idealized, Lorca's mythology implicates him again, as it did earlier with the faun. This time he is the "enemy of the satyr," and opponent of heterosexuality. We are expected to accept his hostility as the condemnation of erotic technique, rather than as a sign of impotence. Lorca tries to assure us that Whitman is capable of other means of amorous expression besides the denounced sexual form. Thus we have many reminders of his "virile handsomeness," of his being a "lover of bodies under rough cloth," and that one might "moan in the flames" of his "hidden equator." These physical allusions are among the most sensual in the poem, and yet, they are just as ambiguous as the "rose" of circumcision, which later turns into mutilation. In other words, they are the promise of sensuality cut off before fruition. This is why Whitman is described "moaning like a bird whose penis is transfixed by a needle." Regardless of Lorca's idealization, Whitman's hatred of the satyr derives from his own inadequacy. His grief is as obvious as the mutilation is painful, and his moan gives final evidence of the secret lamentation that underlies the apparent praise-singing of the ode. Lorca's poem is an unconscious eulogy of disfigured potency.[4]

Why Whitman must be castrated is self-evident. Lorca does not want to face the fact that a secret compatibility exists between the poet and the perverts who identify with him and point to him as one of their own. Moreover, Whitman's ambivalent position in the ode as a gentle idealist and masculine lover threatens the poem's entire argument. He comes perilously close to the abyss of violence, so characteristic of the homosexuals.[5] For example, what difference is there between "the comrade who would place in your breast the tiny pain of an ignorant leopard," and the man with "flesh made for the lash, the heel or the bite of animal tamers"? There is no difference, except that the first experience belongs to Whitman's life, and the second to a degenerate's. But both are victims, both are subjugated to the passions of animalism, and both relinquish their male role for the passive submission of a woman. Furthermore, Whitman is just as much a part of the ugly social scene as are the condemned perverts. He dreams of escape, of being a river, but his aspirations are fed on "mountains of coal, advertisements, and railroads." And above all, he is recognized by the city's homosexuals as being one of them. This, then, is the same Whitman that Lorca tries to remake in his own idealistic image, even while supplying the proof that denies this image. Lorca's attempt fails, and rather than permit his idol a decisive act of potency, he unconsciously castrates him.

The failure of Whitman to live up to the poem's ideal is the central cause of its surrealist crisis.[6] This moment is climaxed by Lorca's banally didactic summation, but it is redeemed aesthetically by the final atmosphere of terror. What happens is that Lorca is on the brink of discovering Whitman's ambivalence, but he is overcome by vertigo because of the truth, and reels back into the black pit of chaos. Thus, reality and dream merge into the nightmare of surrealism. Time is lost count of and becomes a "breeze that comes sleeping in the branches." Reality spins round Lorca, and parts of nature are hoisted and pulled down like backdrops on a stage. Thus, night turns into an uncanny artifice: "When the moon rises the pulleys will roll and bring down the sky." Lorca himself loses control of his faculties. He expects that "a circle of needles will limit memory"—a motif which echoes the castrating needle that afflicted Whitman. Insight into the homosexual world becomes morbid and paranoiac. Mutilation is recurrent in "scratched out eyes," and the flagellation once executed by "animal" tamers is now performed by the moon, who "whips [the perverts] along the street corners of terror."

Thus, the grey tone of previous scenes merges here with the sterility of death, as bodies "decompose beneath the clock of the cities" and "war passes by weeping with a million grey rats." It is useless to point out the illogic. Only one clock for all the cities? And which cities if the locale is New York? But this is a nightmare about the death of time and memory, the postmortem of a past ideal, the obliterated recollection of a poet-lover. Lorca's bad dream is caused by a vice that exists in every metropolitan area, as his list of cities shows. And hence, a single clock serves them all, because the nature of time is the same everywhere: cyclical, dormant, and ultimately sterile. As Lorca states pithily: "Tomorrow loves will be as rocks, and Time a breeze that comes sleeping in the branches." No better reason for Lorca's fury could be supplied. His angry invective takes on the color of his nightmare, and becomes just as sterile: "Death flows from your eyes and groups grey flowers on the slimy shore." The tight integration of images and themes is again evident here in the elements of beach, moisture, poetry, and futility, all of which have appeared previously in different forms.[7]

In spite of the aesthetic triumph of this surrealist atmosphere, its effect is subdued by Lorca's argumentation. His purpose is eulogistic, and he falls back from the chaos that is brought on by the recognition of Whitman's ambivalence. The nightmare becomes his protection as he gropes dizzily between reality and ideals. What he refuses to see becomes distorted until it no longer makes sense. This critical moment before he regains his balance is the ode's saving grace, from an artistic point of view. But Lorca does recover, represses the nearly remembered insight, and holds firmly to his equilibrium by means of sermon-like statements. He tells us that "life is not noble, or good, or sacred," and that "it is fitting that man not seek his pleasure in the next day's jungle of blood." There are other homilies on tolerance and temperance, and we learn that as long as love is not manifested shamelessly or violently, then humanity may engage in either heterosexual or homosexual relations. As Lorca phrases it, "man may, if he wishes, conduct his desire through a vein of coral or a heavenly nude." These are among the less fortunate lines of the poem, although they are necessary for the poet's sanity. And this reasonable state of mind, complete with repressive mechanisms, is fundamental to Lorca's surrealism. His poetic consciousness remains outside the thematic substance of the ode. In other words, his rational manipulation of symbols is limited, and the symbolic meaning of some themes acquires an ambiguity that escapes the poet's awareness.

There is no doubt that Lorca understood the symbolism of his imagery. Nevertheless, the artistic configuration of these symbols runs deeper in meaning than the original significance intended by Lorca. The best illustration of this occurs in the last strophe, where he successively alternates: his idealization of Whitman, the New York nightmare, and a wish for the arrival of an Arcadian idyll. At the very moment that he denies corporeal traits to Whitman ("soft clay or snow," "disembodied gazelle"), he surrounds the pastoral Hudson banks with sociological chaos: "a dance of walls agitates the meadows and America is submerged in machines and grief." Lorca does not seem to be aware of the contradictions. He wants to think of Whitman as a nonsensual ideal, yet his description is full of physical allusion. He wants to depict America's urban decay, and yet his prayer is that "the strong air of the deepest night remove flowers and letters from the arc where you sleep." He hopes, in other words, that the same city which he rejects will be instrumental in fulfilling his ideals. As stated in the final couplet: "And may a black boy announce to the wealthy whites the arrival of the kingdom of corn harvests." The pastoral dream is glimpsed and retained in symbolic imagery, but the totality of symbols reveals an unconscious irony never intended by Lorca. His wish is to turn a dream into reality, but his poem separates nightmarish reality from dream.

Chapter Six

Biocultural Prehistory
(Lorca)

Thus far, I have shown how Lorca transformed the aseptic garden of dehumanized art into an urban jungle of basic emotions. His interest in aesthetic abstraction in the ode to Dali was exchanged for an impassioned attack against social corruption in the ode to Whitman. This change from an artistic to an ethical orientation was accompanied by a deepening obscurity in his imagery. Whereas the metaphors dealing with aesthetic principles seemed even-tempered and intellectual, those concerned with cultural values were charged with disturbed feelings. Moods and psychological distortion became more evident, and the edges of reality dropped suddenly into nightmare. Nevertheless, the surrealist vision was limited by a fairly traditional framework of logic and references. Language and image were bold and sometimes hermetic, but meaning did not break down into nonsense. Furthermore, the underlying social commentary consisted of an orthodox plea for justice and reform.

When we examine Lorca's third ode, the one addressed to the king of Harlem, we see how completely surrealistic its treatment is. It goes to the roots of New York's social and moral problem by digging into the most elementary layers of culture. Here Lorca finds the irrational sources of human society, the biological drives that unite all races in prehistory, but that also divide them violently in the social stratification of urban life. This biocultural view is, by its very nature, different from realism, and Lorca stresses this by using absurd and chaotic images taken from the primeval world. Thus, the ode proceeds where the georgics of technology stop. It describes the primitive forces in Negro life, which rise to the surface and spill onto

the delicate texture of white civilization. The city's advanced industrialism represses a barbaric essence: the Harlem slum. The latter
erupts despite the repression, and the ensuing conflict of energies is
depicted by a shifting platform of jungle and city images that end
in vertigo. The result for the poem's structure is that it becomes an
amalgam of Afro-Saxon motifs, with allusions to wild animals and
modern artifacts in the same context. Meanwhile, they produce a
psychological tension that grows strained with the expectancy of
death. In all of this, the metropolitan idiom remains wordless and
strident, without coherence.

Lorca's lament for the black man's subjugation has, at certain
moments, the appearance of a social commentary.[1] But its occasional
rhetoric is outweighed by its surrealist metaphors. This does not
mean that the ode is valid only to the extent that it can make moods
and images, as in Aleixandre's poetry. However, were it not for the
metaphorical treatment of its central myth, its social attitude would
at best be commonplace by today's standards. This myth concerns
racial purity and innocence, and it is elaborated by an imagery that
corresponds to it in primitivism.[2] The role of the social themes is to
give the myth contemporary relevance, but this only supplements
the effect of the images. As a result, the ode's main achievement is
found in the psychological impact of its metaphors, although the
latter's full significance can only be understood in relation to the
social question.

The issue, then, is that modern culture has destroyed the native
innocence of the Negro. This idea is expressed by a concrete imagery
that portrays white civilization as the purveyor of contamination.
American women are loud, mercenary, and profligate, and they
"carry babies and coins in their wombs." Others are ostentatious
and giddy, like "trembling little Jewesses filled with bubbles." The
motifs of money and liquor show the depth of corruption, even to
its prenatal form. Similarly, white men drink "whiskey of silver," an
allusion to the debauchery under attack by Lorca. This is the original sin of the industrial world, whose tempting fruit is preferred to
the Negro. Thus, we find "the blond vendor of aguardiente, and all
the friends of apples and sand," engaged in economic and moral
debasement. Their women bear within them the seeds of an evil
technical culture, while they themselves form a ruling caste bent on
sterile pleasure ("apples and sand"). These are the people who have
exploited "the waiters and cooks and those whose tongues clean the
wounds of millionaires." Consequently, Lorca condemns them,
urging that the solution must be "to beat with closed fists," "to kill
the blond vendor."

The racial exploitation just described is aided by the obvious condition of skin color. But beneath this surface reality, there are more primal motives of color consciousness. It is not enough to identify the vendor as white, for there are all degrees of whiteness. Hence, he is identified as a blond, the most perfect racial type of his group. By doing this, Lorca sets a biocultural pattern that is followed throughout the ode. He converts the sociological approach to the interracial problem into a depth analysis of the psychology of race. In this scheme, both blacks and whites exhibit a range of skin shades that begin at the borderline of color and diverge to their respective extremes. Thus, blondness and jet blackness exemplify the purity of the two races. At the same time, they converge toward a midpoint: the mulatto. But the Negro can never become white, despite the fact that the only culture he knows is a white one. It is this factor which works behind the mechanics of economic injustice to separate the races.

Cultural conflict, therefore, has its roots in biology, which in turn conditions a number of mental attitudes. One of these is the anguish of living in a physiological trap. The Negro strains to be released from his color, but manages only to increase his awareness of the barrier. As Lorca puts it, "the mulattoes stretched gum, anxious to reach the white torso." In their desire to overcome the limits of race, mulattoes have become evolutionary contortionists. The biological permanence of their skin prohibits any alteration in the development of race differences. Nevertheless, the emotional impetus to change is there. Thus, Lorca expresses this desire in terms of basic facts of evolution. He sees that New York rests on a presociological principle which involves physical and psychological necessity. It functions according to a system of racial communications whose primary signal is a man's complexion. Even if the disadvantaged Negro has evolved toward a lighter skin color, he still has not passed over the line. This is the only implication of the ode: that the present social relationship between blacks and whites contains a biocultural structure. The inaccuracies of this theory might well be pointed out by anthropologists, although Lorca did not intend to suggest any extensive commentary on the problem.[3]

The first cultural criterion that we find, consequently, is the biology of race. The blond vendor reminds us that he is the product of an indelible hereditary pigmentation. But he also introduces a second criterion for understanding the meaning of civilization, namely, its corruption of nature's life sources. He plays the role of a seducer by selling alcohol to the innocent, thereby stimulating them artificially beyond the limits of natural intoxication. What was once a healthy form of pagan revel turns into a metropolitan madness of drunkards and bums. Here, all men are victims, regardless of race, as their bodily vigor is sapped by alcoholism. Far from exalting the spirit, the drunkenness of New York's white culture degrades it. And yet, if the fault is anyone's, it is the white man's, as represented by the blond vendor. This is where Lorca's vision differs from the Romantic notion of the noble savage. His idea is that social evils are a part of white civilization, that the corruptors of men are white. Hence, he is not concerned with Man's loss of rustic simplicity, but with the black man's loss of innocence in an alien culture. While the white man may have fallen into decadence in comparison to some earlier paradise, he did so on his own self-destructive initiative. The Negro, however, has not only been transplanted from an African culture, but he has been further degraded by the customs of a different racial milieu.[4]

This fall from grace is described by metaphors that show nature being undermined by artificial forces. New York's corruptive sophistication lurks behind the discontinuance of natural processes. The denaturation of nature is intended to parallel the Negro's gradually stiffening spontaneity. For example, his loss of a pristine cultural life is expressed as: "the beetles drunk on anisette forgot the village moss." This means that the normal lethargy of the idyllic past is forgotten in the current drunkenness of the city. The abnormal association of insect life and alcohol reflects the Negro's misplaced life in New York. Both he and the beetle have forgotten their innocent original state, and have succumbed to the lure of the blond vendor. In general, the link between the Negro and wild life is one of the ode's most vivid motifs. Some of these allusions testify to the choked and petrified vitality of nature, again corresponding to the Negro's fate. References to "drowned wasps" and "ivory salamanders" reduce reality to unnatural concrete states. In addition, they approximate the harsh logic of the metropolis: money, silver, monocle. That is, the disruption of natural life has its counterpart in the corruption of white culture as revealed in its social comforts. On the other hand, the Negro is culturally isolated from this medium into which he has been transplanted. His roots are as artificial as the alcoholic stimulant given him to drink. Even his clothes are a poor imitation of an alien way of life, and they produce "a false sadness of faded gloves and chemical roses."

In themselves, Lorca's concepts of alienation and natural life are inaccurate, and yet they contain much truth. What makes the ode unusual is that their sociological value becomes visible through surrealistic methods. The cultural standards that we have discussed are too profound to be judged by moral and economic criteria. They go straight to the organic life of New York bioculturalism.[5] Lorca describes the functions of an organism, giving a biological diagnosis by means of metaphor. Thus, he analyzes the white city in terms of its people's reproductive system. The American girl whose womb spawns coins as well as babies is a perfect biocultural synthesis of New York life. This urological vision is one of Lorca's best surrealist innovations. It not only adds a trace of cold scientism to the image, but it dehumanizes life in keeping with the denaturation theme already mentioned.

In contrast to the clinical analysis of white sterility is the method of demonstrating the Negro's superior primitivity. This is done by characterizing Harlem as an independent subculture within a deficient civilization. Harlem is a separate offshoot, but one whose roots feed back into the white metropolis that poisons it. She retains her original racial constitution, but receives nourishment that causes some monstrous changes in her makeup. For example, one can hear the "noise coming across tree trunks and elevators," from wood to metal, from the natural jungle to the asphalt one. Furthermore, automobiles in the neighborhood are "covered with teeth" like mechanical animals, a clear reference to the grillwork on the front of cars that might menace pedestrians like the frontal attacks of a wild beast. Primitive and modern worlds are so fused that it is hard to tell which is more barbaric. Lorca suggests that the colored passersby harken back to their African forebears, who climbed trees instead of ascending by elevators, and, although this is hardly a realistic concept of Negro history, we see even now that their king recalls a predawn era as he "beats the rumps of the monkeys" with his kitchen spoon.

Hence the poet's lament over "disguised Harlem," the fact that her true cultural structure has been masked over and hidden by foreign strains. This does not imply that Lorca prefers Africanism or barbarism. It does mean that the infiltration of civilized elements into the native folkways of Negro life has worked adversely. The superimposition of a modern veneer on an essentially naive group has had some tragic effects. This is why her vitality is likened to a chemical rose, for her life is as artificial as her newly learned sadness. It is not natural for the Negro to wear a melancholy face, and this "false sadness of faded gloves" belongs to the same motif of disguise and metamorphosis. Since the Negro has inadequately assimilated the habits of his new environment, he seems to be masquerading, or at least imitating the wrong models. Moreover, his essential characteristics are in danger of suppression. Harlem is a district "menaced by a mob of headless suits." In other words, Negro identity is threatened by a larger group of faceless people who rule without heads and who have no substance beneath the outer appearance of their clothing.

These ideas have a great bearing on Lorca's surrealism. He views the white city as fundamentally sterile, its women showing only a metallic fruitfulness, and its men living as mere decapitated mannequins. These images are in the mainstream of surrealist techniques in Spain, although in Lorca alone do they embody so many social connotations. Furthermore, they help convert the atmosphere of the setting. Since the white urban dwellers suffer from this lack of vitality, their milieu is easily turned into a dream state. Lorca sees everything through "grey layers," and the animalistic automobiles "float" in this colorless stratification. The scene deforms its realistic details —"dead horses and tiny crimes"—by exaggerating and muting them at the same time. Thus, the muffled quality of the nightmare is achieved without detriment to the abrupt breakthrough of violence and chaos.

The Harlem slum itself is the locale for the shifting levels of meaning that support the main surrealist construction of the ode. These levels extend from their point of contact with white society, down to the Negro's mythic ancestral experience. As a result, the theme of metamorphosis becomes prominent, as forms reappear on different planes with new attributes. Lorca's intention throughout is to show the injustice of the Negro's cultural uprooting. Thus we find that Harlem's insect life has come under the benumbing spell of alcoholism, and that the king is transformed into a cook with a ladle for a sceptre. The days of Negro prehistory are recalled by the allusion to the crocodile, which in former times was left unmolested in the swamps (a motif which I will discuss shortly). Now, however, the crocodile is subjected to an eye-gouging at the hands of a king whose ancestors would have allowed it to sleep. This victimization by a figure of authority symbolizes the Negro's own humiliation by the white populace. The king is really a "prisoner with a janitor's suit," and the anguish of his "oppressed eyes" is socially derived. Thus, the crocodile and the Negro are identified, with the latter coming to resent his condition. Even the disfiguring of the reptile is symbolic, assuming a form of self-punishment as the king recognizes his past origins and strikes out against his present subjection.

As the themes become intertwined and confused, the fallacy of acculturation becomes increasingly clear. The Negro belongs to another culture, and can never be assimilated into the white man's civilization. This idea is so obviously wrong that no rational argument is made for it in the ode. Let us also bear in mind that the white man's understanding of the Negro was minimal in 1929. Nevertheless, this point is made intuitively, and what interests us is the fact that it is made with a series of chaotic and senseless images. An identification is sought between the natural environment and the Negro's biological heritage. These are pitted against the white culture that has transformed them. Thus, the violence done to nature and the Negro are alluded to by figures of repression, splitting action, and flaming light. They suggest the folly of believing that Negro life is successfully absorbed into the larger culture. For example, the physical setting contains the latent power that the Negro himself conceals beneath his black skin. Fire lays "dormant in flint-rock," and an "impassable wall" challenges the Negro's strength. His blood grows turbulent with repression, and is ready to burst into view. Thus, the blackness of night and of man's complexion are equated, and caused to be split by light and passion. This is where the theme of breakage occurs. In nature, "the night had a cleft" through which the starlight appears as "ivory salamanders." And in Harlem, men who are halted by the wall seek "its crevice in order to find the infinite mask." In other words, the Negroes attempt to penetrate the cultural barrier in the hope of finding some kind of redemption. But Lorca is saying that salvation by acculturation is a fallacy. To enter the alien city culture is to put on a mask, even though it has the semblance of infinite freedom. Negro destiny lies elsewhere, determined in part by its lost cultural heritage. Therefore, warns Lorca, the present sham of the Negro's life in the metropolis will be exposed. He warns that "the marrow of the forest will penetrate the fissures, to leave on your flesh a light trace of eclipse." That is, the ultimate power of the jungle will be revealed, and the real meaning of racial history will become known in Harlem.

In the above imagery, the concept of greatest significance is the idea of uncontainable energy that bursts the vessel that holds it. The primal energy is ultimately derived from the jungle experience of Negro ancestry. It is also intimately related to the ode's central preoccupation: the blood symbol. In a poem about the Negro's liberation, it is easy to see why his blood would play an important role. What is difficult to understand is why the physical properties of blood are given such prominence. For example, Lorca blackens the associations around the color of blood by adding deeper hues to its redness. He also links the viscosity to the thick consistency of other natural elements, like black slime. And in one stanza he describes blood as being "made of pressed esparto grass, the nectars of

subterraneans." In all of these references, the most elemental qualities of organic life are found to share a common basis. At the lowest
level of primitive existence, this meeting point of vital fluids represents the substratum of living reality.

Lorca's intention, it would seem, is to evoke the earliest moments
in the history of biological life. The Negro's blood is likened to the
sap of "pressed esparto grass" in the primitive forest. Thus, his
ancient blood heritage is established in terms of jungle vegetation.
Blood is "the nectars of subterraneans," the precious liquid that
quickens the instinctive life impulse of plants and animals. The sap
of life lingers underground in dank sweetness, oozing forth from the
thick, fertile mud, or dripping like nectar when the grass is crushed.
This takes place at the dawn of the evolutionary process, where there
is no clear distinction among awakening physiologies. Further up
the scale, human blood is associated with the sap of trees, the
marrow that will "penetrate the fissures, to leave on your flesh a light
trace of eclipse." Man's growth, like a plant's, is compelled by the
surging of bodily fluids within. His body is a tree trunk, his veins
are fibers, his blood, sap. This common origin with plant life is even
visible in the "chlorophyl of blond women," a reference to the
chemistry of surface color.

Once the physiological analogy is made, Lorca tries to forge the
link between blood and culture. He does this by means of the notion
of biological eclipse. The metaphor of the eclipse describes the dark
rush of blood that breaks through the Negro's artificial condition in
Harlem.[6] Thus, it symbolically represents the overshadowing of
modern civilization. The idea that the jungle's marrow will penetrate the fissures of the cultural wall indicates that instinct will
triumph over urbanism. It leaves "a light trace of eclipse" on the
Negro's flesh, the appearance of instinctive tendencies on the social
veneer. In other words, the racial energy of the black man will dominate. It is his "blood that comes . . . to burn the chlorophyl of the
blond woman," and his impulses that demand release. Thus, when
the jungle marrow—his own blood—reaches the surface of his skin,
the mark left on his flesh is truly an eclipse of culture. It is the
fading of a glove, the congealing of stars into salamanders, the
"drowned wasps" of a battery gone dead. This phenomenon of
shadowy eclipse proves to be appropriate, since it suits the darkness
of skin, mood, and jungle that are evoked by the Harlem king.

Nevertheless, the triumph of primitive forces is not fully
assured. The repression exercised by New York's metropolitanism
has been quite effective, and this is the cause of Lorca's lament.
Consequently, he uses the eclipse metaphor in a reversible role.

Interchangeable with the Negro's racial vitality is his emotional congestion. He has a reservoir of feelings which are dammed up without an outlet. His blood is "trembling inside the dark eclipse," the result of the anguish brought about by social oppression. Thus, while his blood does pose the threat of eruption, it is now only a "deaf and dumb, crimson violence within the penumbra." Its intensity grows violent for lack of release, but it is repressed to the point of docility ("trembling," "deaf and dumb"). Hence the reversibility of the eclipse image. The latter stands for both aggression and submission, an overshadowing of either civilization or of the Negro's own strength. When the king of Harlem is subjected to the humiliating occupation of janitor, he lives under a cultural shadow which itself is the penumbra of the deeper obscurity of his hidden blood.

Since Lorca dedicates a substantial middle section of four stanzas to the blood theme, it is not surprising that still other aspects of the eclipse are evident. The use of light, for instance, is manipulated for the purpose of showing just this reversibility of the blood's strength and weakness. The ambiguity is expressed in an allusion to Negroes "crying confusedly among umbrellas and golden suns." We have already seen what the denaturation of the natural world accomplishes in the poem, and this includes the motif of light-darkness. Here, the Negro vacillates between light and shadow, just as nature transforms its illumination and energy: stars-salamanders, drowned wasps-battery. Even the conventional surface brilliance of the moon turns into the "asbestos" quality of rough porousness, while the "celestial moon" itself appears with the pincers of Cancer.

Most important is the contribution made by the eclipse motif toward understanding Negro freedom. This is done by continuing the cultural mythology which was discussed earlier. The Negro is advised to seek "the tatooed sun that descends along the river, bellowing, followed by alligators." This is the black man's sun, darkened by the emblematic tattoos that are the signs of primitive group affirmation. In addition to this cultural trait, the sun is endowed with an animal characteristic which is seemingly appropriate to the jungle environment. Its nativist regression is as suitable to the Negro's mythic past as the denatured asbestos moon is to his present environment. Thus, the sun retains an elementary force that is capable of freeing him from the illusions of civilization. It does not hold forth the prospects of imagination and intellect, and, in fact, it "slides through the forests sure of not encountering a nymph." In other words, the sun's energy has a destructive meaning in the Negro mythos. Far from the stimulating idyllic fantasies, the sun "destroys numbers and has never come across a dream." It represents a sobering view of metropolitan society, and shows a darkened face that corresponds to the dark blood of the Negro. The sun adopts the tatoo ritual of an elementary culture, and it also suffers an eclipse of its productivity. Its tribal markings have dimmed its shining face, and its clarity is obscured by the symbols of the modern world: "Forgetfulness was expressed by three inkdrops on the monocle." Thus, the sun stands midway between two civilizations, marred by the artifice of today's culture, and obscurely lighting the path back to Negro prehistory.[7]

These, then, are the functions of the eclipse image. In its biological role, it is bound up with racial evolution (blood). Its social aspect reveals the barren artifice of contemporary New York (monocle). And its mythic vision conceives of the Negro's return to cultural grace. Here the "great central sun" illuminates the road to salvation which the Negro is urged to seek. Since he is deprived of tranquility even by the natural elements, he must escape his current environment. The "wooden south wind, oblique in the black slime" wreaks damage indiscriminately on man and his manufactures: it "spits at broken boats and drives nails into one's shoulders." Moreover, it randomly mixes "fangs, sunflowers, alphabets," sweeping away the cultural rubble of past and present life. The wind reminds us of nature's uprooted state, a condition in sympathy with the Negro's alienation. Against the wide expanse of nature, the Negro's biological repression is boldly stated: "Blood has no doors in your night, lying face up. There is no blush. Furious blood beneath the skin, alive in the dagger's spine and in the bosom of the landscapes." With the increased stifling of racial vitality, the underground surge of Negro character becomes more concentrated. Its violence, therefore, is in direct relationship to the natural world from which it originated.

Lorca solves the problem of expressing this irrational concept by the use of surrealist diction. As we will see in the chapter on Alberti, this diction consists of the borrowing of terms from an altogether different realm. In this case, the realm of chemistry supplies the vocabulary, and we find that blood can "oxidize the trade wind," "dissolve butterflies," and "burn chlorophyll." These chemical properties are not inherent in blood, but are modeled on the processes of deterioration existing in nature. Furthermore, the suppressed flow of blood has occurred underground, "in the bosom of the landscapes." But instead of being a sweet source of life, the blood becomes the "nectars of subterraneans," acid and corrosive substances that burn, rust, puncture, and rip the life around them. The long suffocation of the Negro's vitality finally causes it to turn against nature and consume her. The inner pressure is now too much, and it poisons the blood by perverting its life-giving powers. Now, the attack on nature is total. Beginning with the "tanks of polluted water" that arrive at the king of Harlem's dwelling, the infection spreads. Little boys "with a flush of stained frenzy" imitate the eye-gouging scene as they "crush little squirrels." Nature retaliates as the wind "breaks the veins of the dancers," and the mutual acts of mutilation continue until even the future is affected. Here, the king's death is predicted: "bristling flowers murder our Moses, almost in the bulrushes of heaven."

The confusion of unnatural states is everywhere: oozing trees and synthetic roses, pincered moons and decomposed butterflies, crushed stalks and broken veins. This is nature's nightmare, just as the Negro's eclipse is part of Harlem's surrealist dream. Natural monstrosities are made commensurate with the enormity of the cultural crime committed in New York. And at bottom is the suggestion that the only expiation possible is by contaminating nature to the same extent that the Negro's racial energy has been vitiated. It is too late to dream of returning to the primeval innocence of evolution's dawn. Nor can the mulatto "reach the white torso." What is necessary is the release of pent-up, poisoned emotions, even if the result means destruction. After all, this has been the effect of civilized life on the black man. As Lorca states it, "the woodcutter does not know when the clamorous trees that he cuts expire." In other words, the white culprit has systematically decimated the black forest without regard to feeling or consequence. And in this image the ode's entire biocultural theme is metaphorically stated. Here is the white man who has cut down life for his own convenience; and here are the Negroes, whose tissue and organs have evolved from primitive roots, stems, and trunks of the black forest. The phrase "clamorous trees" makes the message graphic and suggests the evolutionary line from plant to animal life. Now it is time to repay civilization with similar violence, and the event will take place under the shadow of this evolution. Thus, the poet counsels the Negroes to "wait for your king beneath the vegetal shade, until hemlock and thistle and nettle bring down the final roofs." With this prophecy, the vision of a racial victory over culture is complete.

The surrealist techniques that develop the biocultural theme—also surrealist, as is seen in the chapter on Dali—are extremely effective. Most notable is the enormous sense of space and motion in the poem. It is as if the shut doors and constricted arteries of Negro life have somehow exaggerated the value of air. Thus, when the explosion occurs, it is with a manic lust for space. This spatial dimension becomes the framework of the Harlem nightmare, whose themes are paranoia and escape. But before discussing the nightmare, we must remember what kind of reality is causing the fear. The peculiar feature of Negro life is the alienation of the self from its concrete environment. This is depicted by means of images based on inert objects that have a special effect on the alienated mind. For example, most such objects remain beyond the perimeter of normal emotional response. They are perceived, but they rarely involve us in any affective experience. However, since the Negro is psychologically estranged from his reality, commonplace objects evoke feelings far beyond their usual limits. We have already mentioned some of these: the storage battery, the spoon, the elevators. All were invested with the uneasy and dislocated mood of the scene. The most important example is the "insomnia of the washstands," which alludes to the dripping faucets that cause sleeplessness.

What is strange about this image is its reversible condition. Its metaphorical meaning is that the dripping washstands cause insomnia. And yet its direct meaning, qua concrete object, is that the washstands themselves are sleepless. This second meaning is entirely in keeping with the Negro's nightmare reality, where neutral objects may acquire human or animate traits. As I indicated in the chapter on Solana, to attribute animate qualities in this way constitutes paranoiac activity. Indeed, the full context of this insomniac image reveals how deep the illusion of persecution is:

> The blood is coming ... to moan at the feet of the beds before the insomnia of the washstands, and crash into a dawn of tobacco and high yellow.

Nowhere is a human presence alluded to; and yet, the ensemble of inert objects creates an emotional atmosphere for itself that belongs more properly to the haunted Negro.

Similarly, the sense of space plays an important role in the feeling of persecution. It is used as a psychological counterpart to the need for escape from the nightmarish scene. Thus, the blood just alluded to comes "along the housetops and roofs, everywhere." Or else, we find "roses fleeing along the edges of the final curves of the air." This sense of openness helps to allay the persecutory fears, and is aided by the very motion of the objects. The geometry of movement is irregular, occurring on the different levels. There is a feeling of urgency to move in every direction: "One must flee, flee along the street corners, and lock oneself in on the upper floors." People search "along the streets or in the angles of saltpeter." This precision in the spatial setting is offset by the grey vagueness of the situation; both correspond to the ill-defined yet acute terror of the Harlem hallucination.

Sometimes the escape has a fantastic quality, like one of Chagall's flights over houses or to the moon. Curves traced in the air describe arcs from earth to heaven, and lead to disturbing scenes: "Medullas and corollas on the clouds compose a desert of stems without a single rose." Thus, the shadow of Harlem life is never cast off completely. Its sterile existence is summarized in this image by the desert of stems, which makes escape a futile act. The Negro's nightmare world is now provided with a vivid cosmology. As other motifs of barrenness recur, we recognize the paradox of his volcanic but fruitless energy. Blood no longer symbolizes life, for it "looks along a thousand paths for flour-covered deaths and ashes of spikenard." Instead, reality is a desert located anywhere in space: in New York, on a cloud, or in the mind—hence the "thousand paths," the obsession of moving space which extends from street to sky as a defense mechanism against fear.

Thus we return to the nightmare's essence: paranoia and escape. We are kept awake by the dripping of the sink, and yet the sink itself is considered an insomniac. We hear a moaning of blood at the foot of the bed, but it is our own racial captivity that torments us. A dream is dashed to pieces in a "dawn of tobacco and high yellow," because nicotine and the desire to alter one's racial condition are mere evasions of reality. All of these cases demonstrate how a subjective state of mind is projected upon a neutral environment. The Negro's fear and despair help him to imagine that he sees in objects what he is unwilling to face in himself. But this method does not work, and so he needs to escape. The nightmarish mood is due partly to his flight and to the erosion of his mental security. His blood finds "rigid skies slanting down, where colonies of planets roll along the beaches with the abandoned objects." Here, too, he projects his sense of isolation upon the empty beach. In his fantasy, the Harlem king reaches to the planets, but he also imagines an abandoned beach where he may find solace through identification. His logical disintegration is complete, and he evokes disorder in every moment of his racial experience. Whether in escapism or urban reality, the exact mixture of desolation and psychosis is used to complete the surrealist nightmare.

Chapter Seven

From Bioculturalism to Critical Paranoia
(Dali)

The biocultural vision in Lorca's surrealism is just a brief intuition
when compared to the biological prehistory of Salvador Dali. His
paintings are a rich compendium of myths whose twisted roots lead
down to the forgotten subsoil of organic life experience. This complex mythology is partly reproduced in literary form by his novel
Hidden Faces.[1] Here, as well as in other prose writings, the painter
becomes a more intelligible practitioner of the surrealist mode and
provides the basis for a wider theoretical understanding of his
paintings.

   Hidden Faces is a slow novel written in baroque prose. Its intellectual position is ambiguous, due to the odd mixture of reality
and myth in its narrative. But there are two fundamental myths,
transplanted from the paintings, that give Dali's overall work unity.
One concerns totemism and the intuited bond that relates plant and
animal life with human existence. Closely linked to this myth are the
resultant insights into the evolutionary process. Thus, the novel contains scenes with perceptions of instantaneous duration that lay bare
the "anamorphs" of a living being. The second myth elaborates the
notion of death and regeneration. This is done by means of a dialectical association with totemism. I will discuss the meaning of these
concepts shortly, but what is important to recognize now is that the
ideological themes of *Hidden Faces* receive mythical adumbrations.
For example, at the novel's conclusion, the young American couple
stands at the beginning of a new life cycle, like a modern Adam
and Eve. This cycle represents man's evolution toward progessively
more sophisticated cultural states. Mechanized civilization is the

final stage in this development, but it is also the instrumental factor in man's death. War turns into a destructive fertility rite from which a new species vigorously arises. Furthermore, the masks of certain social ceremonies are torn away, exposing the real faces of the performers. And yet, this final unmasking is an exposure of naked flesh, the revelation of sincerity and even of innocence. Hence, the novel ends with a new Adam and Eve, who recommence the cycle of life.

All of these themes are controlled by the two basic myths already mentioned. In one sense, a woman's "expectant figure resembled that of a chimera, a celestial Madonna's face attached to the equivocal, full-curved and half-animal body of a sphinx" (211). The description is made in a dimly lighted room, where shadow and gloom permit Dali's fantastic imagination to modify at will the original contours of the woman's shape. It turns out that his will is to distort the figures into a totemic image of a sphinx. Nevertheless, these features are not metaphorical details invented in order to execute a chimerical portrait. They are subordinate to the ideological aspects of Dali's mythic truth. The woman is realistically reported to us by a mentality that is abnormally aware. In this hyperconscious state, sudden flashes of intuition seem to illuminate certain hidden truths. One of these truths is the arcane reality of totemic identification.

Dali's purpose is to bring to the surface the subliminal truths of a tradition no longer remembered. His technique of disfiguration does not deface what is visible as much as it actualizes what is invisible. Since ordinary perspectives yield the usual representations of existence, a distorted lens will bring into focus the inconspicuous and, hence, usually ignored aspects of that same existence. For example, when one character, seated with guests at dinner, uses for a lens the concave and convex surfaces of the silverware, he gains a hypnotic insight into the process of evolution. The faces of his friends become

> unrecognizable, while reassuming by virtue of the fortuitous metamorphoses of their rapid deformations . . . the most striking resemblances with the vanished personalities of their ancestors, mercilessly caricatured in the polychrome images . . . (24).

Thus we find that Dali's images are both simplistic, in that they make unnoticed features stand out, and also abstruse, due to their intellectual symbolism. In this case, the symbolic concept is that of ancestral visitations, with its implication of perpetuated guilt. Dali's preoccupation here with primitivism and atavistic tendencies is part of the entire biological orientation found in his paintings. The novel form merely makes it more explicit. Using an elite dinner party as the scene, Dali exposes the guests' momentary regressions with deliberate irony. Going further, he suggests that their faces are no more than conventional surfaces that for the most part conceal an ugliness which civilized man had supposedly discarded eons ago. The faces are "caught in the ferocious meshes of anamorphosis, twisting, curling, extending, lengthening, and transforming their lips into snouts, stretching their jaws, compressing their skulls, and flattening their noses to the farthest heraldic and totemic vestiges of their own animality." Although not a moral judgment, the passage alludes to man's false veneer and to the fact that his bestial nature is seldom repressible. The glimpse of truth is a "demonic flash," an interval in which one sees "the dazzling teeth of a jackal in the divine face of an angel, and the stupid eye of a chimpanzee would gleam savagely in the serene face of the philosopher" (24–25).

Since the narration unfolds in the shadow of World War II, the humorous teratism of Dali's early paintings acquires a sobering cast. The novel points out that during times of stress, such as war, a kind of animality erupts in human behavior. Primitive inclinations presumably lost in the long evolutionary march turn out to be no less than suppressed qualities of human nature, too inherent not to manifest themselves under unfavorable conditions. Man's social role, so admirably civilized when not tested by tension, proves at critical points to be a flimsy mask behind which lurk characteristics that epitomize the physiology and behavior of lesser animals. Dali's totemism, therefore, reveals that the refinements of the species and the advances of a technical civilization are merely dominant genetic traits in human beings and society. This confirms, at the same time, the existence of baser traits in man and culture which persist in recessive form.

But there is something beyond the perpetuation of a bestial heritage with its attendant moral blemishes. Dali's biological analysis of existence also attempts to reveal a kind of consubstantial bond that unifies all forms of life. He suggests that the evolution of awareness begins at the most minimal level of unconscious mineral states and viable organic matter. From there it extends to the protoplasmic complexities of higher vegetation, and thence up the zoological scale. At one critical stage, there is a vacillation at the nebulous frontier where animal life differentiates itself from botanical growth and emerges from the latter. The intuitive affirmation of this common origin is, of course, present in the vast Occidental mythology about men who assume the forms of flora and fauna. Several motifs in *Hidden Faces* express the same idea, as in the episode where the heroine stretches her legs, and the knee bones crack in unison with the logs crackling in the fireplace. And again, we read that "the Count is the living incarnation of one of those rare phenomena of the soil that elude the skill and the resources of agronomy—a soil molded of earth and blood of an untraceable source, a magic clay of which the spirit of our native land is formed" (3).

It is not coincidental that the heraldic escutcheon of the hero's household is a tree-woman. This emblem illustrates Dali's idea graphically, for it is an elaborate fusion of branches and limbs, trunk and torso, with a woman's face in the center of the foliage. But these allusions to man's phytogenic nature are also the basis for aberrations in the sensibility of the novel. Thus, Dali's stylistic extravagance is determined by this theme, and everywhere we see references to insects, rocks, vegetal formations, viscous substances, and other protomorphic varieties of life. Even in the novel's eroticism, its decadent tradition is perverted by the preevolutionary identity of life:

> In the place which the strip of cork had left bare in the middle of the tree trunk now appeared a kind of delicate skin—silky, tender, sensitive, and almost human, not only because of its color which was exactly that of fresh blood but because these trees stripped of their costume of cork strikingly suggest the bodies of naked women with their arms raised to the sky in the noblest attitudes, and by their bold lines and the smoothness of the rounded reliefs of their trunks they imitate the most divinely and ideally flayed anatomies in the world of sense perception, while yet they have their deep roots in the earth. The mere presence of a naked cork oak in a landscape suffices to fill the evening with its grace (407–8).

Thus, the most morbid elements of fin-de-siècle art are here transformed to suit the primal fantasies of phylogenic sexuality. This follows the general pattern of reaction against post-symbolism, in which the subjective aspects of descriptive sentimentalism are objectified. Here, the perception of an erotic mood follows tradition in its analysis of violence and perversion. But the frame of reference is uniquely Dali's, whose personal obsession with sex is projected outward in a detached form. Nevertheless, we can reconstruct the metaphorical relationships on the basis of his paranoiac reaction. This surrealist technique will be discussed in detail later, but it is evident already that the comparison of trees and women requires a certain projection of disturbed reactions. Dali willfully imagines that feminine curves are found on trees because he wants the environment to respond to his obsession. In any case, the botanical analogy follows the biocultural method of describing man's evolution.

Atavistic tendencies are shown not only by metaphor and lens-studies of faces but by cultural phenomena as well. One of these is war, which Dali depicts as a revelation of basic truths. War can be an experience of the most fundamental reality—the struggle for survival—or of great fantasy. It is destructive in its pitiless removal of the adornments accumulated by civilization since primitive times. But it is also intellectually constructive in that it forces man to face those adornments for what they are—disguises. Everything becomes a simple case of black or white for the aviator portrayed in this novel. During the moment of violence, his abstract thinking ceases and his consciousness is limited to the immediacies of tangible reality. In terms of life's evolutionary process, this mental confinement constitutes an atavism. Just as war is a manifestation of cultural regression, so too is the mentality required for this state of violence a return to animal perception. The aviator's responses become instinctual, and he is more aware of his physical presence and of the sensorial phenomena around him. Never does he transpose his experiences into abstractions.

The aviator's own account of what happens to him when he flies is indicative of the pure biologism of his situation. He declares that the important thing is "to feel yourself become once more a drop of albumen, of instinctive and vulnerable life in the center of a mica shell in the middle of the sky! Instead of thinking, your brain functions; the systole and diastole of your heart, the chemical combustions of your liquids nourish the wings of your plane . . ." (136). This odd reversal of roles shows how drastic the view of reality is. The fighter pilot sees himself as a vulnerable fetus instead of as an aggressor. He is a passive, instinctive organism back in his shell—a fragile womb where he feels secure enough to wage his war on culture. His regression, therefore, is ambivalent, for he retains enough of his acting role to be the nucleus of his protective egg. That is, he is the one to provide nourishment to the womb that envelops him, rather than the other way round. And at the same time, he is relieved of responsibility by reverting to an organism that functions without self-awareness.

As we read more of the account, we understand the purpose of Dali's bioculturalism in his surrealist aesthetic. He has split his vision in half, giving a genuinely biological analysis of contemporary life, and saying that this analysis belongs to the techniques invented by that same contemporary life. Therefore, the analysis is as weak as the sophisticated mind that conceived it. Nevertheless, Dali is the author, and he cannot attack his own creation. Consequently, he uses his aviator to express this anti-intellectual conviction. The pilot represents the image of Dali's split vision. On the one hand, he illustrates the biocultural analysis by regressing to the evolutionary stage of egg albumen. And on the other, he flatly affirms this regression over contemporary forms of culture. He claims that in the plane "you feel really yourself, from deep inside your viscera to the tips of your nails—you are the eyes and entrails of your plane, and then there is no more Paris, no more surrealism, no more anguish, do you hear? All your fears, all your remorse, all your theories and laziness, all the contradictions of your thought . . . disappear to give place to the furious jet of a single and unique certainty, the continuous and cracking sheaf of fire of your machine gun" (136). Thus we have the negation of the very surrealist technique that exposes the primitive roots of modern life.

Despite these inconsistencies, the diagnosis of war as a cultural disease remains clear. Dali uses the biologist's vocabulary in making this point, for his purpose is to trace the anatomy of cultural phenomena as if they were composed of vital life substances. But since the phenomenon of war is a regressive deformity, the substances described are like the repugnant tissue of some aborted growth. In one scene, "the swollen and irritated epiderm of the sky" is covered with antiaircraft "carbuncles." The bullets,

> hard and shiny like scalpels, flashed their deep incisions in all directions in the form of crosses, bursting the loathsome yolks of eggs fried in boiling oil with the tumors of explosions, bespattering the stars with all the thick pus of their dense and bloody smoke and smearing the clouds with the entrail-vomit of shell bursts (242).

This kind of vocabulary is appropriate for the description of a tumor operation, not a war. Yet, from a biocultural perspective, they are both part of the same degenerative process. In this major sense, Dali's attitude toward war neither conciliates nor condones. His narration of the bombing of Málaga—omitted in the Spanish version—is chilling, but still displays the humanity of a surgeon at work.

The foregoing descriptions are in keeping with Dali's cyclical view of evolution. According to this action, regression and development succeed each other in a constant process of destruction and regeneration. The aviator feels like a drop of albumen in a shell and behaves with primitive amorality. Yet, his destructive acts are no more harmful than the adventitious growths produced by a technological civilization. In this truth, Dali's position is similar to Lorca's even in its metaphor ("the mechanical vermin of industrialization" [229]). Thus, the embryonic airplane becomes a symbol of withdrawal and the instrument of rebirth. War not only annihilates the old order but also produces a new social species. Such an attitude reveals a pathological awareness that reality is a tumorous growth. But this type of mentality also allows for the assurance that healthy tissue will follow the extirpation. Nor is there any moral issue involved in the life process. Even the word "sabotage" is regarded as a purgative force in war's revitalizing effect.

Behind the biological laws of life and society is the metamorphosis of myths corresponding to evolutionary change. Society provides its ceremonial masks just as much as primitive groups do. And these rites have their effect on the physiology and psychology of the modern organism. For example, the novel's heroine is a creature who is constantly transformed and rejuvenated by beauty parlors. Both through nature's endowment and "an innate sense of imitation," her face can reproduce the expressions of man, woman, and even animal. "Plunged in the mythology of fashion shops, she expended all her mimetic faculties in contaminating herself at will with the virtues and attitudes of the divinities of the day . . . in the frenzied race of her depersonalization, [she] spent the treasures of her energy in resembling all the pretty women of her period, while keeping of herself only what was strictly necessary to remain alive" (63-64). The blend of animal and human traits is not only a fact of evolution that can be expressed mythically. It is also a product of modern ritual. Civilization develops its own mythology, which reflects new transformations in body and spirit. The loss of human facial characteristics in an atavistic vision is now paralleled by ceaseless changes in face, hair, and clothes. The instinct of the first is matched by the promiscuity of the second. Most important, the ceremony is really an exchange of masks, the wearing of a new face and personality for different occasions—hence the meaning of the title *Hidden Faces.*

In the modern metamorphosis, man's face and personality evolve according to the laws of culture. This is why the faceless figure and the mannequin are so typically surrealistic in theme. In this novel, the aviator has his face swathed in bandages when he first meets his bride after the war. Later, his name changes as they set out to make a new life. The loss of identity and the myth of how it is regained are both part of the new cultural evolution which

Dali is anxious to set down. This record, with its antecedents in biological prehistory, extends to the psychology of a more sophisticated age, and finds its natural expression in surrealism.[2]

Expression, of course, leads inevitably to language, and the language of this surrealist novel has its humorous side as well as the repugnant elements already seen. Dali's style is flamboyant and excessive, but it sparkles with the irony and imagination that are associated with his other prose and his paintings. In one portrait of a lady, he writes that she "possessed a small brain molded of newspaper pulp, irregularly sprinkled with lugubrious black squares combined with the dirty-grey ones half-effaced and dreary pencil-scribblings of a crossword puzzle left lying around" (59). This kind of extremism registers clearly the satirical aspects of surrealist and Dadaist styles. But the references to materials used by painters— papier-mâché, newspaper cuttings—show how closely the painter's mentality is linked to the writer's. In another passage, describing an anxious woman waiting for the telephone to ring, she watches it "slumped like a motionless sleeping white lobster, stupidly caught on its fork, incapable of coming to her rescue" (62).

These instances are characteristic of Dali's remarkable verbal talents. Despite his outlandish statements here and in other contexts, the sum total of his prose writings represents much more than eccentricity and narcissism. They show a command of scientific terminology that is rare for an artist. Indeed, his literary rewordings of the paintings are vaguely suggestive of a philosophy of life, and, as we have noted, his novel is an explicit reflection of his surrealist vision of organic life. Thus, even though the titles of his canvasses are extravagant, they and Dali's prose glosses of them reveal significant poetic insights into the nature of art and existence.

If we pause to consider some of these epithets and phrases, we discover the essential unity of Dali's vision. His work is aimed at the integration of psychic and biological experience by means of the mythology of paranoia. The exact nature of this paranoia will be discussed later. As for biology and myth, their effect on Dali's prose has already been seen. Furthermore, it should be noted that he transforms the classical myth into a surrealistic nightmare. This effect, which is most visible in the glosses, is paralleled by the conversion of epic adventure into introspective experience. Dali deforms the bold exterior world of mythical antiquity, and he revitalizes its symbolism in accordance with the psychoanalytical dreamworld of modern man. Thus, his triple method of distortion, psychology, and literature (as opposed to painting) recapitulates the natural metamorphosis of a creative spirit. Dali's use of words to explain plastic images betrays his need to make the inexpressible verbal. But instead of following the episodic framework of classical myth, he finds a substitute in the concern with formal technique. At the same time, he turns to deformation to show how myth changes when applied to contemporary life. And finally, his obsession with psychology reflects the turning inward of man's attention from the episodic world while it also serves as a medium for inventing modes of deformation.

Dali's surrender to the power of rational language provides several lessons. First of all, it shows how fragile a single artistic form can be, whether the latter is literature, music, or painting, and how incomplete an artist can feel when he expresses himself in only one of these art media. It also reveals that surrealism is essentially a failure as a means of communication, since its difficult imagery encourages the painter to translate it into words. And finally, it becomes clear how deeply the roots of surrealism extend into the unconscious, for just as the dreamworld is subjected to verbal analysis, so too is its artistic counterpart, surrealist painting, now restated in linguistic terms.

The nature of this restatement becomes apparent when we study Dali's commentary of his paintings. Here, his intention is to state the irrational in unemotional terms. This does not mean just a logical rewording, for Dali is required to deny his emotional life at the very moment that he sees the emotion depicted in the nonverbal surreality of his paintings. In other words, he contemplates his emotional experience in plastic form, and at the same time transforms it into the language of cold reason and science. True enough, his explanatory rubrics do not sound very coherent. But they stand at a distance from the plastic image and try to explain its absurdity in a rational way. Since this is done verbally, the result is once removed from the irrational plasticity of the image. And since the explanation uses a pseudoscientific terminology, the effect is an even further withdrawal from the original experience.

This rationalizing process pretends to be serious, but if it really were, it would be self-destructive. That is, the effect would be to nullify the subjective character of the surrealist vision. However, this danger is avoided by Dali's irony, which lurks behind everything he does publicly. The very fact of the statements' scientific precision introduces a facetious element. For example, the gloss of *The Great Masturbator* states that "eroticism is an infinitesimal part of the inner world," an idea which must be dealt with on psychological grounds. But the statement goes on to affirm that "after Freud, it is the outer world, the world of physics, which will have to be eroticized and quantified." This lack of logic and continuity is exasperating, until we realize that the real function of the gloss is to connect the worlds of psyche and phenomena. Thus, the shift from psychology to physics is justified, with the erotic element becoming the common link between the two concepts.[3]

Nevertheless, there is a certain guideline to Dali's thinking, especially with regard to his own work. The difficulty is that he speaks in metaphor, and often elusively. But it is obvious that his concept of the imagination is the nerve center of his creative activity. Regardless of rhetoric, this idea is clear:

> Paranoia has the permanence and the analytical hardness of granite. The quicksands of automatism and dreams vanish upon awakening. But the rocks of the imagination still remain.

Exactly how the technique of critical paranoia operates will be discussed at the end of this chapter. What emerges from the quotation is the notion that behind the irony and the illusion of objectivity stands an intelligible idea. When one thinks of the preposterous titles of his canvasses, one tends to discredit this as a possibility. For example, *Atmospheric Skull Sodomizing a Grand Piano* means nothing. Yet in the gloss, Dali explains:

> This vision is a retinian product, an hypnagogic image of pre-sleep, occurring in the course of a siesta, contrary to the images resulting from the effects of mescaline, which can never reproduce instantaneous memories. Unlike other hallucinatory systems, this painting offers a complete argumentation with unity of time and development similar to the fundamental characteristics of Greek tragedy.

There is no doubt that the obscurity of vocabulary in the above passage weakens its analytical value. Nevertheless, its intent is plainly to uphold the critical paranoia method over other systems of aesthetic perception. Its talk about Greek tragedy and hypnagogic influences are merely side issues in this key idea. True, such influences also support the notion of paranoia by calling attention to time as a dimension that can make surrealist images more comprehensible to the waking world. But the main point is that Dali can rationalize his hallucinatory system despite the exotic terminology. Indeed, his word choice might even be defended on the grounds that new and obscure experiences require a corresponding vocabulary. In any case, Dali did not intend to destroy the basic irrationality of his paintings by restating them logically in these glosses—

hence the slight tone of extravagance and absurdity mixed in with the intelligible aspects.[4]

The tendency to dismiss the theoretical side of Dali is unfair, especially when considering the articles he published in Catalonian and Spanish vanguard magazines during the 1920's. These articles are serious and without pretension, and are useful for the ideas that they were soon to be reflected in Spanish literature and in Dali's own work. The essay of most concern here is called "Reality and Surreality," appearing in 1928.[5] Its thesis is that there is no organic or functional difference between reality and surreality, but that each is contained in the other. It is up to the observer to perceive each according to his mode of perception, for the latter is what influences the configuration of the external world. This fundamental subjectivist concept later became the basis for the technique of critical paranoia.

Dali conceived the role of automatism to be the achievement of the "definitive extirpation of the naturalist residue." This meant that it was necessary to make sure that cognitive modes did not arbitrarily separate the two kinds of reality. For example, if the observer's imagination were excited, he would actively influence the form of reality caught by his eye; but by the same token, his utter passiveness could also be the occasion of an unusual form. It was this latter case that interested Dali with respect to automatism. He felt that the suddenness of a perception determined the degree to which conventional reality might be distorted. He referred to a kind of sensorial receptivity that was far removed from the active intervention of the imagination. During this condition, the abrupt and unexpected sight of an ordinary phenomenon might be converted into "the most disturbing, concrete, and detailed of magic arrangements."

This does not deny the importance of imagination. But what is involved is an instant where reality is captured in a form of perceptual inversion. Take, for example, a situation in which the roles of a cart and animal are reversed. Instead of creating a stereotyped image of the animal and cart in motion with an awning fixed to the cart, the sudden abandonment of intelligence might lead to a vision of the awning in motion and the cart and animal fixed to it. Dali calls the conventional representation "antireal," whereas the new image is called "surreal." Here, then, is the cornerstone of critical paranoia, which is Dali's own style of surrealism.

From this it is clear that the elements of reality are not as important as the relationships that the mind establishes between them. This point contradicts Lorca's analysis of Dali's work to a certain extent because, as we saw, objects were supposed to have acquired supreme value in themselves, according to the new aesthetic. But the contradiction is not serious, since nowhere is private emotion involved in representing reality. Thus, where Dali is concerned, there is little need to transform the shapes of existing objects, or to invent new ones in order to depart from the normality of reality. The phenomenal world suffices, untouched by subjective feelings. The artist simply utilizes real objects in strange contexts and relationships. This is important with regard to technique, especially because Dali is scorned for his so-called draftsmanship. But the photographic quality of his paintings is a logical outgrowth of the process just described. As his article explains, there is nothing more favorable to the "osmosis established between reality and sur-reality" than the photograph. The camera provides data that make us revise the exterior world, turning the latter into an "object of doubt and at the same time [filled] with more unusual possibilities for the lack of cohesion." Dali exalted objective facts over "intellectual impressionism," a term which includes all species of aesthetic subjectivism. In this sense, he even opposed the self-styled vanguard literature of his day, because he said it fell victim to experiments in expression that led to vague, grotesque, and absurd art forms.

In contrast, Dali upheld the "live emotion" of "strictly objective transcriptions." These, he felt, did participate in the poetic knowledge of reality. This was a persistent aim in Dali's aesthetic, although the notion that perceptual relationships define reality might also produce grotesque results. However, it was obvious that the beautiful and the ugly were categories made defunct by the "osmosis" of reality and surreality. Accordingly, Dali cultivated his "loving capacity for the most cruel and unexpected relationships." The latter were also "pathetic because of their lush sterility," a paradox whose converse—"useless morbid fecundity"—suggests how deeply the castration theme is ingrained in the surrealist mode. These relationships, however, never lost their objective link with reality. Normal cognitive procedures could be retained while still invoking surreality. For example, a horse and rider might change into a logical yet eerie series of relationships. The reins could become extensions of the fingers; the wind could affect hair on the arms more than hair on the head; and the hair could become thick roots that fix the figures to the ground. Such a situation is not absurd, but merely an evasion of accepted rational order. In fact, Dali claims that our conventional way of putting things in order has done violence to the world of objects. Moreover, there is a world beyond our imagination which can be reached only by distinguishing between conventional value and real value. Dali was soon to exploit the transformations of the natural world that were possible under this distinction.

The difference between conventional and real value is fundamental. The first results from the preestablished categories of the mind, and the second from the cultivation of "biological excitations of instinct." Like the metamorphoses seen in Lorca's ode to the king of Harlem, this technique prefigures Dali's own practices in painting and the novel. It was termed a "cruel and jovial revision" of previous aestheticism, as, for example, when a rose hanging from a delicate stem was compared to a huge, deathly hand hanging from a slender arm. Admittedly, a sense of aesthetic horror would replace the old artistic pleasure. But the price would be worth it in terms of genuine insight into reality. Distortion was a matter of establishing illogical relationships between things. The natural world, therefore, remained untouched, and Dali counted more on illogic than on the disfiguration of line. In fact, the feeling of uncanniness depends largely on his precise delineation of figures in absurd relationships. And here too, the status of photographic techniques becomes prominent. The pictorial element strengthens its role as a reproductive agent, and reduces its "creative" role in painting. Graphic representation of reality has no bearing on the accuracy of a statement dealing with this reality. In other words, the truth about reality is determined by what associations are formed among the photographic details.

Dali's theory of art, consequently, has a dual nature, consisting of the polar operations performed by psychological and formal techniques. We find this separation suggested in another of his early articles, "Photography, Pure Creation of the Spirit."[6] Here, he argues that the formal process is detached from the phenomenon of inspiration, and is comparable to the "unconscious calculation of the machine." "Unconscious" does not mean subliminal activity, of course. Rather, the idea is that both the machine and practical technique lack a self-directed purpose. They are simply the instruments of a separate intelligence, which the artist knows as "inspiration." Thus, Dali can talk about "the new manner of spiritual creation," which is photography, because in this medium all the phases of artistic activity are "put in their proper place."

In this new method, the use of fantasy consists of keeping one's eyes open, observing carefully, and inventing unique relationships for the phenomena one sees. However, the individual may sometimes minimize and even repress a few components of the scene that

he is watching, simply as a normal mechanism of psychic adjustment. Consequently, the passionless photograph of, say, a bathroom
will represent more accurately than the naked eye the "cold morbidness of the white sinks." So too with the "magical, unreal
exactitude" of an electrical apparatus. In both instances the individual's feelings diminish the disquieting aspects of the scene in
order to make an adjustment to reality. Man compensates for the
brutal nakedness of his eyes' image by subduing and altering those
elements. This is why they seem unreal when attention is called to
them. On the other hand, the camera makes no selection or evaluation. It records all that it sees without emphasis, giving equal weight
to every facet of the scene—hence the strangeness of a bathroom
when seen surrealistically, and in this context let us recall Lorca's
sleepless sinks. Hence too the meaning of the term dehumanization,
since the world of inert objects is suddenly elevated to the same
plateau of interests as man himself. Thus, Dali exults in photographic fantasy, which he finds more satisfying than the subconscious
process. His justification for the minute detail and ocular precision
of his work is that they are the very source of the surrealist experience.

Inspiration, as the second factor, is also indispensable. Dali
does not deny that an imaginative power of association is just as
necessary for surrealism. But part of this ability resides in the artist's
unlearning the normal habits of vision. He must see the world as
the camera does, and relate some of the repressed elements in a
more plastic way. This is the technique known as critical paranoia.
Dali describes the method as a spontaneous form of irrational knowledge. This implies that there are other forms of irrational knowledge
which are not "spontaneous," and indeed, Dali did not want to
include such faculties as intuition or the unconscious, with the
latter's fixed symbolism. It is true that he exploits these other areas,
but they provide long-term ways of knowing rather than instantaneous ones. The unconscious, in particular, cannot furnish spontaneous knowledge since its dream symbolism is a prelearned and
deliberate form of expression. Dali does mean that his irrational
knowledge is based on a sudden, paranoiac association of sensations.
He calls this a critical and interpretative association of delirious
phenomena. What happens is that an abrupt perception will take
reality unawares, or rather, will catch the observer off balance, making him suddenly see things in a new way, like a camera. During this
instant, the components of reality do not have the opportunity to
fall into place according to the observer's emotional equilibrium.
Thus, the strangeness of the configuration proves to be disturbing.[7]

Critical paranoia, therefore, is the cultivation of this new way of looking at the world and developing it pictorially. Of course, the method is not propitious for all elements of reality, and so Dali specifies "delirious" phenomena. By this, he means all elements that appear disturbing and out of place during the first moment of perception. As Breton once observed, paranoiac delirium retains complete clarity and order in thought, will, and action. What is abnormal is the nature of the association, which the normal person finds unreasonable because it consists of an error based on emotion. Thus, both the perception and the representation are coherent, but the association is absurd. And it is precisely the reasonable tone in a paranoid's statement that is so frightening. Similarly, the photograph, and Dali's graphic exactness in painting, emphasize the deformation.

Dali's method of making himself paranoid consists of not engaging rationally with the world during his initial encounter with it. At every other moment his perception is tranquil and normal, but for the first instant he suspends it, allowing certain aspects of reality to stand out as if they were pursuing him. This does not mean a real chase, but rather that they appear to be engaging with him. That is, he imagines that these intensely perceived elements are reacting to him, developing attitudes toward him. We saw how this worked in Solana, although there most of the imagined attitudes were aggressive. In Dali, they are simply elements that take the initiative, assuming guises which the senses ordinarily could not imagine. For example, most people at one time or another have convinced themselves that a particular cloud formation or a series of cracks in the wall actually do form a face or some other real shape. This prosaic experience is the basis of critical paranoia, which Dali goes on to develop in its most profound mechanisms.

Other passages in Descharnes' book contain images and neologisms that indicate how the paranoiac method is linked to bioculturalism. Going further, Dali joins these approaches to the description of natural phenomena by means of scientific terminology. For instance, he speaks of a "colloidal" origin, or a "hyperxiological" sky. Absurd images thus strike roots in the real world. The best example occurs in the gloss of the painting where a woman poses with a square section cut out of her back, *The Weaning of Furniture Nutrition*. We are told:

The wall-piercing eye must cut out a limpid space in the flesh of reality. If this space is cut from the back of one's own nurse, there will result, as if by magic, "the weaning of the edible piece of furniture." The absence of a loved person leaves in us a sentimental vacuum. The absence of a bedside table would leave, in its place, a transcendent, philosophical-visceral void.

This piece of nonsense is the best kind of surrealist writing that can challenge the active mind. It invites us to engage in a form of paranoia of our own. The eye alluded to is the same as the hypnagogic, masochistic, and narcissistic eyes mentioned elsewhere in this book, and it is akin to the eye sliced by the razor blade in *Le Chien andalou*. It is the generic surrealist eye that transforms the reality it sees into the absurd world of impossibilities. This is why it is called a wall-piercing eye, for it accomplishes what reason judges to be impossible. At the same time, the eye is part of a human body that reacts psychologically to its environment. It changes another human being into an obstacle, and a woman's back into a wall. A paranoid would likewise consider the nurse to be a confining individual, no doubt, a wall that he had to break through in order to escape. In any case, a woman's flesh becomes the flesh of reality, the conversion of a solid world into a soft, penetrable substance that can be torn asunder. This is the fantasy of a mind desperate for freedom, an eye so alert to the prospect of escape that it will change reality to suit its psychological needs.

This type of absurdity is comprehensible, since its genesis lies in a simulated, self-induced psychosis. Yet, Dali moves on to a conceptual type also, one created by words instead of mental or plastic images. This conceptual absurdity is a natural extension of fantasy to the realm of abstraction. Hence the complete absurdity of the idea that the "bedside table would leave, in its place, a transcendent, philosophical-visceral void." There is no meaning here, just as there is none in certain details of the original painting. And it is at this point that surrealist prose fails where its plastic counterpart remains successful. For whereas the irrational in painting can remain aesthetically significant by virtue of its sensorial effects, its literary analog cannot. When linguistically irrational prose is empty of metaphor, it has no redeeming asset. This is why Dali has incurred so much derision in the later years of his career. He has taken to supplementing his irrational art with a prose that seems pointless by comparison. And yet, we must remember that it is only through his writings that we can gain insight into the technique of critical paranoia. Thus, out of the philosophical-visceral void of Dali's language emerges a psychological method for finding true meaning. This is one paradox of Dali's that is not difficult to accept.[8]

Chapter Eight

Surrealist Rhetoric
(Alberti)

When we turn to Rafael Alberti, we find that two of the aesthetic tendencies noted in the chapters on Dali and Lorca reach their maximum expression in his surrealist poetry. One of these is Dali's use of scientific terminology, which in Alberti becomes a more general preference for allusions to the world of technology and artifacts. The second tendency is Lorca's muted social awareness, which is briefly paralleled in Alberti's surrealist period before the latter's poetry turns into the prosaic blare that it later became. Part of Alberti's work, therefore, occupies a very important position in the Spanish surrealist mode because it stands at the crossroads of hermetic and realistic art forms. Its lexicon of references to the industrial world points the way to a reality beyond nightmare. But its private vision still remains too subjective to be of service in the resolution of social problems. Nevertheless, the fact that surrealist diction can become a stepping stone to a less distorted poetry is significant in itself.

The development of Alberti's career follows a pattern away from "pure poetry" and toward social commitment. In this respect he joins company with Lorca, since his later works were also written for the theater. Although these plays are not as deeply grounded in everyday reality as are Lorca's, they do represent a gesture of literary sociability. Still more committed are the poems composed after 1931, which involve impassioned pleas for social liberty and justice. In addition to this, Alberti became a Communist, thus repeating the ideological evolution experienced by most French surrealists. By doing so, he lost his effectiveness as an artist. And yet

121

whatever value persists in the artistic remnant of these works, it is due to the traces of surrealism that are still visible.

The gradual penetration by the real world into Alberti's verse occurred in two stages. First, it transformed his early poetry from an elaborate baroque edifice into a place more inhabitable for his subjective self. And second, it changed the latter's surreality into a violence that was subsequently relevant to the chaos of the Spanish Civil War. This second stage was a transition to the later propagandistic poems, and will be discussed in detail later. As for the first period, its obscure Gongorism was abandoned for an equally cryptic personal baroque that was expressed in the collection *Sobre los ángeles*.[1]

Despite the difficulty of *Sobre los ángeles,* each poem reveals a sense of real and profound anguish that could not be detected earlier. Alberti appears to be drawing closer to emotional reality, no longer hesitant to explore his feelings toward the phenomenal world. However, as his interest in purely formal images ebbs, it leaves a vacuum in meaning. The poems seem distorted because their obscure imagery is divorced from the meaning which is now expressed by personal lyricism. Whereas Alberti's earlier baroque poetry was significant for its formalism, this new poetry is meaningful because of its emotions.[2] Nevertheless, the difficult images are retained, although they are no longer as important as the poet's feelings. The latter, however, are somehow displaced from the imagery. Thus, the poems remain with a metaphorical structure whose meaning is misshapen. Alberti devotes considerable energy to the psychological aspects of the self, but he does not eliminate the unemotional imagery. Consequently, the reader faces the double complexity of feeling and image, and tends to regard the image as a vestigial element.

It is this situation which accounts for the extreme difficulty of *Sobre los ángeles.* There is a divorce between feeling and metaphor. The rhetoric involved in conveying emotion also helps to build the labyrinths of Gongoristic abstraction. Language is not free to serve human feeling realistically because its repertoire of images is still hermetic. Thus, the poet's steady drift toward reality is not intelligibly articulated, for his metaphors still belong to a nonrealistic realm. As his subjectivity becomes more pronounced, the gap between it and his rhetoric increases. The result is a perplexing poetry of strain, jarring sentiments, and uncertain semantics. Such is the general atmosphere of *Sobre los ángeles,* and the primary reason for its inaccessibility. The reader is conscious of a dramatic lyricism which obviously comes from the poet himself, and yet communication with the poet is blocked by a linguistic superstructure.

This tension between Alberti's real emotion and the meta-phorical artifices around it makes *Sobre los ángeles* a surrealistic book.[3] What is involved is a disparity between the emotional symbolism of a word and the actual image the word evokes. Take, for example, the phrase "the explosion of the mechanical rose of the world."[4] This metaphor has an imagistic appeal in its poetic context, namely, the role of machines in the modern world, but the image is fantastic in relation to the feelings it awakens. There is scarcely any perceptible relationship between symbolic and natural meaning here or anywhere in *Sobre los ángeles*. However, one year after this collection, in 1929, Alberti began to modify his imagery so that it approximated the reality he was describing. As he moved away from his inner world and toward real life, he saw the latter as increasingly twisted by social chaos, and scarred by the machinery of technology. To describe this he used a vocabulary whose overtones were full of violence, victimization, and dehumanized scientific symbols. Thus, he preserved a certain marginal surrealism even as the number of realistic themes began to increase. By 1931, when Alberti began to write *El poeta en la calle,* he had abandoned his linguistic nightmare for the realities of the Spanish Republic.

What is of interest to us, then, is Alberti's rhetoric at the intersection of surrealistic imagery and social reality. This meeting place is important for several reasons. It shows how heavily the poet's vocabulary relied upon the scientific world, a dependence which is representative of the surrealist mode in Spain in general. And it also illustrates the influence of modern social conditions upon the aesthetic principles of surrealism. Moreover, it locates the center of balance between these principles and the emerging neorealism. In other words, we are given a historical perspective from which to view the turning point of surrealism from its hermetic state to its precursory phases before the rise of a new literary school.

A good example of this transitional stage can be found in the poem entitled *Sermón de las cuatro verdades* (1929). Its content is dense and tortured, as might be expected, but for the first time a surrealist writer here proposes to deliver a moralizing lecture in verse form.[5] The fact that the sermon is incomprehensible does not matter. What is unusual is the supposition that poetry should be didactic. Indeed, the notion that didacticism and hermeticism are compatible bedfellows is itself a paradox in literature. This is stranger still when we consider the ideologically disinterested character of the surrealist mode as we have seen it thus far. Yet Alberti proposes not only to instruct us with statements of obscure significance, but to reveal a set of truths as well. He asks us to accept, with absurd logic, the premise that it is possible to arrive at objective "truths" in the relativistic world of surrealist poetry, where associations are subjectively presented.

Here, then, is the beginning of a new ethical and cognitive orientation in surrealism, where poetry is assigned the direct task of instruction. Not even in Lorca, whose odes embodied specific moral values, was there any intention to teach an ethical truth. This does not mean that Alberti's poem makes an explicitly intelligible commitment. But the title *Sermón de las cuatro verdades* does suggest a significant shift in his concept of poetic function.[6] This incipient case of doctrinal writing is significant in the light of his later poetry, which, by contrast to Lorca's, verged on the propagandistic. Strictly speaking, Alberti's message is not political. His aim, as he states it, is: "I am coldly going to reveal to you what a basement is like from the inside" (295). This spiritual cellar represents more than the bottom of Alberti's troubled soul. It also symbolizes a reduction, as we will see—the pandemonium of the physical world reduced to its technological components. Thus, the symbolic use of objects provides a glimpse of the external reality which was eventually reached by Alberti, even though his primary treatment of this material does not produce a realistic sermon.

The poet's desire to communicate by means of a discourse reveals his assumption that all sensitive men suffer equally. Yet he does not express this idea directly. The concept of suffering, as a human value, is diverted by a priority of references that place the inanimate world into the ascendency over ideas. For example, "bricks and debris grow disheartened," and they "harass the purity of the sandals that sustain the boredom, ill-humor and weariness in man" (298). Although the poem was obviously conceived with human pain in mind, its verbal structure subordinates this pain to the inert realm of matter. Moreover, the lifeless world acquires the characteristics of man's sorrow. Thus, the dejection felt by rubble, and the purity inherent in shoes, are made to supplant what was originally a human experience. It is up to the reader to reverse the referential framework, and relocate the psychological and moral positions in a more logical way.

Alberti, of course, sympathizes with the attitudes found when this relocation is made; it is simply the logic that he opposes. In his cracked mirror of reversible values, he is able to perceive emotions indiscriminately, whether they are in men or in objects. The technique is similar to Dali's critical paranoia, where the artist imagines that the meaningless configurations of rocks and objects are really expressive of attitudes. But Alberti's mirror is illogical for another reason. His submerged awareness of reality tells him that human misery is a universal fact. The social chaos in human life reflects the larger violence of matter in the universe as a whole. Thus, he tells us to "not abandon the one who swears to you that when a dead soul gets drunk on Earth, his soul imitates him in Heaven" (299). That is, whatever is absurd on earth will also have its counter-reflection in the universe. No aspect of mind or existence is free from the contamination of illogic.

At this point, the idea of man's suffering and absurd condition is not the exclusive concern that it later turned out to be. Alberti's method of referential inversions is also important, and it holds our interest even more because it is typical of surrealist rhetoric. Were it not for this rhetoric, Alberti could not speak so easily of moral and spiritual qualities among objects: sad fermentations, innocent stars, disconsolate cigarette butts. What will become Alberti's undisguised commitment to real problems is, at this moment, still a recessive screen of associations. For example, when he calls a break in the circular orbit of a star a "slander," the absurdity does not lie in his semantic usage but in reality. Alberti knows that life has scrambled the categories of values and conditions. As a result, the ethical and sentimental traits of living things become interchangeable with the inert qualities of matter. The illogic of this has nothing to do with language difficulty. Thus, the true meaning of absurdity must be conveyed by a comparable confusion of phenomenal conditions and affective-moral characteristics. Alberti does this by the misapplication of value judgments. This technique preserves normal linguistic construction, but plays havoc with commonsense experience.

The mirror universality of the absurd is a concept implied throughout the *Sermón*. We read that "the corruption of the heavens took place on the same night that the vinegar invaded the [wine] casks and rumpled the blankets of the virgins" (299). In this case, the state of human corruption is alluded to by the decomposing properties of vinegar. Alberti's rhetoric builds upon the associations of vinegar with other chemical activities, and from there goes on to the processes of inert matter. He refers to unfermented juices, the acidity of decomposed must, sodium chloride, volcanic sulphur, and other corrosives. All of these tend to dehumanize the atmosphere, which is otherwise charged with the tragedy of man's fall. This is how Alberti constructs his surrealist mood. He dislocates the human condition from its causal elements, and introduces a situation that parallels it in the nonhuman world. At the same time, he destroys the logic of relationships by replacing a natural set of causes with an absurd one. And finally, the ultimate absurdity is the insertion of human anguish into an inorganic context.

This juxtaposition of the organic and the inorganic is part of an overall aesthetic with many forms of transvaluation. One of these is the principle of reversibility, which is used in the area of meta-phorical relationships, as we have seen. Another occurs in the area of causality, where a similar disjunction serves to heighten the sense of torment and the absurd. And still a third method involves anti-thesis, in which ugly and degrading elements reveal the highest goals of poetry. All three techniques can be traced ultimately to Alberti's latent ideology, but they are more prominently the instru-ments of a coherent aesthetic. This is particularly true of the last-mentioned antithesis.

Here we discover that artistic beauty can be evoked from the depths of decay. For example, the poet states that "the excrement of birds contains the darkness of infinity and the head of a wolf" (297). The two elements of eternity (infinity) and violence (wolf) are universal factors in man's condition, and yet, they are also found in vile and insignificant places. But Alberti is not trying to create beauty out of aesthetic perversion, as did Baudelaire and the post-symbolists. He goes beyond this, using decadence as a point of departure. Thus, he declares that "the heavens' perfection will commence" with "the mole's sloth," or with the "acrid yellow breath coming from the dry saliva of a mule" (298). After this initial step, he goes on to adapt a scientific perspective for the creative act. In other words, just as an earlier generation stylized ugliness, so too can a new aesthetic now arise from the technological breakdown of reality. A rhetoric derived from modern technology, with words borrowed from the everyday workings of the scientific revolution, can provide a poetic vision beyond the scope of naturalism and post-symbolism. By liberating science from its utilitarian role, Al-berti allows it to transcend value judgments. In this way, it enters the realm of art. Science is no longer viewed as a means of deter-mining a fixed number of rules concerning existence. Instead, it makes possible an interchange of an infinite number of elements. Consequently, surrealist art is able to depict a free-form universe haphazardly fragmented by an indifferent science.

Such a fragmentation is also aided by perceptual means, as well as by scientific language. Here, then, is another difference between the flowers of evil and Alberti's mechanical rose. He practices a dis-cordant type of sense perception that is beyond the symbolists' derangement of the senses.[7] Beginning with a psychic attitude that permits him to withdraw from his human condition, the poet slips into the world of things. In this way he can imagine, for example, that footstools have legs like men, which are "bitten by the shadows" of a room. The normal perception would be that of shadows stealing over the stools and wrapping them in darkness, but Alberti sees them as being ingested and spatially swallowed by the devouring darkness. In this same passage, the projection of living character-istics upon lifeless things is given an emotional and even moral reinforcement. That is, a mosquito is accused of avarice, and dust grows disillusioned because it accumulates in a lovely room without anyone to trace fingerprints upon it (298).

These affects and attitudes have little to do with the sensorial reality of the situation, but rather, they serve to record Alberti's chaotic sensory perception. At the same time, the meaning of nor-mal valuation and perception is destroyed by the psychological humanization of objects. In other words, there can be no realistic significance in describing emotional and ethical states among things. This, then, is the difference between Baudelaire's flowers of evil and Alberti's aseptic, mechanical rose. In the first case, the trans-valuation consists of converting a moral evil into an aesthetic good. In the case of Alberti, no value formation is possible at all, because the condition is itself absurd. What the poet does create is a sen-sorial discord, whose very absurdity becomes the instrument of a psychological mood.

If we examine the mechanisms of these surrealistic perceptions, we discover that their discord is due to the reversibility of sensations. For instance, an image like "the damp and concave silence of the wine cellars" describes an acoustic fact in terms of tactile and spatial references. It is true that sound, or in this case, the absence of sound, occurs in space, but so does light, for that matter. Actually, the dampness and concavity are not traits of the silence, but of the cellar, although the inversion is effective. But Alberti goes further, and writes that "above the damp and concave silence of the wine cellars, ten echoes chase each other, detached from the corpse of a man as he bumped against a surface too refractory for light" (298). This is a completely irrational statement as far as the phenomenon is concerned, since it is impossible. Yet from the standpoint of per-ception, the fusion of sensory functions and the disregard for order create a new image. Light turns into sound echoes, and the relation-ships between mass and light remains a mystery. On all counts, therefore, reality is transformed, even though the presence of a scientific word ("refractory") seems intended for objectivity.

There is one final aspect of Alberti's mechanical rose which is central to his aesthetic. This is the concept that surrealist sensibility must depend on the new mechanics, no matter how grating to the senses it may be. Indeed, the harsher and less refined the perception, the more synchronized the work is to modern anguish. One of the

Sermón's four truths is precisely this idea: "A star diluted in a glass
of water gives back to the eyes the color of nettles or prussic acid"
(296). The star, once a source of beauty when contemplated either
directly or by reflection in water, is now diluted in the style of
chemical reactions. Alberti expects the modern reader to accept this,
and he admonishes "those who are unaware of the screech of a
saw against a nail" to flee (295). His warning is a bold declaration
of what the surrealist sensibility is, a series of aesthetic effects derived
from the tools, materials and acids, and precision instruments of
technology. The contemporary age can only be understood by dislocation and the scientific representation of the latter. It does not
matter whether we stumble against a shadow or a piece of furniture,
for the pain will be expressed mechanistically in both senses. At any
rate, substance and insubstantiality are one and the same, when
viewed in the refractory light of the reversibility principle.

It is clear, then, that the mechanistic expression of anguish
requires a special rhetoric. This language is so different, that for a
moment the reader forgets how traditional man's sorrow really is.
Alberti's sermon is understood directly, being addressed to people
who still wish to communicate with their neighbor, to those who
have, "on screwing in a sparkplug, felt in the most intimate part of
their fingernails the instantaneous electric shock of another soul."[8]
(295). The Romantic sentiments have not changed, but the modes
of expressing them have. Thus, kindred souls recognize each other
nowadays by means of their experience with the artifacts of the
modern age. If they have felt "the insistent rubbing of a hand
against the rusty bristles of a brush," then they can communicate
with each other (296). Compassion is a metallic affair, an ionization
of steel hearts, uttered through soldered tubes by tongues made of
concrete, iodoform, or even broomsticks (297).

To the poet, every sensitive individual is submerged by ma-
chine-made objects. Men stand behind electrified doors, desensitized
by a hyperrationality that turns experience into absurdity. In Alberti's mind we are like dead insomniacs, no longer capable of
feeling or dreaming. As sleepless corpses, we are subjected to "nocturnal attacks by ten red-hot pokers" (297). This is another version
of the nightmare of the senses that we saw earlier, where the echoes
were emitted from a confrontation with light. Now, however, perceptual confusion turns into a form of death to the normal world,
but it opens the gates of surreality to those whose sensitive nerve-
endings have become frayed wires. In terms of reality, such a condition would be called desensitization, and so it appears in Alberti:
"A soul might have inhabited my body if the blood hadn't carried

it . . . to be submerged in echoless contacts: like that of a leg which has fallen asleep against the sordid wool of a bedspread . . ." (297).

This last allusion is an accurate testimony of the disrepute into which the senses have fallen in surrealism. They are not only unreliable but they are better off muffled. Without them, the materials and apparatus of the machine age can probe the depths of terror more extensively. With the poet unable to distinguish among various categories and phenomena, he advances an aesthetic of comparable confusion. In Alberti's phrase, "my soul is just a body which is deceased for having touched against and fused with living and defunct objects" (297). Man's most spiritual faculty, the soul, turns into a corporeal entity, and then suffers a death of the senses. What triumphs in this general anesthesia is matter itself, and here we must recall Lorca's aseptic laboratory. Substance in all forms emerges intact, neither perceived with limited sensibility nor classified by genre or function. The primacy of existing matter is restored, and becomes the aesthetic premium for having eliminated the pleasures of the senses. By the same token, the result of suppressing the rational mind is the identity of substance and nonsubstance. Thus, human sensibility is suspended in all areas, emotive as well as intellectual, while at the same time, the poem achieves a total fusion of reality and nonreality. And this is exactly what surrealism means to Alberti, a fusion of realities in which the poet suffers the despair of not controlling his environment.

This despair is a good sign when viewed from the standpoint of Alberti's future realism, because it reveals his desire to understand and dominate the world around him. Although eventually he succeeds, for the moment he is trapped in a seizure of creativity whose aesthetic climax denies the senses. It is as if the phenomena of surreality are beyond the grasp of perception, not because they are spiritual, but because they are too real, too primitive in their reality. Indeed, among the fusions effected by Alberti is one which joins the realms of organic and inorganic matter. Not unlike the atavisms of Lorca and Dali, Alberti's world exists on all levels of the evolutionary scale, from humanity to minerality. Moreover, these levels obey a reversible interrelationship. Man's physiological character is traced back to its vegetal origins, while morphological avatars assume modern roles.

The best example of how forms are reduced to their primeval simplicity occurs in Alberti's pleas to "help me to dig into a wave, until my hands turn into roots and my body sprouts leaves and wings" (296). Here, water is illogically equated with earth, and a biological impossibility is sought in the request to be all stages of

life at the same time. As in other instances, this wish negates all
human sensibility. Its antitemporal attitude is also clear, confirmed
by the statement that "once my ancestors predicted that I would be
an only tree in the midst of the sea." Alberti's renunciation of his
human condition is followed by the integration of his existence into
the whole of surreality. His life is dehumanized, growing more
similar to the materials and utilities of civilization. The diminution
of modern life is measurable against the rising tide of allusions to
industry. The closer man comes to the state of being inanimate—
as a chemical, machine, or piece of clay—the more these attributes
are confirmed in his environment. Thus, the progress made by technology is matched by comparable regression of humanity to the
point where they both reach the same stage of dehumanization.

What remains, therefore, is a vestige of human consciousness
and a heavy flood of "things." The human spirit is persecuted by an
irate nature in league with culture, with the result that "the coastal
sands, joined with boiling oil, fly to cauterize the shoulders of man"
(295). Nature revolts against the individual, and assumes an artificial role symbolized by the oil-acid image. Similarly, technological
culture usurps the role of nature, attacking man with its instruments: "My soul is pierced by the crab of burning pincers and
compasses" (296). This image encapsules the entire complex of rhetorical and symbolic references that have been analyzed in this
chapter. The metamorphosis of the crab into a precision instrument
is reversed by the atavism of the instrument, which lapses into
primitive violence. The pincers recall analogous objects: spikes,
fingers, metallic tubes, and other materials in the poem that caused
abrasion and pain. And the allusion to "burning" continues the
motif of corrosion and acidity. The total effect, consequently, upholds the ultimate truth of the *Sermón,* namely, that the merger of
realities occurs by the law of reversibility, and is expressed by technological rhetoric.

Chapter Nine

Esperpentism
(Valle-Inclán)

The same road that led Alberti and Lorca from aestheticism to social awareness was also traveled by Ramón del Valle-Inclán. In his novel *Tirano Banderas* (1926), he perfected an aesthetic theory that wedded politics to certain distorted aspects of the surrealist mode. This theory took the form of a highly original genre which Valle-Inclán called an *esperpento*.[1] As we all know, the word itself denotes a kind of grotesque nonsense and absurd fright that uses sarcasm to mitigate terror, and lessens tragedy by means of caricature. But *esperpentismo* as a literary technique is more than just deformation. It is a distorted picture of reality that is based on a special vision of the history of Spanish culture. This socio-political attitude is as crucial to the *esperpento* as the principle of morality was to Goya's *caprichos*.

Some critics will question the linking of esperpentism and surrealism.[2] But even if we were to find little thematic or formal similarity, we would have trouble selecting a better word for characterizing the *esperpento* in European terms. It is possible to call the work expressionistic, but this word is both historically and semantically confusing when applied to Spanish literature.[3] The fact is, however, that there is a good deal of similarity between the *esperpento* and surrealism, both theatrically and in some narrative sequences. For instance, they both uphold the principle of irrational logic. Whatever absurd and grotesque elements appear in them are treated as if they were natural, a part of the rationality of everyday life. Furthermore, the *esperpento* relies upon the breakdown of intellectual categories. That is, it causes certain generic distinctions to collapse, as in the case of the confusion of men and animals in the technique of animalization. In addition, the *esperpento* presents a nightmare version of reality, and at times modifies the dream mechanism for its own purpose. And finally, it depicts the crisis of personality, including the problems of nonidentity and ironic self-consciousness.

All of the preceding characteristics of the *esperpento* confirm its relation to surrealism, especially insofar as *Tirano Banderas* is concerned. It is true that the novel has a coherent structure and an ideological position. In fact, the reason that it ranks above Alberti's social-minded poetry is due to its psychological and formalist aspects, and not because it avoids politics. Nevertheless, whenever form overshadows subject matter, it is because the technique is surrealist and occasionally even cubist. Valle-Inclán's themes are socially realistic, but he raises art above argument. Thus, intellectual and political issues become mere surface in the novel: dialog, action, narrative, realism. They are important because they hint at a deeper reality, the characterological core of society. Political revolution and economic misery are symptoms of a disturbed cultural psychology, but they are best understood in artistic terms by modes of structure, perception, sense association, and personality.

Consequently, when we read this novel, or such *esperpentos* written for the theater, like *Luces de Bohemia,* we are struck with how disfigured they make social reality by means of their experiments in distortion.[4] And yet, the aesthetic behind this experimentation is the result of Valle-Inclán's confrontation with cultural reality. His theory of art is based on a particular method of analyzing the character of the Hispanic world. This method begins with an interpretation of history, and states the premise that Spain is a grotesque deformation of Europe. That is, if Europe is the standard of historical normalcy, then Spain's fundamental experience with the norms of national progress has been failure. Spain has never solved her problems because her genius and talents are disorganized. And if a popular hero should appear to lead the nation forward, he would suffer from the same defects that mar the culture which nourished him.

The main deficiency is found in personality, according to *Luces de Bohemia.* Spain creates the type of hero whose willpower is weakened by his knowledge of the reality around him. As his will to action is discouraged, it is compensated by an attitude of pride, haughtiness, and even of insolent bearing. The hero recognizes a disparity between the ideals of his role and the defective situation of the culture that resists him. He also recognizes a discrepancy between his own abilities and the acts he attempts to carry out. As a result, he develops a kind of desperate cynicism which negates all ideological positions, and which judges every form of activity to be a farce. This means that ultimately, such a hero can take no action at all. Valle-Inclán's interpretation fits in well with the attitude taken by his other contemporaries, the members of the Generation of 1898. But his conclusion is unique, in that he claims that the Spanish genius is incapable of producing a tragic hero. That is, if a national version of Hamlet were to appear, he would be timid, foolish, esperpentic, anything but tragic. A classical hero in the normal mirror of European art becomes a distorted figure in the reflection of Spain's warped image. And this is the central idea of *esperpentismo*. The tragic sense of Spanish life can only be presented by an aesthetic that is systematically deformed.[5]

Although Valle-Inclán credits Goya with originating the *esperpento,* he himself was the first to conceive of this art form based on a theory of culture. His idea was that human experience can be rendered artistically by a progression ranging from the tragic, to the comic, to the farcical, and on through the burlesque, the grotesque, and finally the *esperpentic.* Regardless of how valid this gradation may be, the two extremes are clearly incompatible. This does not mean that the *esperpento*'s hero is unworthy of a tragic characterization. But the situation in which he finds himself cannot be considered tragic because its causes are ridiculous ones, involving an abnormal stupidity, incompetence, or awkwardness. This is one type of deformation, where the origins of a potentially tragic situation are foolish or absurd. The interplay of these contrary elements evokes conflicting emotional responses in the spectator, who recognizes the incongruity. Sometimes he is drawn into the disparity by the author, and this self-consciousness, which exists outside of the dramatic framework, converts the tragedy into absurdity.

Another *esperpentic* mode is the grotesque parody. An ordinary parody is the type of exaggeration which mocks the original subject by emphasizing its most characteristic features. But whereas the normal parody is deliberately derogatory, its grotesque counterpart is serious in purpose and effect. In one case, the parodist tries to make a humorous mockery of his subject. By contrast, the grotesque parody injects a serious element into the ridicule, giving the exaggeration an ulterior motive beyond mere humor. This transcendence of the original mockery is never quite complete, and so the serious intention falls into ambiguity. In addition, the *esperpento* acquires a dual perspective. From the standpoint of the character, who is unaware of what constitutes serious norms, the situation is tragic. But the observer cannot accept the hero's dignity without a smile, since he has a basis of comparison outside the artistic framework. Thus, life is comparable to a "tragic mummers' dance," or to a "paltry stew," or to a "sad little candle." Yet, none of the analogies escapes the tinge of grotesque humor. And this extends from a simple scene to the general description of Spain's cultural values. Consequently, everything that is noble is transformed into the tragically ridiculous: heaven is represented as a bazaar; death becomes the painted face of an old hag; and religion is a dotage.

The final mode of deformation involves the concept of art as a reflection of life. Traditionally, when we speak of art holding a mirror up to life, we mean that artistic norms are used to depict reality in accordance with a system. But this cannot be considered a mirror reflection of life, because art is only a representation of reality and is not identical to it. Therefore, the application of aesthetic norms is, by definition, a stylization. And stylization of any kind means deformation, in the best sense of the word. Nevertheless, the result does not seem to be distorted because the aesthetic is applied systematically. This is why art is said to be analogous to a mirror, with the reflection of life that it produces showing verisimilitude.

However, all of this supposes a "normal" reality, one which is reflected by an ordinary, plane mirror. It would be absurd to think of using a concave mirror, since the result would be deformed. But what if the reality to be depicted were Spain, which is a *grotesque* deformation of "normal" Europe? Clearly, the ordinary mirror would be of no use. It could reproduce the deformities of its model, but it would not have the means for rendering them grotesque. In other words, a straight mirror has norms that are suitable for a society that stands erect and unwarped. But a deformed reality requires a warped mirror to reflect its aberrant norms faithfully. Spain is not merely a deformation of Europe but a grotesque deformation. On this point Valle-Inclán is subtle but very clear. A plane mirror is sufficient to reflect an aberration from the normal European context. But a grotesque deformation can only be reflected when the glass itself is distorted. Hence the need for a concave mirror, whose norms best reproduce the norms of Spanish society. To hold a plane mirror up to Spain would be like holding a concave mirror up to Europe. The use of a different set of norms would distort the image of reality in each case.

This, then, is the theory of the *esperpento*. Insofar as it affects certain aspects of *Tirano Banderas,* it places the novel within the

surrealist mode. This does not mean that the entire novel is surrealistic, although we will be hard put to find another term to describe it. Indeed, what is most difficult to accept about the novel is
that it purports to describe a reality which by nature is incredible
and apparently unreal. Although the political situation is authentic,
the characters behave like caricatures. And the scenes reveal a
physical and moral confusion that is abetted by the fragmented
narrative. These incongruities are caused by Valle-Inclán's private
vision of the Hispanic world, a vision which, as I have noted, constructs a cynical and farcical framework for a supposedly realistic
story. Occasionally, his presence obtrudes into the account, like the
hand of a puppet-master suddenly visible in a moment of intricate
technique. When this happens, the plausible setting is turned into
an obvious stage, and the once-convincing personages become oddly
unreal. Such moments are not frequent, and they constitute deliberate self-exposures on the part of the author. His intention thereby
is to cast ridicule on his subject as an intellectual protest. Not only
does he accomplish this but he also violates the scene's credibility
and creates a momentary sense of absurdness. These and other
devices contribute to an *esperpento* with strong surrealist features,
as will be seen.

The cornerstone of this novel's irony and absurdity is the
element of self-consciousness, which shows up either in the author
or in his personages. At times it consists of an unexpected wink at
the audience, as when the narrator begins an action sequence with
the exclamation, "It was like the trick of a melodrama!"[6] Or else
the self-awareness is found in a book caption ("Dramatic Guignol");
or in the narrator's view of activity: "they all found themselves
caught in the action of a dramatic harlequinade" (II, 3, ii); or
finally, in the description: "he bowed with a pompous and sceno-
graphic curve" (VII, 3, iii). All of these cases involve a complicity
between author and reader. The reader is shaken from the artistic
deception to which he has succumbed and is reminded of the artifice
of the situation. This interruption is not always pleasant, since he
might have been persuaded by the fiction, and so he is unwilling to
accept the author's realistic judgment.

As for Valle-Inclán, his intrusion suggests that he is impatient
with his craft, and with the real world that it represents. Thus, he
heaps ridicule on the former in order to reveal his true feelings toward the latter. His destructive act is shocking by traditional art
standards, for it undermines a convincing show by dragging out the
hidden stage props. But when we remember that he is more interested in the real world than in his creation, the subversion is com-

prehensible. In fact, it is the reader who has betrayed reality by allowing himself to be lulled by the artistry of a novelistic world. In contrast, the author reminds himself of his original purpose in having undertaken the novel. Thus, he shatters the fictional spell by calling attention to its artificiality.

When the deception is exposed, the characters' natural movements suddenly become stilted. What is cruel, however, is that the personages go on acting as naturally as before, without knowing that the audience is now disenchanted. And yet much is gained by the technique. We partake of the best kind of irony, seeing the characters erroneously take themselves seriously when, in fact, they are only part of a Punch and Judy show. And we are successfully alienated, which is the author's purpose. Moreover, the rude awakening from the pleasant illusion of reality is followed by something more valuable: a sudden insight into the absurd. It is as if we had been passive members of the drama until the director whispered for us to come backstage. We then tiptoe out of the scene and join the larger reality, which can never be represented by the unsuspecting actors, who think they are real.

Thus, in great measure, Valle-Inclán produces a schizophrenic reading experience. We know that this is a true-to-life novel and not a puppet show, and yet he insists on destroying the illusion. As we watch, for example, the apprehension of a certain character, we are suddenly told that he "had the petulant and worried look of a comedian in the wings who is waiting for his entrance on stage" (II, 3, iv). The individual is not aware that he is simply an actor, and neither were we until a moment ago, when the author so insistently shifted the focus. But eventually, the original perspective returns, and we are obliged to sit in two seats at the same time. The author has his cake—a convincing novel—and also devours it, by destroying the authentic quality of the realism. What remains in this self-aware dualism is an ironic detachment in the midst of a serious situation. This in turn precipitates a grotesque atmosphere.

The steps involved in this technique require that the reader have a knowledge of literary history. He must recognize, for example, the foolishness of a scene where an inept sentimentalist pours out his sincere Romantic rhetoric to a prostitute. The man's speech is studded with stereotypes, after which he "sobbed, and his paid companion, to console him, gave him a kiss straight out of a Romantic *feuilleton,* pressing against his mouth her own heart-shaped painted mouth" (III, 2, v). The incongruity stems from the inappropriate language, which the reader perceives with his dual focus, and from the speaker's unawareness that his words are misplaced. Moreover, the description is so blatantly artificial that it cannot be reconciled with the lovers' emotional sincerity. The reference to the heart-shaped mouth recalls the slick pulp magazine illustrations, which were vulgar to the point of being Kitsch. Thus, we find a serious love scene presented simultaneously with its parody.

There is one more factor in this scene which displaces the subject matter from its context. Since the artist is conscious of his role, he displays a certain irony in the choice of diction. This can be noted in the faint lack of harmony found in the language. For instance, a normal description of a character would allow the man's qualities to correspond to his personality: "He had the sputtering pathos of four candles, the sentimental and heroic eloquence of the tropical regions" (IV, 5, ii). None of these traits is out of place, because the writer has not consciously tried to show off his style. In contrast, the opposite effect occurs when he deliberately displays his technique: "Suspended in an alcoholic cloud, he came out of the dream into a hilarious reality. He noticed the woman and rose to greet her with a jocund gesture, crowned with the laurels of Bacchus and Mars" (IV, 3, iii). The difference is that the second description tends to lift the subject out of its context and give it a split identity. The colonel depicted here belongs to two realities by virtue of the language, even though he physically appears in only one reality. That is, the classical allusions would usually serve as a means for clarifying the condition of the subject described, and amplifying its vividness. But here, they operate in a contrary manner. They do not refer to the colonel's real condition, but instead force him back into his dreamworld. Thus, the allusions detract from the realism of his real world by assuming a mock-heroic function.

The development of self-consciousness is accompanied by a psychological dissociation in the novel's atmosphere, with the result that the real setting becomes unreal. Sometimes this is directly due to the undercutting of reality by the intrusion of a self-conscious stylization. This happens in one scene which tells of a "gluttonous figure foreshortened so disproportionately that it almost parodied the gluttony of Saturn" (IV, 5, ii). The word "foreshortening" hints at a geometrical technique which is used more extensively elsewhere, as we will see. Here, it furnishes the perspective of caricature in opposition to the novel's real dimensions. Hence, the profile is intentionally exaggerated, while the parody of the Saturn myth removes the figure still further from reality. Thus, in one brief moment of angle-shifting, an unreal effect is produced because the observer is abruptly caught up short and is detached from the scene's psychological unity.

More frequently, however, the displacement occurs internally. The general uniformity of mood is gradually transformed by new discordant elements. However, one of these elements becomes dissociated, while the rest remain united. For example, in the following carnival scene, it is the cat that is dislocated:

> Echoes arrived of the evening festivities. Strings of little lanterns danced in a row along the street. At the end the wheel of the merry-go-round was turning. Its luminous, hysterical, strident scream hypnotized the cats on the edge of the eaves. The street gave sudden winks, in concert with the noise and the acrobatic exercises of the wind on the lantern strings (VII, 2, iii).

This is a traditional fiesta, but a subtle counterlogic begins to tip its equilibrium, and imperceptibly a disruptive atmosphere forms. The stridency of sensations increases in volume progressively from echo and dance to screams, winks, and acrobatics. There are no human beings on the street, and although acrobatics would be expected at a carnival, they are performed by the wind—also unseen—not by people. The narrator speaks incongruously of a concert of noises, and he gives the scream a visual quality instead of an acoustical one. Finally, the linear advance of the lantern row is checked at one end of the street by a disc in circular motion. In all of these details, the principle is to carefully derange the normal perception of things without this being noticed. Thus, like the cats at the margin of the scene, we are unwittingly hypnotized by the gradual change that goes undetected. And then suddenly, at the end, we are the ones who are dislocated from the harmony of illogical elements.

The carnival, of course, is one of surrealism's favorite media for communicating its special uncanniness. There are a number of reasons for this, the most important being that it constitutes an evasion of reality which can be exploited without the artist's having to resort to a fantasy of his own. With the carnival as a technique, the writer does not have to abandon his realism in order to make a surrealistic statement of reality. Instead of using dream, distortion, or fantasy, he merely describes a carnival realistically, and the evasion is accomplished. But once this real element of existence is selected for use, it presents us with a difficult problem. We have no way of knowing whether the carnival is depicted realistically, or whether it too has been subjected to deformation. Is this a carnival or a carnivalesque representation of one? The question is not an idle one, for it holds the key to the artist's mental state. If Valle-Inclán has created an aesthetic transformation of a real-life carnival, then he provides a basis of comparison between normality and its evasion.

And, in truth, he does reveal that he has not succumbed to the carnival mood, but, on the contrary, is alienated from it.

This alienation is precisely what makes Valle-Inclán's fiesta surrealistic. The carnival is not the same for the people caught up in it as it is for the observer who is estranged from it and is struck by its absurdity. Although the outsider it not literally hypnotized like the cats, he is just as cut off psychologically from the carnival's inner mood. Since he cannot participate in it, he perceives it differently, and this affects his aesthetic re-creation of the scene. The best example of this transformation of an already absurd reality can be found in the use of light. In most passages, Valle-Inclán delights in all varieties of illumination, from the direct luminosity of impressionism to the prismatic decomposition of cubism (I, l, vii; II, 2, i; IV, 6, iv). But when his desire is to deform the environment—in this case, the festival scene— then light is subjected to a denaturing process.

If we examine the lighting technique, we discover that its denatured quality appears when the carnival is contrasted to ordinary reality. Life is defined as a "terrific everyday stupor," which is dispelled during the festival season by a "tragic and time-devouring fury." At this special time, the confusion of hawkers' shouts, guitars, pennants, and lanterns merge into a "luminous hubbub," which causes a "lighted vertigo" consisting of a "heat of light and darkness." Thus, even though light is but one element among many, it manages to influence them all. Every element falls into the category of either hubbub or of vertigo, and yet these generic terms are themselves qualified by the light. The effect is to throw a "succession of violent and tumultuous images" into angular relief. The presence of light adds to the turmoil without lending to it the properties of color or brightness. Light is perverted, its intensities and hues ignored, and its illumination exploited for a negative evaluation of life. In other words, the light is used for its garish disguises of "life's obscure and desolate throbbing." It does not redefine reality or provide a meaningful escape from it but, rather, shows that there is no desirable alternative to life. In Valle-Inclán's pessimistic view, the only difference between reality and the carnival lies in the degree of movement.

From this we must conclude that what is described is not an objective carnival, but the author's re-creation of one in accordance with his ideological motives. The distinction is important, for we must bear in mind that it is not necessary to subordinate aesthetics to ideology in order to produce a surrealistic effect. This carnival, however, is determined by a modification of Valle-Inclán's usual light technique, and by his cultural ideas. Elsewhere, he juxtaposes "chromatic dynamism" and "chromatic cruelty," thus shifting from an aesthetic position to an ethical one. Within the total context, this dynamism consists of only one part light against three parts other sensations, and the next sentence refers to a "caliginous marasm" whose components are acoustical.

As the description of the carnival develops, Valle-Inclán's distortive purpose becomes clear. He causes his "enervated" figures to be "unified in an expressive and monotonous synthesis." This impossible sounding paradox is typical of the author's dual intention. He wants to capture the dullness of daily life and yet make it expressive by means of his art—hence a synthesis of seemingly incompatible elements, along with a value judgment that borders on the surrealistic. Later, Valle-Inclán finds in the carnival atmosphere certain qualities of temperament which symbolize the reality he wishes to distort. "The dances, the music, the lantern cords held an absurd exasperation, and annoyance of dazzling chimera" (IV, 6, vi). The author's impatience with the failures of real life are here projected upon the carnival disguise. Furthermore, his suspicion of the reality of existence causes him to focus carefully on the chimerical quality of the fiesta. This emotional transference from reality to art could only be effected by a personal aesthetic, not by a casually objective description of a carnival.

The subordination of aesthetics to ideology occurs again in a revision of cubist techniques. Ordinarily, the function of cubism is to make an objective statement of its subject, doing so in the mathematically equivalent terminology of art. To the unpracticed eye, of course, the representation appears to be distorted, but this is not because of the artist's own subjectivism. The viewer is simply unaccustomed to looking at reality in this way. Valle-Inclán, however, is interested in deforming his subject, and so he revises the standard cubist technique to serve his intention. For example, the flashing lights of a candelabra reflect several figures in a mirror with "an oblique and disparate geometry" (VI, 3, iii). Another scene tells how a moving figure enters "disturbing the golden symmetry of mirrors and consoles" (I, 2, ii). And elsewhere, this same idea of motion as a disruptive agent is repeated: "The flutter of a reflection unhinged the walls of the Green Chamber" (III, 2, vi). In all cases, the concept of space implied is one of permanence. Reality has a certain order, which seems fixed until a moving element enters to destroy it. Space does not appear to be flexible or instrumental; it is just there in a fixed, almost object-like fashion. Nor does the phenomenon of motion act to unite areas or volumes. Motion is unable to harmonize them by lending a sense of rhythm or flow. It simply breaks reality down.

Thus, space is used just as light was, to represent the original reality before its deformation. Motion not only parallels activity in life but also life's failures, because its appearance marks a deformation of the situation. Hence, original space is equivalent to normalcy in life, which, when disturbed by the futile action of Valle-Inclán's characters, results in the displacement of the normal arrangement of things. But instead of paying attention to this arrangement, either before or after the displacement, the author concentrates on the act of disintegration itself. He is not interested in the details of his subject once they have been deranged, but, rather, in capturing the moment of cubist dispersal in itself. In one example, a few staccato sentences are enough to convey the very instant of disintegration: "A convulsion of lights dying out. The midway shattering into angles. A cubist vision of the Harris Circus" (II, 2, v). After this, there is nothing more. The scene is transformed into pure motion by syntax and selectivity. There is little emphasis on the visual, in spite of the token gesture paid to light and to the term cubist.

The above scene is suited to the *esperpento* because it goes beyond the cubist intention to display all the facets of a subject. Valle-Inclán's description rejects the governing rule of multilinear cubism: stasis. Instead, it uses absolute motion, since the artistic motive behind the representation is not analytical, and even less synthetic. Its purpose is a victory over space and line by an act of disintegration— hence the selection of a moment when the lights are going out and the lines of the midway are breaking into bits. Although this effort might more properly be called futurism, the term is less important than the principle which links the entire vision to the *esperpentic* aesthetic. And that principle is the devaluation of space in favor of sequence, mutation, and confusion. Thus, in the larger sense, the scene serves surrealist ends rather than cubist ones. That is, the essence of the dreamworld is the emphasis on the visual symbol rather than on space. And even when surrealism uses spatial values, such as in depicting flight and vertigo, the purpose is to symbolize the emotions of the inner character: fear, desire, confusion.

Actually, it should not surprise us that an apparently cubist scene turns out to be surrealistic, for this also happens in painting, as in the case of De Chirico. A good example of the technique in this novel occurs in one Chagall-like sentence where "at intervals, the enormous eye of the horse received a light during the play of moving silhouettes that cut the circle of candlelight" (IV, 7, iv). We can immediately imagine a section of an eye upon which are superimposed the broken outlines of shadows cast by the candle. It is so much like the fantastic horse's head in Chagall's painting that, coincidence notwithstanding, the same aesthetic principle is in force. This consists of removing a subject from human perspective and redesigning it without reference to normal proportion. Of course, such a technique can simply be regarded as nonobjective, and our example here indicates nothing more. But in view of other instances already examined, it should be clear that Valle-Inclán's purpose is to deform, not to analyze.

This usurpation of cubist analysis for the benefit of *esperpentismo* acquires a different value within the same technique of silhouette drawing. In a prison scene, for example, the sun's rays are shown through the high window bars as they "split the square jail-hall into triangles." Some of the men move in search of "sunless triangles," while being aware of death's proximity, an identical destiny for them all that fixes "a single accent in the diversity of faces and expressions." As other men sit, "the triangulated light of the jail placed the figures' emaciated appearance in bold relief with a modern and cubist modulation" (V, 3, iii). Since the triangle image has no variation, it is evident that Valle-Inclán did not intend to emphasize cubist details. On the other hand, he did want to depict human tragedy—an old theme—with a "modern" modulation. By disfiguring the traditional face and capturing a new angle in the anatomy of pain, he creates the *esperpento*. This is only one effect, and a partial one, but combined with others, it ushers in the surrealist atmosphere. At times, the mood is precipitated by the natural environment, as when the moon, "wearing a cloud as a bandage over its eyes, plays blind man's bluff with the stars" (VII, 3, vi). Or else the moon appears with braggadoccio, swaggering in the spirit of the carnival below it. But in all cases, fantastic and cubist motifs are never developed for their own sake, but as props for an ulterior motive.

As a whole, the *esperpento* reveals a difference between the stated theory of a mathematically applied deformation and the practice of it. The novel, although strict in organization, is not consistent throughout. This inconsistency contributes in part to the uncanny situation that purports to be true. For example, the concept of stasis varies. As we have seen, static conditions are rejected in the cubist passages. However, when Valle-Inclán desires a feeling of temporal paralysis, he dispenses with space altogether: "Forms, shadows, lights multiplied and entwined, inducing a caliginous and dazzling oriental vibration that is formed by opium and marihuana" (II, 1, vii). Purely visible, or visual, elements are converted into motion, and then they seem to escape from space, going from vibration into narcosis. Thus, reality is evaded by an understatement of its sense data and dimensions. And at the same time, the scene is infiltrated by a nonspatial sensibility, which creates a dreamworld induced by dope.

The result of this loss of primary experience is that other perceptions, as that of chronology, tend to be exaggerated. Eventually, these grow so far out of proportion that they lose their definition and significance. Such is the case in another episode of drugged awareness:

> Time seems to have prolonged all action, absurdly suspended on the apex of one minute, stupified, crystallized, neat, inverisimilar, as happens under the influence of marihuana (II, 3, iv).

Here, a transition is effected from a world perceived through narcotics to a new world of abstraction. This distortion of time indicates how far reality is stripped of its basic structure during the surrealist transformation. No longer do we find traces of sensation or measurement. Color, line, action, and thought are all neutralized. The sense of sharpness in the words "crystallized" and "neat" fail to refer to anything concrete; they are illusions fostered by the excruciating awareness of a single moment in time. However, this too is lost in the eventual breakdown of meaning produced by the stupor of drugs. The only value offered by the apex of time is that it provides a framework for the nonexperience to take place.

Slowly it dawns upon us that Valle-Inclán considers reality itself to be a nonexperience. The drugs are merely a pretext for revealing this truth artistically. Consequently, we find similar effects of alienation and the "dull sensation of somnolent irreality" occurring after some whiskey drinks (VI, 1, ii). In fact, the simple, abject misery of life is sufficient cause for experiencing a nightmarish intuition of the world. This is best illustrated by the motif of the beggarly blind man. In one episode, he plays the guitar, accompanied by his singing daughter, while the garish saloon becomes a scene painted the color of lividness. The piano is "blind" because it is encased in black canvas during the day, and its keys sound "hypochondriac." And yet, these traits belong to the father and daughter, the latter also being noted for her "dead girl's face" and the "funereal" tray she carries. Moreover, the guitar music is fingered in "livid scales," while "the livid voice, in the livid illumination of the deserted hall, screeched out in inverisimilar high pitch" (III, 1, iv).

The insistence on inverisimilitude, along with the accumulation of vaguely disturbing details, points the way to the surrealist mode. It does not matter that the scene is taken from life's sordidness, for people like this blind guitarist are not really living. The episode bears no resemblance to livable reality, either in the transference of human traits to nonhuman objects or in the reduction of color and music to a single-toned travesty. Although this situation is a rather obvious picture of death in life, its technique becomes the key to more subtle forms of dehumanization, as we shall see. Here, the human factor is quite recognizable; the only disfigured elements are the human experience and sensory phenomena. But even now, the essential vision of grotesque tragedy is already outlined.

It is interesting to note that Valle-Inclán's stylized cubism is integrated into the more traditional, post-Romantic sensibility. This is why the passages under discussion retain their human interest even while evading reality. A number of devices are used which combine the cubist and modernist approaches, often with strange results. We find fireflies "inflaming their dance of lights in the blurred and lunar geometry of the garden" (II, 3, vii). Or, another garden has a "gallant geometry of fountains and myrtles," columns of cypresses, and "immobile clauses" of reflecting pools. This same setting is contemplated by aristocrats whose eyes are like blue porcelain and whose stilted postures come straight from a minuet (VI, 2, vi). The style and details of these examples reveal how self-conscious Valle-Inclán was in manipulating different techniques. He was clever enough at it to succeed, but the high artifice of such scenes adds one final note of discord to the *esperpento*.

One might say that Valle-Inclán's eclectic use of many styles is proof of his esteem for them. But when it came to creating characters with these styles, he showed an apparently deep disrespect for the human personality. The cruelty and pitiless sarcasm of the author's characterizations make him seem to be unfeeling. Just as exaggeration in style leads to mannerism, in character-description it ends in caricature. In this regard, Valle-Inclán is particularly fond of animalization and even mummification of his personages.[7] One reason for this is his desire for humor, although this is often a secondary consideration. His main intent is to highlight a particular attribute that is unique to the individual under scrutiny. By concentrating on a peculiar trait, and by naming it whenever the personage appears, Valle-Inclán develops a characteristic exaggeration that is not only amusing but has a grotesque function as well.

The most important category in this technique is the use of animalization. Since there are so many examples, it is pointless to list them all, but these three are most typical: "a snout rocked by a goat's laugh"; "dwarfed, oriental hands . . . an enslaved smile, and the oblique eyes of a serpent"; "from the remote window, perched in the immobility of a sacred crow. . . . " Throughout the novel, the most classic instances involve the tyrant Banderas, who is often portrayed as an owl or some other bird of gloom. In all cases, the shadow of Goya is perceptible, although not dominant. The painter's moralistic tone is lacking in these animalizations, and in its place is Valle-Inclán's pleasure in perversity, his desire to ridicule and contort the faces of his creatures. The rationale behind these portraits is twofold. One is essentially a political judgment: that the dictatorship has forced an inhuman existence upon victims and victors alike. The other involves a vision of the absurd, the fact that the social situation in the novel is so incredible that it requires an equally unbelievable mode of expression in order to be artistically effective.

As we have seen, animal motifs have served other Spanish surrealists also. But whereas Dali and Lorca used this method in order to explore their concept of the chain of life, Valle-Inclán's search goes in a reverse direction. His *esperpento* shows the petrification of human life. In other words, his treatment of human features displays them in an atavism to rock and mineral states. And at the same time, he casts these immobilized features into an artistic representation. For example, individuals are described regressively as having the "rotund belly of a Tibetan idol," or a face like a "taciturn mummy with green saliva," or a head "as bald as a large onion that shone like a Buddhist belly." Thus, the characters are immobilized in an earlier form of existence or in an ancient cult. In addition to promoting an aesthetic of unreality, these comparisons create an art within an art. Since the characters are often handled like puppets, the additional stylization of their forms into art objects creates an interior duplication within the novel. Elsewhere, a note of preposterousness is added ("his turkey-like roundness"), where realistic details carry the portrait into the realm of caricature. Other examples of parchment heads, wooden stick figures, and ivory skulls demean the value of human life in various ways, but always with the central purpose of confirming a grotesque theory of existence.

The concept of grotesquerie as an aesthetic goes beyond the practice of surrealism and cannot be discussed here completely. However, insofar as the *esperpento* is concerned, the grotesque consists of an ironic distortion based on a dehumanizing principle. Without this suppression of the human factor, there would be no surrealist deformation in *Tirano Banderas*. Nor could there be any genuine *esperpento* without an element of pessimistic irony residing in the distortion. For example, any personage who is described with the "automatism of a puppet" cannot really enjoy a fully human status in the narrator's eyes. And this is frequently the case in this novel. The systemization of the actors' movements is partly the result of literary technique, as we have seen. But more important, it is also the emblem of their reduced human role. As people, the characters seem to have lost some of the qualities that would have assured them of at least a semblance of participation in a coherent existence. But instead, the individual is not a believable man, and his plight does not rouse us to many strong feelings. There are exceptions, of course, but not many. In general, the character's voice acquires a "machinelike modulation." Thus, when he calls out, he is heard as one more noise emitted from the nonhuman realm.

However, the reader cannot help feeling that there is something terribly wrong with the situation. These people are not automatons and dolls, but individuals who are made to suffer a dehumanizing transformation. The artist's systematic comparison of human with mechanical parts becomes a relentless degradation and mockery. It reveals his personal attitude toward his creatures, as well as their own inherent characteristics. Consequently, their metamorphosis is the result of the author's analysis of their interior lives, just as much as it stems from their social condition. The personages are hopeless not only because of their failures but because they have lost their dignity at the hands of their creator's disrespectful treatment. Valle-Inclán scorns the external gestures that are man's last recourse to self-respect, and he condemns the moral failure of their psychic world. They are dissected and analyzed from the outside in, from voice to inner spirit. Hence, they are all like a certain character in the novel who had a

> thin voice, like a broken-down piano, and the rigid mobility of an automatic doll, an intractable spring action, a private life of coiled wire. He smiled in a dark and mannered grimace (VII, 2, ii).

Valle-Inclán's personages resemble T. S. Eliot's hollow and stuffed men, lacking the vital substance or spirit that once linked them to the world of meaning. But they are different, too, in that they have been moved off-center through no fault of their own. It is as if their gears have slipped and their lives no longer mesh with the real world around them. And here is Valle-Inclán's diabolical irony. He is saying that the world also moves mechanically, but that as long as one keeps his wheels meshed, everyone is satisfied and no one is the wiser. But as soon as the inner spring is pulled out of shape, one's entire mechanism is exposed for the cheap trickery that it is. In this discovery there is an element of sadness, and on occasion the author permits himself a moment of compassion. He can, for example, mitigate his technique of animalization by giving a downcast man the expression of a whipped dog; or he will find a "baroque and statuary pathos" in a sinewy figure (III, 3, v). But for the most part Valle-Inclán lets little stand in the way of his ruthlessness in stripping men of their prerogatives as human beings. This is justifiable in isolated cases, like that of the degenerate Spanish minister, whose facial cosmetics, egg-like eyes, and smile of "inverisimilar elasticity" lend themselves easily to the idea of masks and dolls (I, 2, iii). But the novel's widespread deformed dehumanization can only be explained by Valle-Inclán's personal theory of the concave mirror.

Here, then, is where cultural and political concepts gain stronger impetus in the *esperpento* than in the surrealist mode as we have seen it thus far. Social ideology is not necessarily a part of the surrealist's repertoire, although there is often a close connection. But *esperpentismo* is both an outgrowth of an ideological position, and also the aesthetic medium for expressing it.[8] And conversely, the raison d'être of the *esperpento* aesthetic is a cultural or political theory. Thus, the compassionate moments just referred to are not so much displays of Valle-Inclán's emotion, as they are frank admissions of his intellectual role vis-à-vis the aesthetics of his novel. For example, he sketches in the "ambiguous expression of compassion and disdain in the funereal face" of a dying old man, a description that fits the author's attitude perfectly. But the statement seems insufficient for contemporary art, and incompatible with the notion of Spain as a grotesque deformation of Europe. And so Valle-Inclán twists the ambiguity into a definitive deformation, without withdrawing his personal position: "The waning of that buffoon in misfortune had a certain grotesque solemnity like the mummers' dance burials that conclude the pre-Lent carnival" (V, 1, vii).[9]

What is of interest here is not the incongruity of misfortune and buffoonery, for this juxtaposition is a standard technique for creating the grotesque. The point is that the author has endowed grotesqueness with solemnity because he himself regards Spain's condition with gravity, even though her destiny may be ridiculed by Europe. There is little amusement in the *esperpento*. Its comedy never occurs in pure form, and laughter is never light-hearted. Humor is always sarcastic, black, and slightly demented, its bitterness being derived from the sad thoughts concerning Spanish life, and its madness stemming from the reckless dehumanization of the characters.

In addition to this cultural theory, another reason for the *reductio ad automatum* is the notion of absurdity. Although this idea is now associated with existentialist philosophy, its earlier roots in the surrealist mode were deep and essential. The dreamlike atmosphere of many settings created a sense of the absurd, but in *Tirano Banderas* this effect is achieved primarily through the "wretched sense" of life that is counterpoised against unrealized heroism. This happens in one of the novel's prison scenes, where a youth feels the "humiliation of his life" due to his political indifference. His condition reaches a crisis when existence becomes to him "absurd, unconscious like the postures of dolls that lie forgotten after a game" (V, 1, vi).

This sort of diction has become rhetorical by today's standards, but in 1926 it was one of the first literary counterparts of what the surrealist painters were doing with their mannequins. The purpose of such imagery was to express the absurd without losing some of the emotional overtones suggested by the traces of human tragedy. The attitudes struck by dolls do not in themselves arouse any feeling. Only when they evoke a human condition in the contemplator's imagination, do they create an illusion of human kinship. Pathos materializes after the viewer recognizes this similarity, although he is then overtaken by a sense of the absurd upon realizing that these are, after all, only dolls. Nevertheless, absurdity cannot arise without a prior equation between dolls and life. Unless the viewer first establishes a psychological identity with the figures, his sense of the absurd will not be awakened.

Nevertheless, the creation of absurdity is not due to pathos alone. The author's ideology and aesthetic both control its formation. Thus, Valle-Inclán's skepticism about Hispanic culture leads him to invent special techniques of dehumanization. Inanimate objects are elevated to the order of human semblance, and human elements are reduced to the level of lifeless things. It is this ideological point of departure that distinguishes the dehumanizing process in the *esperpento* from that employed by other surrealists. Yet, Valle-Inclán never falls into the obvious routine of propaganda, as did Alberti. In fact, it is historically interesting to note that his merger of political and aesthetic awareness was repeated years later by the French surrealists.

There is one final aspect of the absurdity of *Tirano Banderas* that brings the novel into the aesthetic scope of the surrealist mode. Its linguistic modifications are among the most drastic to be found anywhere outside of automatic writing. Without losing complete syntactic and semantic control, the language matches the revolutionary experimentation of the *esperpento*'s dehumanization. A few of Valle-Inclán's reforms are now of parochial interest when compared to European standards. Some of these include his preciosity far beyond the artifices of modernism, his expanded use of slang, and his lexicographer's interest in the regional speech of Latin America. But from the standpoint of surrealist aesthetics, the most important factor is the disintegration of language. Just as the novel's characters were stripped of traditional value, so too is the linguistic stature of the prose broken down by a number of clever techniques. The use of narrative fragmentation, hyperbole, interjection, and the obscurity of meaning all contribute to this disintegration.

The best description of the mechanism involved occurs in the description of a narcotic hallucination (VI, 3, i). The Spanish minister is under the effects of a morphine injection, which has paralyzed his speech without impairing the mental processes of language. Thus, we find in his egg-like eyes "the fluctuating signs, the toboggans of thought," which initiate the descent into a pit of disparate images. He goes sliding down "rapid toboggans of shadow," and reaches a "stillwater of consciousness." The downward journey shifts from toboggans of thought to toboggans of shadow, or from the mental process itself, to some larger penumbra within the arena of consciousness. Having reached bottom mentally, the minister's thinking mechanism can begin to assess what surrounds it. Let us note that the diction in this account is similar to the kind of submergence described by Aleixandre. Indeed, there is little difference in the structure of both subconscious worlds. The most significant feature is the reproduction of inner motion and space. In other words, instead of a wide color range, what is duplicated subconsciously are the dimensions of reality.

The drug addict's inner world reveals that "images had an isolated and ecstatic value, a livid and cruel relief" which enables one image to be distinguished from another. Hence, the technique is far from impressionistic not only in its lack of chromatism but in its linearity. Moreover, since everything is an illusion, spatial values are fallacious. In order to correct this, the principle of dimension is removed from its normal association with space, and is linked to the thought process. That is, the concept of space is transferred to the function of words themselves. This does not mean that words are used to re-create the sense of space, but that they are themselves subjected to it phenomenally. Thus, we learn that "some words, between angles and grammatical breaks, linked themselves together with epigraphic vigor." Words are no longer images that represent objects and their spatial dimensions. Words form their own relationships in space, become volumes in their own right within the hallucinatory depths of the mind. Consequently, although the pit is full of images, the latter do not have their former spatial relationships. The words that once represented them are now autonomous, set free by narcosis, and delineating their own volume with the "numbers of a broken grammar filled with angles." As the mind is liberated from reality, there is an equivalent release of the word from its role as a symbol.

After the breakdown of rational thought, an additional loss occurs in coherent language structure. To remedy this, a new sense of order is required. Valle-Inclán furnishes this by means of geometrical order in space. Thus, "polyhedrons of thought" are inscribed within the inner stage of drugged consciousness, where "acrobatic clauses linked by a hidden nexus" perform. Hence, language reaches a level of ultimate perfection or purity. Normally, mental perceptions are given significance by syntax and verbal image. When syntax loses its meaning under the influence of drugs, then the image becomes the sole agent of the mind's perceptions. But since the entire vision is hallucinatory, there is no real object requiring representation. The imagination simply produces a mental image. Word images, of course, are usually symbols that represent objects which exist in reality. Therefore, in the hallucination, the word takes precedence over the imagined image, and preempts the spatial role once held by the object and its image. That is, what was normally a spatial relationship of objects becomes a geometry of words that substitutes for grammar.

Nevertheless, there is more than linguistic geometry in this vision of the absurd. Further along in the drugged condition, "thought, diluting itself into a vague, jocose emotion, transforms itself into successive plastic intuitions." The idea is phrased imprecisely, but it means that with reason having slipped away, the mind becomes vague, and then irresponsible. This accounts for the jocose or frivolous emotion that is felt when the mind is set free from the rigidity of logic. Clear sentence formation is replaced by a "vigorous mental graphism, and an absurd logic of the dream." Here, then, is the essence of surrealist imagery. The dream never appears logical by the standards of the outside world. And yet dreams contain all the elements of the real world, albeit in absurd contexts. Moreover, the nature of dreamwork is plastic and visual, in accordance with reality. Thus, in order to represent oneiric imagery, a certain logic is necessary which we call absurd by realistic standards, but which is logical for the dream. Hence the term "mental graphism," a grammar of images that obeys the rules of dream logic, and expresses its meaning visually instead of with verbal order.

The dream technique is used only once in *Tirano Banderas*, but the overall effect of hallucination is often present in the incongruous descriptions already described. The result is a novel that attacks the traditional groundwork of literary analysis. The critical perspective, language, and narrative devices employed by conventional novelists come under the destructive scrutiny of Valle-Inclán's *esperpento*. By inventing this genre, he is able to both mock and mourn the culture that he depicts. And paradoxically, by undermining the normal methods of novel writing, he creates the only puppet show that must be produced by conventional narration in order to remain puppetry. The net effect ought to be depressing, due to his concept of man and Hispanic culture. But instead, the novel is exhilarating, and for the same reasons that save it from the propaganda which mars most social realism. And this is its aesthetic genius, the requirement that it be read on surrealism's own terms: with the logic of the absurd.

Chapter Ten

Intellectual Fairy Tales
(Gómez de la Serna, Jarnés, Arderius)

Although *Tirano Banderas* is the most important novel in Spain using surrealist techniques, it is only one of a series that appeared in the decade between 1920 and 1930. Most of these other narratives play a minor aesthetic role in Spanish surrealism, and their interest to critics is largely historical. But there are three novelists whose works reveal a significant cohesiveness in perspective, irony, and concept of reality. Their fiction veers away from deformation in favor of a playful fusion of fantasy and abstraction. By combining imagined and real events in mixed sequences, their method results in what is best described as an intellectual fairy tale. These writers are Ramón Gómez de la Serna, Benjamín Jarnés, and Joaquín Arderius, and I will deal with one novel by each in the sections that follow.

I

Turning from Valle-Inclán to Ramón Gómez de la Serna is like going from the theater to the circus: one leaves a demanding and significant experience for an idle and formless spectacle. One normally thinks of Ramón's novels as adventurous and extravagant feats of humor and style. In content, they are usually without much intellectual substance or psychological interest, and they reveal little structural experimentation. But their ingenious word plays and analogies, as well as their antic comedy, give them a special place in Spanish literature. Nevertheless, one suspects that after Ramón's creation of the *greguerías,* his reputation thrived more on flamboyance and monstrous prolixity than on sound literary merit. In any case, those novels which exhibit surrealistic tendencies do so without deep and disturbing transformations of reality, but rather by humorous eccentricity and preposterous situations. One such novel is *El incongruente* (Madrid, 1922).[1]

Implicit in this novel is an awareness of the whimsical foundation of modern society. Ramón suggests that despite the seriousness of European life, the innovations brought about by the twentieth century are modish and, when carried to their logical conclusion, absurd. As he observes in one prophetic statement, "some day they will devise a citizens' exploitation for advertising purposes, and unnoticed, will inscribe on everyone's backs the latest ad released by the Great Universal Agency" (18). This expectant gloom concerning man's future, phrased with a fashionable ironic judgment, typifies Ramonian humor without yielding to frivolity. It conceals what by now is a stereotyped vision of contemporary uniformity. But in 1922 the idea was still fresh, and the vogue of advertising was not as yet an integral feature of modern living. This idea, needless to say, is that people are nameless and have a single face, suffering democratically the burdens of the collectivity.[2]

Given this tacit concept of mass man, the kind of novel which can be written is somewhat predetermined. The hero Gustavo appears without a personality, and the characters around him are never described. For example, "Gustavo knew that no woman is different. There are only houses, balconies, and rooms that are different, or furniture of another kind, or oscillating positions . . . " (33). At the same time, the lack of human variety in existence is compensated by a new intimacy between man and objects. The depersonalization of the human world will be represented by a novel, not of characters, but of quirks. The people around Gustavo are shadowed in grey, and the protagonist himself is depicted as a series of oddities manifested in episodes. He has no well-defined personality, but he does have an inventory of foolish responses, which appear when stimulated by the proper circumstances. This is why he relates to situations and things instead of to people. As a result, the novel as an art form is perforce limited to anecdotal material and cannot move into the area of emotional activity. Hence the lack of human interest and vitality in this work, and the reason for Ramón's reliance on verbal liveliness or bizarre episodes for the illusion of narrative cohesion.

Even more notable than the psychological anesthesia of the novel is its indifference to structure and action. Just as life is the blank reflection of a faceless individual, so too is the novel a monotonous mirror of identical acts. And since the protagonist is devoid of personality, there is nothing to distinguish one event from any other. Consequently, it matters little which anecdote in his life is narrated and which is omitted, for the only difference between them is the type of inanity described. All episodes are absurd, and none is molded by character. Therefore, to write about every one of them is merely to give a catalog of incongruities. In fact, at one point Ramón does make just such a list. But in general, the narrator concludes that "better than making an inventory of them all, one should gather some of them together incongruently, with a seriousness independent of the chapter heading" (18). In other words, the novelist should adopt the technique of haphazard selection; the hero's disposition is uniform anyway. Moreover, the structural arrangement of these random incidents ought to be gratuitous. Precise chronology is unnecessary because Gustavo's life is composed of abrupt changes and incongruities which make narrative organization superfluous. In fact, "the very story of his life and the choice of chapters must be an incongruity" (11).

Thus, before one reaches the truly surrealist passages of this novel, one finds the basis of its aesthetic to rest on deliberate madness and disorder. This does not mean that Ramón is an irrationalist or subjectivist, but he does rely for effect on the preposterous humor of the absurd. His narrative structure is illogical for the same reason, although it has bearing on other aspects of the novel too. One of these is the effect of time on the central figure. Among Gustavo's silly problems is the fact that he can never find a Thursday. No matter where he goes, it always seems to be a day other than Thursday. Here, then, is a practical counterpart to the author's negligence of narrative form. The main character is displaced from time, removed from the normal sequence of events. This means that the novelist is fundamentally unimpressed with the temporal value of his story. The absence of Thursdays from his hero's life is equivalent to the random selection of incongruities. Both cases illustrate the uniform absurdity of life, but neither one requires the concept of time for corroboration.

Even so, chronology is not just a historical phenomenon that gives order to a story. It also concerns minutes and hours. Here too, Ramón slights time and strips it of its function. For example, he describes a clock on a building as having "a mirror dial that appeared illuminated, like electrically lighted clocks, but its hands were motionless, as if painted on the crystal" (108). With this stationary image, the paralysis of time is accomplished, and one more example of temporal deformity is added to the history of surrealism. The image is striking because it seems to be oblivious to the emotional possibilities of destroying time. The description is cold and detached, in keeping with the novel's total lack of human interest and intimacy. There is virtually no psychological impact to Ramón's sensibility and image creation. Similarly, the graphic forms which his ideas assume are as intellectually aloof as his preposterous humor is absurd. That is, neither image nor humor evokes more than the most abstract of responses in the reader, even though both deal with themes that trouble modern man.

Nowhere is this deficiency more visible than in the clock image, which lies flat on the prose page like a color cutout pasted onto a montage. Its visual quality is satisfactory, although two-dimensional, and it is a suitable analogy to the author's idea. But it remains just outside the border of plasticity, fading into the black and white symbolism of abstraction. And despite its reference to the technological world, the image falls short of tangibility. Nor does it reflect the novelist's interest in the problem of time, or invite the reader to become emotionally involved. In contrast to surrealism's most disturbing versions of deformed time, this one by Gómez de la Serna is as harmless as a pleasant fantasy, and, like his circus humor, provides a "nice" way to spend a few moments. He is so free of the hauntings of time that he describes how "the clock's tickings couple into lively pairs. Sometimes two ticks chase each other and unite like flies in flight" (16). Here, then, is superficiality at its most unexpected, for the surrealist modes most frequently cultivated are abandoned for the arid realm of impersonality and simple design.

Nor is there much depth-probing of Gustavo's dream life. An itemization of his dreams is given, including those where he turns into a table, a fish, and a Negro idol; where he climbs the marble stairs of a palace full of queens; where sudden changes in light are accompanied by a colored ball bouncing into the scene; and where he sees himself duplicated a half-dozen times, and yet does not recognize himself. Unfortunately, these glimpses into a world of many creative possibilities are never repeated or developed. Thus, whatever seeds of surrealist discord that might have taken root in the novel are scattered in waste. A similar abundance of initial conceptions occurs in the City of Wax Dolls, where windows are made of mirrors, not glass, and where houses appear to be "expressionless" beneath a faltering moon (107). The situation affords little intimacy or probing in depth for the secrets of the city and its dwelling places. Indeed, upon "looking more closely, it seemed to be the dream of a monstrous carpenter, the project of a city that he failed to realize" (109).

And so the list continues, revealing the fertility of Gómez de la

Serna's mind, and his incapacity for sustaining an inspiration beyond its first bright flare. This unstructured work can hardly be
called a novel, but it could have become a contrived mosaic had
there been any thematic recurrence. However, it shows little tendency in this respect. As for the prose, it is fickle but not capricious,
for even a caprice can be built into a loose unification of themes. In
short, *El incongruente* is an abortive attempt at a surrealist novel,
whose embryo is interesting for its budding anatomy of techniques.

II

A more consummate novelist and stylist is Benjamín Jarnés,
whose work, in contrast to Gómez de la Serna's, is unfortunately out
of print and unread. When we examine his novels after 1929, we
find that his surrealism has been fully assimilated into the larger
generic structure of narrative fiction. The surrealist aesthetic is not
fully conventionalized in these novels, but it has lost its flair and
unique boldness. One reason for this is that various experimental
elements are organically integrated within the novel so that no single
feature stands out from the rest. Another reason is that Jarnés not
only uses surrealism as an artistic technique but he also expounds
it analytically in discursive passages and prologues. One particularly
explicit treatment is found in *Teoría del zumbel* (1930), which is
the work that will occupy me in this section.

Like most of Jarnés' novels, *Teoría del zumbel* is characterized
by the ironic method of self-objectivization. By this I mean that
there are two levels of reality in the narrative. The characters are
portrayed in a double focus: as realistically conceived people, and
as the fictional personages that they are. In other words, they are
described as principals in the story, but at the same time, the narrator speculates about them as might a critic, from a perspective
outside the novel's framework. In fact, this artificiality extends even
to the author, who projects himself into the novel as one more member of his cast.

Jarnés' technique works in one of two ways. He either inserts a
dialog in play form, prefacing his speeches with "Me," or else he
adopts the first-person narrator's tone, and enters the action along
with the other characters. The result in either case is an ambiguous
novel structure. On the one hand, we have a genuine novel whose
plot and personalities move with apparent autonomy, despite the
author's strange presence. But at the same time, we are given an
internal discourse on the workings of fiction. The novel offers a
static self-examination, in which the characters and author are

aware of their roles within the narrative and hold dialogs to discuss their problems. Thus, it is not uncommon to see the author step into the action, halt it, and debate with his personages about their future course of behavior.

In one sense, this approach imitates the Unamuno-Pirandello technique of the autonomous and self-conscious hero. Nevertheless, Jarnés avoids the metaphysical issues raised by those authors, and concentrates instead on aesthetic theory. Rather than analyzing the problems of will, destiny, and the nature of reality, Jarnés prefers to see how his novelistic form is affected by reason, emotion, dream, and sense perception. For example, even if the author includes himself in the novel and converses with his creatures, his discussion ignores the relationship between man and his Creator in order to treat the connection between characterization and artistic structure. Consequently, the function of the novel becomes a matter of fictionalizing a certain kind of reality, and at the same time examining this reality with a nonfictional perspective.

Teoría del zumbel derives its title from its central motif, a spinning top which a child winds with his cord and then flings to the pavement. The boy's game is lively and capricious, and he allows the top to spin for some time. When it languishes, he revives it, and finally it loses impetus, falters, and reels about until it comes to a stop. As long as this "childish—and divine—caprice" lasts, the top will keep spinning. In this infantile situation, the boy is the figure of authority and control, and the little world within his power is the game of tops.[3] But let us imagine, as Jarnés does, that the macrocosmic version of this game is a universe full of spinning worlds, with God as the Spinner. In such a case, the laws of motion, equilibrium, and order are not fixed and eternal, but are instead the function of a Player's fancy. If God chooses, he can abandon the game, and a world will topple over and fall. But even while the balance is kept, it is merely the result of playful whim and detached amusement. While there is nothing more serious and perfect than a spinning top, the unpredictable nature of the player is a flimsy axis for so harmonious an operation.

The notion of God as a juvenile is elaborated in a scene where the protagonist, Saulo, is recovering from a delirium after a car accident. God visits him in the hospital, dressed as an old man with boyish impulses. He shows Saulo what infinity and eternity are like, and how divine time consists of an eternal present. However, Saulo insists that he wishes to continue being subjected to human time, rather than dying now in order to gain an eternal afterlife. He adheres to this even when God shows him pieces of string of different lengths, representing the limited life-spans of famous deceased men. An argument ensues, and Saulo is rescued by the devil, who sometimes thwarts God's plans.

What interests Jarnés in this surrealist fantasy are the concepts of divine will and human freedom. His basic question deals with what happens to the top when it is abandoned by the child. Since the top's harmonious motion is left to the whimsical abandon of a young boy, there is something unjust about its ultimate fate, at least from the standpoints of beauty and meaning. Furthermore, there is a similar discrepancy on the human level. Here, a gap exists between man's plans or desires, and his destiny, which is affected by factors beyond his control. And finally, in the realm of the novel, neither characters nor plot are ever free of the author's will. The point made by Jarnés is that these traditionally accepted conditions do not respond to the logic of reality and common sense. The modern era has taught us much that contradicts the seriousness of the universe and its so-called laws. Much of existence is haphazard, and it is absurd for man to have such a sober attitude toward himself and his actions. It would be more realistic for him to view the world as an undetermined composite of possibilities. As far as the novel is concerned, this holds true even more. The author, like God, has no fixed purpose to his work, which means that creation is left to the chance whim of an irresponsible player.

This situation reflects the aesthetic crisis of contemporary art, for it shows how futile it is for the self-conscious artist to be serious. Having realized that he is playing the role of God, the artist must also admit that he often does not know what to create or what rules to follow. Therefore, says Jarnés, why not write a novel in which the creator is ignorant of his purpose, and in which the progress of the narrative is undetermined and susceptible to caprice. Just as the real world is devoid of permanent laws, so too is a work of art beyond the scope of precepts, the one a toy of an infantile fancy, and the other liable to the whims of the artist.

Nevertheless, a work of this sort would for a while gather an initial momentum to operate on its own, just as the top spins free of its cord and escapes from the player's control. Therefore, we would expect the novel to have autonomous sections which develop of their own accord, without the author's intervention. This is why Jarnés tells one character that his novel grew without him, and why the same character calls him an absurd novelist for having abandoned his personages. However, the truth is that when art becomes a game, the only structural law is that of chance. Everything else is not only possible but occurs without the responsibility of the player. Of course, the novelist does write the entire novel, and in this sense is responsible for it. But if he chooses, he can let the narrative falter, permit certain scenes to reel out of focus, and declare a favorable destiny for his characters even while allowing them to pursue less appropriate alternatives. Jarnés does all of these things in his own novel.

A good example of the free-spinning narrative occurs in one dialog between the author and his minor characters. Among the latter is a priest, with whom Jarnés plans the future course of events for the hero and heroine. The priest asserts that God's will must prevail, namely, that Saulo should marry Blanca for the sake of his soul's salvation. Jarnés objects to the folly of attempting to alter a man's destiny by theological means. Thus, he withdraws from the scheme, and writes his own novel controverting the tradition of the logically developed narrative. In it, God is portrayed as an old man who "smiles like a boy who can play with millions of toys," and who has "a chest of human destinies, and cords of different lengths" (204). In contrast to this idea, Jarnés elevates the principle of chance to first importance, with events occurring without much justification. As a result, there is no formal or thematic coherence to the novel, even though its structure is orderly and its content easily understood. In fact, the novel seeks the least probable resolution to its events, in order to emphasize the theory of reality as a spinning top. Existence is viewed in its final, wobbly stage, where everything occurs without direction or meaningful causality. The novelist can choose to let his work flounder or to correct its motion, but neither reality nor its artistic counterpart can pretend to be governed by anything more than a whim.

There are other examples of Jarnés' desire to destroy causal relationships. He steps into the scene when Saulo's friends are about to dissuade him from marrying, and allows the original action to proceed. And when Saulo returns home from the hospital, his servant does not recognize him. Later, the hero finds a new Saulo at his bank, and is told by his former secretary that he is a ghost and must leave them alone. Finally, he drives past the site of his original accident, but this time he crashes and does not survive. None of these episodes has anything to do with characterization, dramatic construction, or any other aspect of the novelistic genre. This fact is important, because Jarnés was a meticulous craftsman who knew the history of the novel and its mechanisms very well. But by the same token, he understood how difficult it is to introduce surrealist innovations in so logical an art form. Since his attitude toward literature had always been theoretical, he was not, as Valle-Inclán was, able to carry out his experiments without justifying them aesthetically. He felt obliged, therefore, to explain the limitations of the novel genre as it existed then, and how its scope could be extended into the irrational. As the novel stood, it presented a universe determined by a responsible legislator—either God or the author. But the discovery that life can be a game helped to encourage art to bend the logic of its dimensions. Thus, Jarnés shows that it is necessary to destroy the narrative sequence and the bond between character and action before surrealist fantasy can enter.

The fantasies themselves, along with the self-conscious humor, are specific traits of the novel's surrealism. We might call their presence a benign deformation, in comparison to the techniques of Valle-Inclán and Dali, where irreality is psychologically disturbing. In Jarnés' work, the humor arises from the author's own pleasure as he amuses himself with tricks of language and commentary on his characters. Thus, the reader finds himself once removed from the comic element, for he sees the novelist smiling at his own irony. In addition to this distilled humor, there is also a concurrence of several levels of reality at the same time. In other words, different kinds of reality appear simultaneously: the fictional scene, the author as character, and the author as author. Not only are the situations humorous but they sometimes become incongruous. Moreover, the direction in which the novel is deformed tends toward absurdity. As we have seen in other chapters, the absurd may be purely linguistic. However, in Jarnés it consists of action sequences, or even motion within a single sequence, that make no sense. Reality is transformed into a lawless caprice, with normal patterns of thinking now reconstructed into an absurd logic. Nevertheless, the confusion of realities is saved from a nightmarish effect by the author's frequent irony.

There are three major surrealistic fantasies in *Teoría del zumbel.* The most metaphysical of them occurs in the chapter entitled "Biography of a Watch." The sequence begins with Saulo staggering drunkenly through a forest, looking for his fiancée Blanca. The trees slow down his progress, and one of them becomes his grandfather, who upbraids his libertinage. Breaking away, Saulo stumbles into another tree, which seizes him and turns into his father. They argue about Saulo's watch, which the family has passed down from father to son, and which traditionally holds a photograph of its owner's wife. But Saulo frees himself, declaring his intention to have one last fling before marrying. As he lurches forward, three frogs mock him, and then two sirens stretch out their arms to him, one of them being Blanca. He descends underground with her, coming out into an open field where spectators, including a band, children, and a priest, are ready to witness their marriage. But Saulo staggers on even further, the watch is projected into the future and dies of old age, and at the end of the fantasy, Saulo falls down and is robbed by a gypsy girl.

The meaning of this sequence is somewhat abstract, but hardly obscure. The central themes of time and escapism are clear enough. Saulo is unwilling to face the duties that correspond to his position as the mature head of the family line. He ignores the tradition of past generations by scorning the true use of the watch, which is to measure the period of his maturity and the moment for taking a wife. Instead, he runs away from these symbols of time and responsibility, and eventually is freed by losing the watch to a thief. But in addition to the abstractions, we find elements of pure fairy tale. The ugly and moralistic toads that issue warnings, the metamorphosis of trees, the enchanted princess revealing herself as a siren, the descent to the underworld, and the happy ending where the entire kingdom is assembled to welcome the hero—all of these are borrowings from infantile and mythological literature. As such, they represent a legitimate source of symbolism and magic realism. Furthermore, in so cerebral a novel as this one, these fantastic elements provide a grace and almost an innocence that make their quaint irreality an effective counterambiance to the narrative setting.

However, it is important to note that the fantasy does not end happily, and this is what makes the episode surrealistic. A fairy tale alone is not an example of surrealism, whereas a fairy tale used gratuitously in a sober context is. In other words, where the entire framework is composed of the magical and the supernatural, the reader must accept the reality presented to him on its own terms and with its own laws. The total representation is without ambiguity and fully logical, and where reason fails, the rule is to suspend disbelief for the sake of pretense. By contrast, the use of magic realism or surrealism requires an incompatibility of two different systems or laws. It is from this divergence or incongruity that the sense of the absurd is produced. Such is the case here, for the situation states a conflict between two realities: Saulo running away in the real world and then being robbed at the end by a real gypsy, as opposed to Saulo descending with the siren Blanca. Each of the two separate frameworks is ruled by its own dimensions and congruences, but their integration results in a surrealistic rhapsody.

If the first fantasy is a good example of beneficent infantilism, the second one demonstrates violence and primitivism. In this sequence the protagonist is Blanca, whose nightmare is described in such a way that we are not aware that she has fallen asleep until after the episode is over and she is awake. The reason for this is that Jarnés skillfully weaves together the unreal details at the beginning of the dream with the realistic details that occur in the scene just prior to it. This fusion is so smooth, that the borderline between realism and fantasy disappears, and it is only after Blanca is fully caught in a web of grotesque fabrication that her departure from reality is comprehended. This technique, then, is identical to that used in Saulo's adventure, for there, too, Jarnés gradually combined the real and unreal in order to ease Saulo's entry into fairyland. But later, Saulo's exit is portrayed as a stumbling out into the real world again, where he drops drunkenly to the ground and falls asleep. Blanca, however, leaves her nightmare by waking up. Nevertheless, in both cases the reader is first led to believe that there has been no actual change in the reality of the situation.

Blanca's nightmare is a composite of erotic and theological symbols reflecting the conflicts of her waking life. The circumstances preceding the dream involve her waiting for Saulo's clandestine visit, and her desire and apprehension about what will be their first act of love. When he does not appear at the agreed time, she is overcome with fears, anguish, guilt, and a sense of betrayal. She feels like Eve, with a serpent around her neck, and when she tries to pray, a tiny gorilla enters to mock her. Other nocturnal beasts, reptiles, and insects berate and menace her, but she cannot run away. The girl falls on her bed and the monsters suddenly vanish. She finds her "angel of modesty," climbs upon him to escape, and in the next instant is running to a lake. But she is driven away from the water by frogs shooting darts from their eyes, and these frogs resemble the men of Sodom. Next, Blanca comes upon her sister, who is lying naked on the ground, and she lies next to her. Just then, Lot appears and stretches out on top of her sister, only it is now her father, not Lot, on her sister. Blanca runs down to the sea, hiding her breasts and abdomen in the water while old men watch her with binoculars. Trying to reach shore again, she wants to cry out for Saulo but forgets his name. The old men turn into trees, and Blanca pulls herself out of the sea by the branches, finding herself in God's Paradise. She wants to rest, but dark clouds gather, and the angel of death roars for her to leave. Dogs chase close behind her, and she is almost lost, but just then her angel appears, tears off his wings, and throws them to her so that she can fly away to catch the four o'clock plane. However, the plane does not arrive, and her wings fall apart. Blanca is then awakened by her sister, who finds her naked and tearing at the pillow.

This long sequence has a number of symbols that stand for the same idea. The basic meaning is that Blanca imagines her imminent sexual life to be ugly and instinctual, and she protects herself against it by evoking several authority figures from her moral past. The animalism and aggressive motifs represent Blanca's fear of sex, and her moral condemnation of it. All of this is no longer very sophisticated to us, although, at the time, it was not very obvious. However, the episode is interesting because its religious transformations give the nightmare a sermon-like tone. In addition, the erotic symbolism is elaborated clearly, an unusual practice for Spanish literature. And the novel is a rarity from the psychoanalytical viewpoint too, since it analyzes character by means of image and fantasy, instead of by dialog and action.

What is peculiar about these fantasies, and especially the third, is that no important difference seems to exist between the realistic and the fantastic. Nor is any apology made for switching levels of reality. Reality and surreality are two modes of the same vital experience as it is lived by the personages. For example, the third fantasy produces a careening landscape when Saulo's car crashes. It is as if he had fallen into a gigantic kaleidoscope and found everything whirling chaotically around him. The reader is confused as to what the events mean, and knows that they are not typical of his normal reality. But from the narrative's perspective, there is no way to distinguish between the realistic and the fantastic. Both realms exhibit coherent sensory perception. The concepts of space and motion remain constant. Language does not change its meaning, and there is no grammatical absurdity. In other words, from the novel's own point of view, events are accepted as happening in a single continuum of reality.

Jarnés constructs his novelistic dimensions in such a way that the narrative progresses evenly from reality to surreality. The difference between the two realms lies in value, not in perspective. The reader discovers that he must attribute symbolic meanings to certain scenes. Whereas the realistic sections are comprehensible on the face value of events and images, in the surrealistic ones he must look beyond the mere representation. It is, of course, true that Saulo's forest episode is utterly fantastic. But we make this judgment from a position outside the novel's framework. From the narrator's own perspective, as well as from Saulo's, these events are really happening. Otherwise, the author would have to insert some artificial device to delineate the boundary between fact and fancy. This is why he does not tell us that Blanca was dreaming until the very end of her experience. We are asked to accept all occurrences in the novel as being real. And this is only possible when a single narrative point of view is provided. The narrator does not separate the categories of fact, daydream, and delusion, and as a result, we are unable to tell where realistic narrative ends and surrealist narrative begins.

Anyone reading the novels of Jarnés would decide immediately that they lean heavily toward intellectualism. But at least in theory, Jarnés was concerned about the dangers of cerebral art. This is borne out in the long essay which prefaces *Teoría del zumbel*. Here, the author explains his views on contemporary aesthetics and its relationship to the unconscious mind. His main thesis is that modern art may choose between dealing with "total life" or a "single life," but that in either case, the artist cannot avoid some form of self-contemplation. In other words, an artist might attempt to write about the general history of mankind in one epoch, or he could do "the monograph of a spirit." But whichever mode he selected, his subjective, and eventually unconscious, attitudes would inevitably influence the result.

Nevertheless, Jarnés as a novelist is unwilling to allow his genre to embrace either of the two forms exclusively. For him, the novel is a field of awareness in which both collective and individual realities come into play. Moreover, the novel represents not only its creator's subjectivity but also the states of mind of independent characters. In this complexity of multiple realities, Jarnés seeks some kind of psychological resolution. He finds it in the unification provided by Jung's theory of the Unconscious, which he cites extensively. According to Jarnés' adaptation of this theory to the novel, the human mind has a structure which is comparable to the many realities of narrative fiction. This consists of a three-storied stratification: the conscious, the personal unconscious, and the collective unconscious. The perception of reality and its temporal phenomena is the function of the conscious sector of mind. In contrast, the personal unconscious is the seat of the individual's past experiences, which have been lost to memory. These experiences have an ancestral counterpart, belonging to the collective unconscious that reveals the prehistoric past of the species.

Traditionally, the novel's representation of reality has corresponded to the conscious mind. The immediate world of perceptible things is what occupies the conventional novel, and not the images and symbols of the universal past. But should art be confined to this reduced area? asks Jarnés. He finds that this first level of reality is almost blinding in its "crude brilliance." The objects we see "can scarcely act aesthetically upon us," and their role is limited to awakening our attention. For Jarnés, "reality is a servant, an entity without personality" whose job it is to stir some beautiful sleeping image in our minds (12). Prime reality is only a stimulus for crystallizing an artistic reality that is found within the creator. This implies a diminished reliance on the senses, which were so intensely cultivated by post-symbolist schools of literature. Indeed, Jarnés' surrealist technique will, on the contrary, depend upon images drawn from his private psychological world. These images are conveyed by methods that do not emphasize sensory perception, but merely use them as initial stimuli to uncover what lies beneath the waking mind.

It is interesting to note that Jarnés likens the substrata of his imagination to a harem inhabited by beautiful images lying in a dormant state. Their shapes are determined by the master's personality, and they exhibit a unique set of meanings in accordance with his subjectivity. In contrast, outer reality is nothing more than an impersonal servant, whose task is to arouse creativity without becoming its raw material. However, this type of aesthetic activity is admittedly quite accessible to talented artists, since they do not wander off into the deeper recesses of the mind. The problem is to descend into the collective unconscious, which means abdicating one's individuality in favor of an imagery of universal significance. The difficulty here is in devising a universal language to communicate what is found in this realm. Jarnés feels that this could only be accomplished by a genius, and that the average artist would achieve "facile successes" by delving into the collective unconscious.

Jarnés is cautious about the use of depth psychology in art for several reasons. It is easy for the ill-equipped artist entering the unconscious world to confuse the personal unconscious with the collective. Jarnés calls such an individual a "pseudoartist," because the latter fails to see the complexities of integrating the three levels of consciousness. This integration is effected by a harmony of aesthetic components which Jarnés refers to as "style." Thus, style is more than the verbal expression of an artist's creative awareness. It extends to an equilibrium among various levels of reality as they are captured by private and universal language. Here, then, is where surrealist fiction enters. The traditional novel dealt primarily with outer reality, and how it was transformed by the writer's subjectivity. On the other hand, the surrealist novel evokes a caravan of internal images that are activated by the real world, which merely serves as an initial stimulus. The pseudoartist does not recognize this distinction, and considers both forms of the unconscious to be rooted in the present. The results of so fundamental a mistake is that his novel will lack style. In other words, his technical apparatus will be inadequate for harmonizing the psychic forces and shapes of his novelistic world.

The artistic genius formulates such a style by balancing reason and emotion against each other. Although the final product is fairly abstract and rational, the artist must have a substantial emotional investment in his work. This, of course, is precisely what Jarnés advocated in his own case. He claimed that it was important for the novelist to get excited, to involve his personality with the object under scrutiny. This meant yielding a part of his inner being to the world that he was about to create. In turn, this implied modifying an already fictional reality into something even more subjective and perhaps irrational. Such an approach had the advantage, from the artist's standpoint, of increasing the expenditure of imaginative and creative energy. Moreover, it counteracted what Jarnés considered to be the pernicious influence of reason in art.

Citing Jung for support, Jarnés explains that man is more than simply rational. However beautiful reason may be, it is only one of the possible functions of spirit that man is capable of sustaining. The irrational, for Jung and for Jarnés, "cannot and should not be extirpated. The gods cannot and should not die" (15). Thus we have the aesthetic justification for restraining reason during the creative process. The existence of godlike forms guarantees the transcendence of art over reality. The gods assure the presence of something greater than visible order, the infinite expansion of real and imagined configurations conceived beyond the scope of reason. Man's rational powers represent only one facet of the phenomenal world, whereas the irrational is found everywhere.

In addition to this aesthetic consideration, there is the question of how the rage for order suppresses the artistic impulse. It is true that the individual's consciousness, as the seat of reason, attempts to eradicate the chaos of irrationality. But it is also true that chaos can provide another form of knowledge. Therefore, what is important is the achievement of equilibrium between reason and emotion. "To feel, when it is a question of reasoning, is bad. To reason, when it is a question of seeing, is worse. Let us not feel the moon's emotion by looking too much, or by calculating her phases, but rather, by seeking it in the bottom of a well where the moon is reflected, where—like any truth—the moon's truth will always be found" (16). This, then, is the value of dream and reverie. The artist, whose traffic in truth depends upon the value of his imagination, requires a certain amount of logical discipline in order to make his vision comprehensible. But this does not permit him to ignore the other

faculties of his psyche when they are more appropriate for appre-
hending aesthetic truths.

And yet, the modern artist has been ignoring just this area of
psychic experience. His principal attitude toward the contemporary
world is ostentatious frigidity. Far from getting excited about things,
he appears to view his reality impersonally, as if his vision might be
obstructed by his personality. In other words, the artist is curious
and attentive to the world about him, but he does not deposit his
emotional energy into the resources of his creative work. As a result,
he tends to acquire the same style, and to treat the same themes,
that his colleagues have adopted. In a group, they all comprise a
collective art movement, a situation which makes Jarnés despair.
For him, an artistic school or "ism" is as rich in potential as a
dead-end street is in visual sights: no matter how curious or inventive one is, the number of new landscapes and objects to be
contemplated is eventually depleted. Such movements, consequently,
are the main censors of individual expression.

At this point, the surrealist aesthetic becomes significant, because it offers an escape from the dead-end. The artist may enter
any of the three-storied houses on the street, or even go underground. Even better, he need not go into the street at all. He can
simply survey everything from his own house, descending into the
cellars of his unconscious and allowing the images encountered
there to perform the real function of thought. In this proposal,
Jarnés follows Breton's pure psychic automatism, in that he requires
the free play of images to remain detached from ethical and aesthetic considerations. The disinterested flow of thought creates a
higher reality, and is an important alternative to the pedestrian
rationalism of modern art. There are, of course, pitfalls, and Jarnés
is quick to point out how the man of mediocre talent turns into a
mass-artist who composes with styleless impersonality. But the artistic genius finds the surrealist mode to be an effective shield against
the destructiveness of reason. It thwarts the contingent of Cartesian
and Valerian men who have endangered the arts with their "invitation to sterility" (20), as they attempt to systematize the creative
vision of existence. Surrealism provides the decisive breakthrough
into an area of infinite expressiveness, where the unique and the
universal can be glimpsed at the same time.

The simultaneity of this artistic vision is important. Because
of it, both the personal as well as the collective unconscious are
manifested. The fault of the modern intellectual artist is that, despite his experimentalism, he is not cognizant of these two levels of
the unconscious. The talented surrealist, however, overcomes this

defect. Of course, Jarnés recognizes the fact that surrealism has developed into a school too, with its own standardized exercises in imagination. It has found the "universal psychic mechanism" which provides for its practitioners the same patterns of style that reason furnished for the intellectuals. Thus, Jarnés warns the new Spanish surrealists against the danger of losing their individuality by drifting into a school of impersonal art. He is distressed, because he feels that the majority of surrealists have produced an identical panorama.

As one solution, Jarnés suggests that perhaps surrealism is a mode for mature men rather than for young artists, a vision for the autumn of life. The very young man will sound the depths, but will return with a mere handful of reflections: recollections of his forefathers, or wonders belonging to the common domain. As for his own gathering of conscious data and unconscious private images, this is not yet forthcoming. But whatever the age, the artist must have a theory of unification. Jarnés recalls Claude Bernard's prediction that one day the same language will be spoken by physiologists, poets, and philosophers, and he wonders if that day is not already on the horizon. He cites the coincidence in time of such divergent approaches to knowledge as psychoanalysis, surrealism, and Scheler's laws of emotion; or the popularity of reading and writing biographies; or the use of dreams as the material for art. In all of these areas, it seems that a single analytical language—or descriptive technique—is being employed for ends so diverse as scientific knowledge, historical fact, and works of imagination.

This convergence of disciplines constitutes an essential truth for all men. It means that fact and fiction are intertwined, and that in the conscious mind it is no longer possible to assert the distinctions between so-called reality and fantasy. The reality of our waking life has become infused with fictional qualities, and this is reflected in the unity of expression just described. This would seem to corroborate the ancient dictum that life is made of the stuff of dreams. But what of the converse of this statement? We know that reality is like a dream, because often we cannot tell one from the other. But it is also true that dreams are made of the stuff of life. In fact, if we enter the dream world, we discover that meanings become clearer, and that forms drop their disguises and appear to us as they really are. For example, the thoughts and appetites which we so cleverly hide from view spring forth with brutal vigor in our dreams. The masks of emotion are removed, and the reality of existence, so nicely fictionalized in waking life, now appears elemental and sharply defined in universal imagery.

Therefore, it behooves the artist to reflect upon whether "of the two halves of this life, perhaps the most fruitful for art is the dream portion, because every unfaithful sign of occurring phenomena disappears at last in it" (22). Reality is so impregnated with falsehood as well as truth, that its totality is like a spinning color wheel (or top), whose colors blend perfectly into an indiscriminate grey. In the dream, however, the mind's agile ability to differentiate shades of feeling and thought is revived, and it makes authentic, even startling, discoveries. Figures and events stand out with chiseled clarity, so that reality appears naked and knowable. This concept of the dream is somewhat idealized and naive, but we must remember that Jarnés is one of the first artists in Spain to think in detail about the psychoanalytical method. Thus, he is disposed toward emphasizing the frank intelligibility of dreams, rather than speculating on their ambiguity, superimposures, and evasive symbolism. As a result of this clarity, he says that "we so often come out of the dream humiliated, with the greatest sorrow at having undergone a terrible examination of our most profound inwardness, an implacable inspection of our being" (23).

Nevertheless, this attitude does not represent an excessive reliance on unconscious mental processes. Jarnés restores the balance to which he so often refers, and speaks of a prevailing "spirit" that integrates the various psychological mechanisms. In other words, if memory is a conscious and unconscious storehouse of images and experiences, and if all this is open to the artist's reach, there must still be an overall technique which rectifies and unites everything in a manner faithful to reality and truth. This technique resides in the faculty of "spirit," which keeps in the individual's hands all control over his understanding of what existence means. In other words, there are no powers outside the individual which can determine the sense of his reality—no chance, or god, or demon to influence him. The dream is the ultimate source of total truth, and the spiritual forces guiding man's intelligence and artistic will are the means for giving order to his reality. Here, then, is the common language of science and art of which Claude Bernard spoke. The correct interpretation of dreams can become the most perfect lesson in human anatomy, revealing the structure of psychic and existential phenomena.

The implications of these ideas for literature are far-reaching. All inhibition must be removed from fiction, since restrictions falsify or distort the truth. Whereas traditional literature concealed the repressed elements of human nature, the new use of dreamwork liberates the psyche, enabling it to express itself with absolute fidelity. This faithfulness to reality insures the discovery of life's highest laws, those which the defenses of waking life hold in disguise. The concept of release, of freeing man's censored sensibility, is essential to great art. Thus, conscious and unconscious life are two dimensions of the same realm, each complementing the other. In one, primitive reality appears with all its splendid and uncontrolled vitality, while in the other, experiences are made rational and civilized. But both aspects comprise a single commentary on an unknown text. And since this textual mystery holds the key to life's truth, neither the conscious nor the unconscious will be anything more than a fantastic blueprint that is attempting to be accurate.

So too with art. The function of art is to decipher the enigma of life by whatever means at hand. There is only one life, one unique reality. This can be approached either rationally or by more intuitive methods. In the first case, these means are science and philosophy, disciplines which correspond to the conscious mind. But reality can also be approached by way of the unconscious, through dream, and with aesthetic principles. These methods, however, provide only partial illumination of the unknown reality that is being sought. Hence, no single technique or approach is sufficient; they all must be employed before any meaningful results can appear. This is Jarnés' theory of the integral knowledge of man, the revelation of man's wisdom by means of his personality. Artist and scientist are one, both in purpose and in technique, just as the conscious and the unconscious are cooperatives in the same quest. The question, therefore, is not which school of thought or art is preferable, or which method and technique should be used. There is only the unified science of seeing and expressing what is experienced. And in this science, every feature of human endeavor is admissible: waking life and sleep, reason and passion, reality and fantasy, philosophy and art.

With this statement, Jarnés reaches his definition of the new artist. Instead of dispassionate, dehumanized art, what must be adopted is the complex spontaneity of sensation. The artist must cultivate this with as diverse means as possible, which does not imply eclecticism, but rather, integralism. The aesthetic movements of the past tend to divide and exclude. Taken separately, these schools are one-sided: Romanticism emphasizing the passionate and heroic in man; realism dealing with the dispassionate and rational; and surrealism unearthing the murky instincts of the unconscious. These movements represent the three modes of human awareness —reverie, waking life, dream—along with their special techniques: imagination, reason, intuitive perception. None of these alone is sufficient to attain cognition, and excessive use of any of them is disapproved by Jarnés. Thus, his conclusion is in no way an exclusive endorsement of surrealism, although it is certainly this element which makes his prologue a milestone in Spanish literature. He sees in modern aesthetics not only the fact that life is a game but that the unconscious can provide another instrument for knowledge. And since art is a form of knowing, it must incorporate this new dimension, surrealism, into its aesthetic canon.

III

Of equal structural consistency as Jarnés' novel is the work of Joaquín Arderius, *Los príncipes iguales* (1930). This modern fairy tale is also full of whim, but there is a clear relationship between its fancy and its surrealist depiction of modern technology. The frivolity of Arderius is directed at the reader's world in a manner which is not like the gratuitous tone of Gómez de la Serna. Just as the post-Romantics flouted middle-class values, so too does Arderius depict a writer who scorns the normalcy of modern society.[4] His attack masks a need to ridicule whatever is not new, but his modernity is revealed in the choice of images. Thus, he shouts his desire to cling to an airplane's steering wheel and "nail" himself into the sky, and then to "stick out my legs from each side of the machine and dangle them, stretching them until my shoes touched the street pavement. One of my caprices, gentlemen. I want to play with the Earth, turning it round and round with my feet, like beetles with their little turds" (30).

In this scatological fantasy, a derisive element enters which is akin to the forms of social protest that we have already noted elsewhere, and yet, which is different. If we compare the image with Jarnés' *Teoría del zumbel,* we can see why. In both Jarnés and Arderius, the world is conceived of as spinning by pure chance, like a game. In contrast, writers like Alberti and Valle-Inclán take fundamentally serious views of their societies. Thus, when Arderius here reduces the dignity of the technological world, he does so by using the airplane, a symbol of the very society he demeans. He dominates his reality, and later turns it into excrement to show his disdain, whereas the serious-minded surrealists deform their world out of impotence.

None of this could be possible without a special groundwork of novelistic theory. The basic premise of this theory is that the novel must be patterned on "the logic of life." This dictum virtually assures the narrative of having some surrealist tendencies, because it eliminates the logical rules of traditional fiction. That is, conventional novels made sense by following fairly strict laws of structural development. The novelist was a craftsman whose calm hand guided a predictable plot, and when elements of suspense and surprise were used, hindsight always showed how well they conformed to the dramatic logic. In contrast, Arderius proposes to make his novel resemble life so closely in its patterns, that the result will be coincidence and confusion. Like Jarnés, his concept of existence is one of an "undecipherable enigma" whose excitement has always been bypassed by the routines of official fiction.

Thus, the new novel will not be "boxed into framed dimensions and definite shapes" (33). Instead, it will pose the major questions asked by the contemporary world, such as, what the difference is between fact and fancy, machine work and art, modern men wearing personality masks and princes imprisoned in lonely castles. These problems cannot be resolved by the older forms of the realistic novel. It is erroneous to assume that appearance is the same as reality, or that the rules of stability, gravitation, and congruency are true. Arderius' novel will dispense with this sensibleness and measurement, and instead will exploit every imaginable kind of madness, disproportion, arbitrariness, and hyperbole. By a "vertiginous inverisimilitude," the novel will reproduce for the reader the same reality that he perceives in his modern anxiety. But rather than taking an attitude of detached irony, the novel will acquire a prevailing mood of ridicule. In this technique, the novelist himself assumes a radically new role.

Arderius projects himself into the novel at the beginning of the action in order to state his artistic position clearly. In this he resembles Jarnés, whose presence as the self-conscious author serves to analyze critically the precepts of fiction. But Arderius is alienated from his fellowmen, and is cast as a foolish figure because he is so different from his untutored contemporaries. Thus, we find him insisting that he is "not a clown" but a serious man, who has somehow been dislocated from his social role. And yet, the only image that he thinks suits his condition is as fantastic as a make-believe story: "I am an isolated tower in the center of a jungle, with all the windows sealed, and where my spirit makes itself phantoms which open the doors at night and go out strolling in infinite solitude" (46).

This Romantic self-image sounds melodramatic in an era of dehumanized art; and yet its meaning is quite opposed to the Romantic aesthetic. Arderius is not describing a melancholy introspection or a tragic stance in the manner of heroic Romanticism. On the contrary, his purpose is to provide escapist fantasies and imaginative methods of analysis for life in the technological age. Consequently, his isolation in a fairy tower symbolizes his failure to grasp the ways of modern science. Nevertheless, these are the only means available to him. He must use scientific techniques just as he used the airplane to devaluate the worth of the culture from which it came. Thus, Arderius declares himself to be a new type of artist, "an ex-man who makes himself fruitful by radiographs assembled with the ultraviolet focuses of his eyes" (38). By means of these "psychic radiographs," he is able to cut directly into the hidden core of things. It is not enough to understand the everyday reality of custom, dimension, and law, for the artist must go beyond this to the irrational recesses of life. Here, however, life's functions can only be examined by x-rays.

The actual implementation of this theory is not nearly as faithful as the novel's introductory chapter would have us believe. In this respect, *Los príncipes iguales* is just like *Teoría del zumbel,* in that the latter's prologue on surrealism offers an approach never practiced by the novel itself. But the central plot is invaded by multiple impressions that occur outside of space and time. That is, the very physical condition of the twin princes and their royal father contradicts the norms of everyday reality, even when the latter is conceived as a fairy tale. The men live in their palace without communication with the outside world. The brothers are near-geniuses, one a painter and the other a poet. And their creative simulation of reality comes to be a very real substitution for the exterior world. In fact, this is so much the case, that the novel is constituted as if the real setting were composed of the descriptions of the princes' art, rather than the actual palace that it is.

This displacement of the natural environment permits an absolute freedom from traditional laws. Its purpose is to give the artist-princes a maximum of individualism in their creativity. But in the act of self-expression, a new statement about reality emerges. For example, when the painter-prince Victor invents and portrays original states of Nature on his canvas, he breaks with the routine mechanics of the earth's operation. His paintings depict vertical mountains of water petrified against the horizon, a contradiction of the laws of physics. But such paintings are restatements of what the planet ought to be like. Rather than reproductions of reality, they are "corrections, and even models for Nature herself" (55). To the painter, "life was not the echo of things repeating themselves into Eternity, but an infinite flutter of improvisations" (56). With each improvised moment, a different concept of the natural world is devised, and, concurrently, another set of rules invented to govern

it. This idea extends to the novel, and is the rationale behind
Arderius' advocacy of the surrealist mode. There is no point in the
modern artist's studying conventional reality when its scientific
surface is so predictable. Thus, he writes *Los príncipes iguales,* with
a minimal "real" setting in the palace, but with many improbable,
momentary scenes that are straight out of the princes' fantasies.

This does not mean that Arderius fails to maintain a coherent
narrative. He uses incongruency with profit, like Gómez de la Serna,
but unlike him, he controls the structural integrity of the work.
For instance, the characters are treated with the same inventive
caprice that marks the ambiguous paintings of the prince. The
butler, especially, is portrayed as a human hybrid, a faun-like man
reminiscent of mythology's fabulous beings. Arderius' intention here
is to reshape the contours of reality, rather than to flaunt us with
a destructive mass of incomprehensibility. Thus, his novel is like
his personage, blending the rational and irrational, the animalesque
and the human, the Oriental and the Western, into an alchemist's
solution of well-mixed components.

What makes this novel a sophisticated fairy tale for adults is
its special absurdity. It combines the make-believe of the children's
world with the dehumanization of modern art. The result is an
atmosphere of fantasy which is no longer innocent or ideal. In
other words, while the traditional fairy tale is also absurd because
of an abstract or inhuman quality, it retains its idealism at the
same time. It can reduce the human element and even deform its
materials, but ideal values are still present: pure virtue, pure evil,
pure courage, pure beauty. On the other hand, Arderius' novel
employs a technique of dehumanization which consists of irony
and ambiguity. For example, one character "raised the ends of his
Chinese eyebrows, setting them almost vertically, and his owl-eyes
danced quickly, as if excited by a few wands, just like hoops turning
on the hands of clowns" (66). In another scene, the brothers appear
to be mannequins (111), and during the entire second half of the
novel, there are cases of mistaken identity, confusion between life
and death, and farcical situations with serious overtones. All of these
examples tend to deny the reality of a given phenomenon. It is,
but then it isn't. When we first apprehend an object, it has one
quality, but the next moment it has changed.

The effect of all this is to remove the novel from the area of
human relevance. Even normal sense perception is altered, as Arderius adopts some of Dali's paranoiac techniques. At such times,
he sees men as if they were beasts, or a lifeless object as if it had
some animate form. One disquieting example occurs as the prince

examines some chairs in a search for a ring. He inspects them as if "they had been the bellies of fabled animals, drugged into sleep by a potion." Thus, the old device of mythical animals and elixirs acquires a new twist by means of critical paranoia. In the same scene, the prince rips out the stuffing from some chairs, "and the wires remained on the floor, like a cyclops' hair torn out from the skull one by one" (146–47). Here, an inanimate object is endowed with animate associations, although in other cases the opposite condition is also possible. For instance, the prince enters looking like a steam shovel that transports blocks, and in another scene, his limbs stiffen into sticks as he turns into a walking gallows (206).

The aesthetic principle behind each of these examples is the concept of reversibility. The fact that roles and appearances can be reversed indicates a peculiar view of the flexibility of reality. It is as if the critical paranoia method has been modified so that the transformation is more independent of the viewer. Arderius differs from Dali in that he plays a game of elastic perception. His basic attitude toward the world is not one of deliberate deformation, but of suspended judgment, in which a flexible or plastic world can shape itself into reversible forms. Arderius also differs from Alberti and Valle-Inclán in the purpose of his dehumanizing methods. Rather than making an ideological statement about social technology, he uses the latter to escape it. That is, his novel harkens back to the magical world of children and fairies, borrowing some of its infantile imagery in order to expand the dimensions of the adult novel. And yet these images retain some vestiges of modern artifacts which link the novel to reality.

As the narrative draws to its conclusion, the various elements of absurdity succeed in converting the setting into an autonomous fantasia. The scenes no longer require the author's distorted lenses in order for us to see them in their fantastic details. Now everything is deformed because Nature herself turns into an old-fashioned witch. This ingenious idea is extremely useful in terms of drawing certain implications about art theory, from Romantic symbolism to sensory perception. The notion of a bewitched world removes the responsibility from the artist's shoulders. He may disclaim all part in the grotesque representation of reality appearing in his work. For example, when the moon emerges as a monstrous descendent of the more vulgarly shaped, commonplace moons of literary tradition, this is not due to art-for-art's-sake flippancy. It reflects the magical essence of the phenomenal world, which heretofore had not been perceived by rational and technological means (176, 183).

Consequently, the novel for Arderius is not so much an artistic genre as a mechanism for releasing the autonomous world from its prison of fixed laws. Moreover, fiction serves the function of dispelling the myths of Truth, Beauty, Wickedness, and all the other idealized abstractions which immobilize reality into unchanging rules and forms. This is why Mother Nature turns into a witch, and why she plays sarcastically with the artist-princes. In one scene, she teaches them this lesson, and like "an old clothes shop dealer, she rents her wardrobe to the Night, so that it might disguise itself" (182). The Night does this often and cruelly, changing masks in order to mock Gonzalo. At first we are in league with the Night against the prince. That is, we understand that the shadows and shapes perceived by him are hallucinatory tricks. And yet, the moment comes when we realize that we too have been duped, that if the prince was deluded by visions, so were we by the words which describe them. Reality frolics with the characters by using its "plastic ghosts" to confuse their perception. But the result is that the reader is also deceived, as Nature causes the air "to vibrate with visionary words" (181).

Here, then, is the essence of Arderius' surrealism. He has shown that Fact and Reality are myths of the scientific age, and he uses an intellectual fairy tale as his method of explanation.

> The globe was filled with Lies. Truth had been condensed into a microscopic lamp which, hanging from the prince's nose, flashed in thousandths of instants, dazzling his eyes with colored lights, and different colors; there was no other truth than the prince's doubt. Not tower, heaven, moon, city, air, nor even the force of gravity—since Gonzalo sometimes felt himself rising and floating in the air, or slowly sinking—nothing showed itself to be sincere (181–82).

Thus, although physical phenomena continue to occur, physical laws are defunct. Time is fragmented into meaningless myriads of experience, and experience is shattered into an equal number of subjectivities. Each man must cast light on his own doubts and be content without a systematic means of communication. This is the meaning of his surrealist world, a reality without ultimate meaning.

Chapter Eleven

The Headless Sirens
(Synthesis)

Throughout this book I have tried to avoid the stereotype of French surrealism in discussing the surrealist works of Spanish literature. As I will show in the Conclusion, there are many similarities between the two surrealisms, and it would seem, therefore, that the precaution was unnecessary. But what I hope to make clear now is that the surrealist phenomenon in Spain can be explained on aesthetic grounds. Regardless of what the role of the French movement was historically, its influence did not determine the process of aesthetic evolution in Spain that ultimately produced literary surrealism. Historical ties are important, but the responses by Spaniards to their own history of aesthetic ideas is, at least in this instance, more important. Ironically, the best proof of this can be found in a work by two Spaniards which was produced, not in Madrid or Barcelona, but in Paris, where the activity of the French surrealists was at its peak. That this work has an obvious historical connection with France cannot be denied. However, I would call attention to the more fundamental attitude toward Spanish post-Romanticism which is reflected in this work, and which is so typical of surrealism in Spain. Even more ironical is the fact that, whereas French surrealism has always overshadowed its Spanish counterpart, it was this work that brought about the most traumatic experience in the whole of European surrealist art.

I am referring to the film *Le Chien andalou* (1929), by Luis Buñuel and Salvador Dali, a work which exemplifies what surrealism meant to Spain and its aesthetic tradition.[1] The opening scene of this film tells the entire story in two symbolic sequences which express the same theme. What happens is that the moon is first shown at night while being overshadowed by a passing cloud. And then, a human eye is exposed as it is being sliced in half by a razor blade. Both of these sequences have the same meaning, and represent in symbolic form the eclipse of Romanticism by a new aesthetic. The moon and the eye stand for the traditional norms of art and reality, respectively, since the one is a characteristic element of the Romantic mode, and the other is the symbol of sense perception. Thus, nature and the light of human knowledge are obscured and deformed by a technique of deliberate mutilation that appears to be rationally controlled, but which commits an absurd act. This is the work of the razor blade and the new sensibility it brings. It allows the sectioned eye to continue seeing, but the pupil will now register a disjunctive image upon the retina. And this kind of perception is just like the sensory dislocation which we have found to be so common in the surrealist experience.

The razor blade itself is a precision instrument which serves the process of dehumanization. Not only does it destroy the balance of human perspective, but it alienates the artist from his own technical efficiency. The razor is psychologically dissociated from emotional reality, and its surgical detachment replaces the intimacy of the earlier Romantic period. This difference is made clear by the uniform mood of tranquility that prevails in the otherwise contrasting sequences of moon and eye. And here we note the divergence of surrealism from Romanticism. In the latter, peaceful and violent emotions alike are bound directly to personal experience. In surrealism, on the other hand, distance and indifference seem to interfere with a totally subjective perception of any mood, calm or violent. One reason for the sense of absurdity and gratuitousness in the eye-cutting scene is precisely this displacement and objectification of the artist's Romantic subjectivism.

We may say, therefore, that a good deal of the Spanish surrealist mode proceeds from this aesthetic transformation, and it is here that we must begin our concluding analysis. This point of departure is the breakdown of post-Romanticism, and especially of Modernism, as a viable mode of expression. As was seen in the chapter on Machado, the Modernist sensibility was the prevailing artistic norm against which members of several generations reacted. Its chief exponent in Spain was Juan Ramón Jiménez, whose poetry assimilated the legacy of Romanticism, symbolism, and impressionism. Whereas Machado eventually left these movements behind, Jiménez perpetuated their motifs and yearnings until the end of his career. His lifelong theme was that which concerned post-Romanticism in general, namely, the reconciliation of the natural world with the poet's absolute subjectivism. What makes Juan Ramón so important for the study of the surrealist mode is the fact that he developed this theme until his death in 1958, without ever doubting either himself or his poetry. This is remarkable when we remember that Machado's Modernism was marred by the grotesque and later evolved into social realism, that Valle-Inclán began as a Modernist and ended as an *esperpentist,* and that vanguard poetry was cradled in Modernism before beginning its deviation. But what is most significant is that Jiménez himself could have turned into a surrealist and didn't. That is, he had certain moments of vacillation, experiences which, had he cultivated them, would have led him to the aesthetic crisis suffered by these other writers. Although Jiménez immediately repaired the cracks in the walls of his Modernist edifice, the other experimentalists systematically widened them until the entire structure collapsed. Thus, by examining certain poems by Juan Ramón, we can determine exactly at what point the Modernist sensibility slackened and the radicalism of the surrealist mode began.[2]

The most fundamental issue for Jiménez was how to reconcile his subjective world with the natural universe around him. This preoccupation had many subtle transformations in the poet's mature verse, but it never deteriorated into the kind of psychological confusion which characterized the surrealist revaluation. As we have seen, the surrealists cast doubt on the reliability of their feelings, and on the perception of reality. Their works, consequently, revealed the hesitancy and distortion of their relativistic world. On the other hand, Juan Ramón never suffered from this self-destructive attitude. He did, on occasion, question the adequacy of his artistic powers, and he experienced the anguish of a tortured spirit. But he did not lose confidence, as did Aleixandre, in the purity of his senses and emotions, or in the value of creating poetry from his responses to nature.

The difference, therefore, between Jiménez and the surrealists lay in the extent of their spiritual and perceptual health. The surrealists were stricken with an intellectual infirmity that caused them to apprehend the dimensions of their reality in a nightmarish fashion. Juan Ramón, on the other hand, had a sickness of soul which turned out to be the healthiest condition for an enduring post-Romantic aestheticism. "Each time life hands me a beautiful flower," he wrote, "I cut it with the blade of melancholy."[3] Thus, he was not only assured of Beauty's proximity but he was able to retain it by means of his emotional life. Moreover, he gained a supreme faith in his lifelong effort to communicate through art his subjective vision of nature. The song of triumph at the end of his career bore witness to this faith, for it proclaimed the mutual transubstantiation of man and the universe.

Nevertheless, in spite of his greatness as a poet, Juan Ramón contributed nothing radically new to contemporary literature from the standpoint of aesthetic history. His sensibility and emotional rhetoric were essentially those of the nineteenth century. So too were his yearnings and representations of reality. He could say—as the surrealists could not—"When cynical emotions approach me, I flee . . . my soul is my landscape" (88). And his technique, unlike surrealism, was merely the outer form of a more substantial, if elusive, Beauty. Once, when chasing a butterfly in symbolic pursuit of Beauty's essence, he wrote, "I nearly catch it here and there . . . but all that remains in my hand is the shape of its escape" (157). In other words, Jiménez had to content himself with form, because he believed that essence itself could never be seized. This contrast between formal and essential qualities was a factor which separated Modernism from the surrealist mode. For Jiménez, if deficiencies existed in the creative process, they were the fault of his formal medium. That is, his words fell short of conveying perfectly the intuitions of his inner landscape, let alone those of nature. The surrealists, on the other hand, were unsure about how to assess the sense data which they received from the external world. Even more, they were uncertain of the validity, if any, inherent in their private lives. Consequently, there was little subjectivism in the authors that we have studied, with the exception of Aleixandre, who was really a neo-Romantic with surrealist methods. In fact, the formal experiments of the surrealists became the best expressions of their intimate experiences, since they reflected the vacillations and chaos of the artistic mind.

Nevertheless, there were moments in Jiménez' career when he too might have despaired of his Romantic criteria. The fact that he did not, and that he was not tempted to overthrow his Modernist ideals, establishes him as a norm against which we may measure the new generation. The younger writers suffered from the same crises which Juan Ramón was able to resolve, but they were unable to handle the problem. Their solution, consequently, was to repudiate his aesthetic with violent changes. Instead of coping patiently with the aesthetic norm and modifying it, they deformed it. The vanguard succumbed to a contemporary disenchantment which Jiménez had also felt but had ignored. Their psychic lives were prone to what he called his "indefinable nostalgia," "weary memories," and "lengthy introspections." Yet, while Juan Ramón searched within himself long enough to conquer his crisis, the others abandoned psychological subjectivism in favor of new answers. They, too, perceived the melancholy afternoon sunlight and its "decoration of fever and nightmare" (95). But instead of turning inward for solace, they chose to project their feverishness upon an environment more objectified (and more deformed) than that permitted by the Modernist. The nightmare was an element virtually suppressed in Jiménez' world.

The difference, then, between post-Romanticism and the surrealist mode lies in the willingness to utilize the aesthetic potential of disillusion. Although Juan Ramón confessed to having a "lethargic dream and stench of the impossible," he cultivated the sweetness of this lethargy in order to disguise his decaying ideal with fragrance. In contrast, the surrealists recognized that their idealistic longing was a fiction of their neurotic inertia. And so they roused themselves by turning their private dream into a more objective art form. Juan Ramón watched with his inner eye as "fantasies whirled among the dry leaves" (95), and he created the substance of his poem out of the emotional malaise of these fantasies. The result, therefore, never left the realm of subjectivism. On the other hand, the surrealists withdrew their feelings from the fantasies, and thus produced an independent construction rather than a direct reflection of the naked soul.

It must be recognized, therefore, that Jiménez did experience the beginnings of the contemporary artist's bad dream, but that he was able to suppress it by maintaining his faith in the aesthetics of post-Romanticism. The surrealists, however, nourished their nightmare and created a new aesthetic from it. Examining the psychology of this critical moment in Jiménez' life, a tenuous line separating the reverie-dream from the nightmare is found. Within traditional bounds are such familiar elements as a "gentle autumn sun," a plaintive piano, and a silent house. But at the same time, the scene is touched by chimera and the fantastic. Juan Ramón suggests that something has gone wrong with his perceptions, even though there is nothing severe enough to be called a nightmare. Knowing this, he leaves the scene saying, "I find myself in a mirror . . . but . . . was it I who was in the room?" (49). The same perceptual confusion which arose during the reverie is now also extended to the poet's apprehension of himself. He is uncertain not only of the world around him but of his own reality as well. The chimerical contours of his surroundings encircle the poet's mirror image of himself, and both elements appear in a quasi-unbalanced poetic description. In fact, if one wished to tilt the balance completely, very little would be required, since both personality and nature stand on the edge of distortion.

The psychological problem involved here is one of disaffection. The poet asks who his real self is: the beggar who roamed his garden this afternoon, or the old man who tonight is dressed in mourning. Jiménez finds everything the same and yet not the same, for his old age marks a physical change from youth, notwithstanding the constancy of his feelings and environs (44). How, then, can he trust his sensibility if he notes an aging in his most visible (bodily) condition? Indeed, the disparity between the present moment and the past instills in him a sense of the unreal. Jiménez knows that some kind of mutation has occurred. And yet, he cannot reconcile the physical difference in himself over the years with his unchanged sensory knowledge of nature. As a result, he feels disaffected from the outside world. He declares that because of this alienation, "the nights of water and snow do not belong to my heart." And so he compensates by creating another set of chimeras within him, and "when everything is frozen, it is springtime" in his heart (45–46).

All of this leads to one central fact: Jiménez is now estranged from the beauty of the external world which he usually feels so intimately. As a result, he begins to create a new beauty that is inwardly engendered. This process is so different from the conditions usually leading to the pathetic fallacy that, in effect, Juan Ramón's normal relationship with nature is ruptured. He no longer finds beauty outside of himself, nor does he need to emerge from the self in order to seek the source of Beauty. When nature is meaningless ("frozen") it is still springtime in his heart. And yet, this moment, in the light of Jiménez' total career, is an exception. His lifelong search proved to be a desire to unify the self with nature, and his late poems indicate that he was successful. Therefore, we must consider an instance such as this one as symptomatic of a fissure which the poet was able to repair. That is, a temporary disturbance took place in his fusion of two realities—self and nature—which was eventually calmed, but which caused permanent alienation when it occurred among the surrealists.

Other instances in Jiménez' poetry confirm the psychological rupture caused by self-doubt. In one poem about a rain storm, several unusual notes are added to the violence ordinarily expected from such a scene. A "bitter and equivocal light" is likened to a sharp knife from the sky, and the "fearful moment is adorned with a strange splendor, delirious and yellow." The afternoon becomes a "fantastic allegory" in which a "false and golden sun persists" among the natural elements, including black waves that are "tragically mad" (92). These details of ambiguity and potential delirium do, of course, draw upon Romantic imagery, but at the same time they also point the way to future aesthetic distortions.

In these and several other cases, Juan Ramón writes about confronting the nothingness of his soul. This concept of *nada* has many ramifications, but its aesthetic importance consists of the conversion of beauty into an ugly lie. The poet had sought loveliness, first in nature and later in himself. But he comes to realize that he was deceiving himself with an illusion, and that his art is nothing more than an "illuminated falsehood." Jiménez expresses this metaphorically in an image of extraordinary self-mutilation. He compares his heart to a blind and trembling bird that has just evaded some cruel children and has flown into a darkened salon. Every so often it tries to escape into the infinite by flying toward the light of a window, only to dash itself against the glass pane. Sometimes it hits the low ceiling and flutters helplessly to the floor. Finally, battered and broken-winged, the bird lays "throbbing with yearning and feebleness," and slowly bleeds to death (122).

However melodramatic or self-pitying the poem may sound, it is remarkably effective and well done. Moreover, it uncovers the destructive tendency that lurks beneath the composure of modern art. The genesis of this self-destructive energy is the psychological crisis already described, and its result is a loss of confidence in the value of creativity. Self-doubt leads to disparagement, and to even more serious forms of subverting both the poet's private world and his artistic effort. Among the surrealists, this propensity to violence was to become objectified almost entirely. But in the case of Jiménez, it was nearly suppressed altogether. When it did rise to the surface, in the rare instance of this poem, its roots were so deeply subjective that it could barely manage a metaphorical disguise.

It is at this point that Juan Ramón and the incipient surrealists who learned from him part company. They all sensed their insecurity, but the surrealists shook it off by turning self-mockery into an attitude of irony toward the external world. Instead of consuming themselves in anguish, they vented their frustrations on more objective elements of reality. Their emotional release was destructive, but it took a sublimated form, whereas Jiménez continued to view his anguish through the subjectivism of self-reflecting images. He used his poems to perpetuate his self-indulgent hermeticism, while the surrealists, in contrast, freed their imagery of all recognizable ties with personal feeling. Thus, even though the motif of bodily deformation is prominent in surrealist literature, there is no case which gives lyrical expression to the artist's own problems in the same way that the crippled bird does for Juan Ramón. This is why the latter remains a fundamentally Romantic figure, and so perfect a foil for the Spanish surrealists. He was unwilling to wrench his imagery away from the self, or to channel his energy into a destructiveness outside of himself. His pathetic, soul-baring attitude prevented any exteriorization of the self-castigating creative process. Thus, his art never achieved the objective status of surrealist distortion.

Final confirmation of the fact that surrealism emerged from a Modernist crisis similar to the one described, can be found in Jiménez' prose poetry. Here, certain passages were written in New York, and it is interesting to keep in mind Lorca's *Poet in New York* for comparison. Jiménez writes that before falling asleep each night he lines the "shore of the river of my imagination" with elements taken from the "best reality." This means that he selects those aspects of the city which will represent the "pure, free, and strong in heart," details that will express the aesthetic ideals of a joyous Romanticism. For this reason, the poet confesses his anxiety lest he contaminate the soft dawn with the "gloomy waters of nightmare," which are found in the "commercial city, Eighth Avenue, Chinatown, the elevated train and the subway." Thus we have Juan Ramón squarely facing the same urban elements which Lorca utilized to create his poetic nightmare. And we have him rejecting these features with the fastidiousness of the aesthete. His rhetoric, in spite of his attitude, suggests a surrealistic perspective: the stream of consciousness, the terrors of modern technology, the contrast between harmony and deformation. But his entire vision refutes the aesthetic implications of the city as it is. In fact, he confesses his desire to "smile in dreams," to "keep life rose-colored" rather than under the harsh light of consciousness, and to avoid further train rides into the "underground of night" (132).

It is clear from the preceding that in New York Jiménez reached the crossroads of Modernism and the surrealist mode. It is equally clear that although he backed away from the vanguard aesthetic, he was capable of succumbing to the dislocated urban scene for at least one moment. He notes elsewhere, for example, that "an invisible reality moves through the subway train," but he can only point to noise and rubbish for details. Similarly, he finds the passengers self-absorbed, "as in a nightmare of fatigue and sadness." Yet, here too, the only symbol that he can devise for them is a rose worn by a Negro woman. It is this white rose which stands for the consciousness of the subway car, and at the same time suggests the essence of eternal spring and eternity. Thus, we find that the components of a possible surrealism are ready to be sprung from their subjectivity, but that they remain fastened instead to traditional symbolic meanings. Details like iron, coal, old newspapers, and chewing gum almost insulate the screeching train against the clean air and infinite horizons beyond it, but, with a rush of artistic housecleaning, Juan Ramón lets in the sunlight.

This contrast with Lorca's conception of the city, and especially of Harlem, is crucial. For Jiménez, the paths of social—and eventually aesthetic—salvation lead to the realm of the white man's values, whereas Lorca suggests that the Negro's own instinctual resources will rescue him from the evils of civilization. The difference can be seen in each poet's formal technique. Lorca simulates the primitive structure of Negro life, while Jiménez preserves his own aristocratic sensibility in a subway snapshot of a Negro woman. And even though both poets develop the implications of their Negro subjects, only Lorca loses himself in the chaotic morphology of industrialization and its effect on biological life. Of course, this disorientation is willfully constructed, and is patterned on Lorca's intuitive response to the nightmarish city that confronts him. But the point is that he alone cultivated this response. This does not mean that Jiménez was oblivious to the potentially surrealistic material in his metropolitan surroundings. Nevertheless, his aesthetic reaction to it remained inwardly locked by personal feeling. He tried to reconcile the ugliness around him with his private idealism, and, consequently, failed to appreciate the aesthetic qualities of this unpleasantness. Lorca, on the other hand, was able to depict his environment with more emotional distance, and he accepted the independence of this reality with the respect of a poet undisturbed by Romantic egoism.

Given Jiménez' retreat from the nightmare of reality, we may conclude that the germ of surrealism was conceived in the gap between this reality and the self. Within that aperture, two psychological positions were possible. One was the stance taken by Jiménez, allowing the ego an intelligible access to nature by means of conventional perception. The other was the surrealist position, which dislocated the self from reality and plunged ahead into the latter's nightmarish aspects. But both choices rested on a single moment of self-awareness. During this instant, all the doubts that plague the creative mind rose to the surface. The artist grew uncertain of himself and his surroundings. He wondered whether the physical world would ever submit to the limitations of verbal imagery. And if so, he wondered whether he had the power to create such imagery. Most post-Romantics, including Juan Ramón, answered both questions affirmatively. The surrealists, however, lost faith in their perceptions, and in their own inner lives as well. Thus, they had to construct a new mode of reality which suited their disposition. But at the peak of self-doubt and frustration, everyone, including Juan Ramón, succumbed to the imagery of mutilation. Jiménez' broken-winged bird became the prototype of the tortured metaphors of the surrealist mode. It reappeared under different forms as an obsessive motif, embodying the most profound and earliest memories of the surrealist anguish.

This early, fundamental experience involved the artist's sense of inadequacy during the creative process. Hopelessly frustrated by the aesthetic means at his command, he is unsure whether the latter are at fault, or whether the failure is his own. His feeling of impotence enrages him, and, no longer able to suffer passively, he becomes violent. The artist tears at both reality and at himself, ripping away the traditional constructions and behavior patterns that are part of creative life. He does violence to the external world, deforming it to fit his surrealist vision. But at the same time, he commits a barbaric act upon himself in compensation for his inadequacy. Finding that he is unable to resolve the problem of self and reality, he distorts the latter and castrates himself. His anger at having failed causes him to act violently and irrevocably. Thus, the deed is at once the expression of self-hatred and the confirmation of his impotence. By excising the very source of creativity, the artist is left with a psyche that conforms to his image of himself as a helpless and unproductive man. But instead of performing the drastic act biographically, as did Van Gogh, the surrealist does it by artistic symbols.

It is no coincidence, therefore, that the motif of self-mutilation is so prominent among the authors discussed in this book. Although the specific meaning in each case depends upon the individual context, the general implication is one and the same. The surrealist distortion of reality is a projection of the artist's deformed self, just as the idealization of nature among the Romantics was a reflection of their inner selves. The surrealist faces his world in a castrated condition, and he represents this state by the violence of his art. This does not mean that there are no other explanations for the aesthetic role of violence. But it does account for the latter's initial cause. The surrealist needs to establish some kind of link with reality, and by mutilating it, he treats it as an extension of himself. This is why Aleixandre builds, in his own image, a universe of vulnerability and spiritual inadequacy, and why his poems are obsessed with motifs of crushed wings and scissors. It is also why

Machado uses the symbolic "weak horn" instead of some other metaphorical expression, and why he fantasies decapitation as his punishment. Finally, it is why Lorca describes a penis transfixed by a needle to imply Whitman's sterility, and why sexuality is repressed or sublimated in Jarnés and in Arderius.

But even more important than the surrealist's self-destruction is his treatment of reality. The eye lacerated by a razor blade in the hands of Buñuel and Dali is a perfect symbol of projected mutilation. Just as a bisected vision will only perceive a dislocated reality, so too will a self-defacing ego find its own deformed image reflected in the external world. Nevertheless, this merely exposes the disfigured source of creativity. It is also necessary that the aesthetic result reproduce the condition of its creator. Thus we find Lorca recounting the decapitation of mythological sirens in the sea of asepsis. This double act of desensitization represents the core of surrealist aesthetics. It turns against the older forms of beauty, and reveals that the artist can no longer succeed with traditional methods. By invoking the beheaded sirens, he creates a beauty that corresponds to his own internal lack. That is, he creates an image that appears perfect to the mutilated eye. And the headless sirens become the symbols of a new sensibility.

This change in sensibility consists of the triumph of matter over the senses. In other words, it represents a shift in emphasis from sense data to the concrete source of these data. Let us recall that the post-Romantics, in general, rejoiced in a sensual and sensorial riot. But their indulgence reflected back upon themselves and their pleasure, instead of extolling the objects which provided those sensations. That is, even while proclaiming their interest in the material world which they contemplated, they simply used it to gratify their senses. On the other hand, the surrealists did not exploit reality for their own ends. Rather than dwelling on sensory experience, they concentrated on matter for its own sake. They diminished the role of color, and scarcely related the functions of line and space to the human element in reality. As Lorca remarked in his ode to Dali, art was composed of a pure steel syntax. All evidence of sensuality was suppressed, and the still-life Venus came to represent everything that was inert in a reality divorced from human participation. So too with Lorca's blind statue, which was lifeless enough without the additional deprivation of sight. But the surrealist obsession with vision and blinding was part of an overall depersonalization of the artist's encounter with reality. Thus, the statue refers back to the observer's sensory perception, invalidating the latter and asserting its independence as pure matter.

This notion of matter triumphing over the senses shows up best in the contrast between the Modernists and such surrealists as Alberti. Although both groups were alike in developing a confused sense perception, the effects were different in each case. In Modernism, synesthesia heightened the value of each individual's subjective experience and exploited the object for its sense data. On the other hand, the confusion in Alberti was meant to cast the senses into disrepute, to demonstrate how unreliable they were before the immutable substantiality of matter. This difference had a profound effect on the evolving concept of reality among the surrealists. They were unlike the heirs of Romanticism, who viewed their art as an idealized reflection of reality, as an image of what they would have wished life to be. For Valle-Inclán, the mirror of art was a concave surface that duplicated an essentially deformed reality. And for Alberti, it was not just the reality of the absurd, but its universality which was caught by his surrealist diction.

In other words, as the artist devalued his perceptual grasp of reality, he revealed an increasing respect for pure matter: objects, artifacts, substances. These he manipulated without reference to sensory logic or rational thought. Consequently, his art held a vision of reality that bore no resemblance to man's percepts or feelings. On the contrary, he saw reality as an absurdity precisely because it had escaped the methodical confines of human sensibility. But by the same token, this estrangement of reality from the senses gave the surrealist license to explore other regions of perception. If the external world asserted its absurd independence, why couldn't the artist invent his own disparity? Specifically, why could he not perceive matter according to other laws: inversely, or by virtue of deranged psychological states? He could indeed, and thus were born the diverse paranoiac techniques of Solana, Lorca, and Dali. Their pathological vision of the world extended the scope of surrealist representation to the outer limits of human emotion. Whereas the senses restricted knowledge to fixed categories, critical paranoia expanded it as far as the individual psyche was capable of reaching.

Once the limitations of sensory information were removed, the surrealist no longer needed to pay attention to reality. He could invent any atmosphere he pleased, making relationships among objects without reference to sense data. His techniques led him straight to the world of nightmare, where an infinite variety of new forms greeted him. The spectrum ranged from the dream mechanism of the unconscious to the use of fairy tales and infantile literature. There were also the elements of carnival, as well as carnivalesque postures that yielded first to caricature and then to more savage practices, such as animalization. Some of these methods belong to the distortions of nightmare, and are borrowed from human experience as well as from the Goyesque tradition. But others involve the grotesque aesthetic, which is a larger category, embracing the surrealist mode. That is, the grotesque informs many sensibilities besides surrealism, just as tragedy or comedy can be found in the Renaissance as well as in Romanticism. However, the grotesque in surrealism is a germinating force as well as an aesthetic trait. It sharpens the surrealist's capacity for self-awareness, and for seeing the possibilities of incongruity. For example, in the *esperpentismo* of Valle-Inclán, both the grotesque and the surrealist aesthetics meet in an ironic distortion based on a dehumanizing principle. And in Machado, the grotesque is a symptom of the gradual breakdown of Modernist art principles.

The surrealist nightmare, therefore, rests on a detailed repertoire of elements. But it does have several broad, unmistakable characteristics. First, it is the result of a symbolic descent. The motif of submergence is striking, both in Aleixandre and in Jarnés, and it even occurs in Azorín's novel *El superrealismo*. This does not simply mean that the artist descends into the nether world beneath reality or that he plunges within the depths of his unconscious mind. The Spaniards showed little interest in self-analysis or Freudian psychology. The act of submergence really denotes a departure from the realm of sensory meaning and from the implications of the social world. It is noteworthy that when the artists return from their descent they enter a new phase of social awareness. This would suggest that the concept of submergence refers primarily to an avoidance of social commitment.

Growing out of submergence is a second characteristic of the surrealist nightmare. The emotional atmosphere is often ambivalent. As an event or scene is described, there is a marked dissociation of feelings from phenomena. Sentiments felt by the reader do not correspond to the events witnessed, either in quality or in level. Indeed, his sense of incongruity depends heavily upon the disparity between emotions and phenomena. This affective dislocation grows more severe with each successive stage of surrealist distortion. First, there is a displacement of feeling by means of abstraction and geometricity, of the kind that Lorca describes in his ode to Dali. Next is dehumanization, the debasement of human life by one of several methods: reducing the human qualities in men, animating the lifeless, or confusing technological functions with human ones. A still more advanced stage is that of deformation, where disfigurement has both a violent and a benign form. In the former category are techniques such as psychological aberration and animalization. Benign deformation, however, is not intended to be emotionally disturbing, and is thus confined to the gratuitous use of fairy tales and infantile attitudes. Beyond this stage of emotional dislocation is absurdity, that is, the logical dissociation of phenomena, concepts, and sequences.

A third and final characteristic of the nightmare is its annihilation of time. Temporality is wholly unimportant to the surrealist. In Aleixandre, the burdens of time are abandoned, whereas in Jarnés, they are evaded by an escape into timelessness. The world of magic and absurdity finds no need for the time dimension, and if someone attempts to measure it, as Lorca did in *Así que pasen cinco años,* the result is emptiness. Thus, it is the apex of a moment, rather than its interval, which controls an image such as Valle-Inclán's. In Lorca, memory and time are blotted out by a needle, and in Gómez de la Serna, one melting clock and another clock without hands suggest that time has no meaning for a mass society.

In view of these three traits, the nightmare presents a curious paradox. Its mechanisms and motifs derive mainly from aesthetic principles. And yet its attitudes of submergence and temporal destruction make it refer dialectically to social reality. The surrealist sensibility turns its back on society, and is drawn away from its rational surface. But at the same time, this implies a certain social attitude. In fact, if we consider the cultural implications of the works studied in this book, we are forced to conclude that the surrealist mode in Spain is fundamentally antiurban. All of the writers give evidence of reacting against the metropolitan experience. Most notably, Lorca builds a pastoral dream to counteract his Manhattan nightmare, and he uses industrial imagery as the materials for his Harlem horrors. By the same token, his interest in cultural atavism is alien to the cosmopolitan orientation of the post-Romantics. Even more extreme is Dali's extensive search among the anamorphs of evolution. His reconstructions of these biocultural forms imply an adverse commentary of modern society. What he gives us is the instinctual, metamorphic vision of the georgics of technology. Thus, we might say that the eclipse of culture is augured by bioculturalism.

Nevertheless, the eclipse envisioned in the surrealist mode is articulated by technological means. A scientific vocabulary is often employed in the midst of irrational sequences, and there is a widespread poetization of the machine. Indeed, the sensibility of mechanization is indispensable to the surrealist, even though he rejects the society which produces it. In fact, by using these basic tools of culture for aesthetic purposes, by transforming reality with the latter's very cornerstone, the surrealist makes his most ironic critique and rejection. He refutes the value of the industrial world, but his judgment is facilitated by all the technical means provided him by this world. Thus, his surreality is the result of a dialectical operation. The dehumanizing power of technological society awakens a nightmarish image in the artist. Yet, he re-creates this nightmare by using the materials and methods of technology for his artistic ends. Consequently, he achieves a symbolic destruction of social reality without having to resort to social criticism.

However, we must recognize that the surrealist distortion does have its roots in social awareness. The evolution from ugly reality to *la España negra* to the *esperpento* is easy to follow. But from there the process reverts back again to the original reality. Machado's external, Goyesque grotesque turns into a historical preoccupation with Castile. And Alberti's mirror of universal absurdity shatters into a myriad of propagandistic fragments. Thus, whereas a Valle-Inclán moved away from modernism to the disguised politics of esperpentism, Lorca advanced openly from surrealist Harlem to the social tragedies of his final years. While Arderius wrote an escapist fantasy as an indirect comment on society, Gómez de la Serna and Jarnés based their intellectual fairy tales on a clear-cut notion of mass man. And a poet like Whitman could represent an ambivalent urban conscience: one that inspired surrealism in Lorca, realism in León Felipe, and class struggle in Alberti.[4]

More than anything, therefore, the surrealist mode in Spain expressed the impact of the city on the artist. His urban experience was impure and traumatic. If we do not sense this directly, it is because we are the children of technology. We see the blight of Harlem, but not the blood in its streets, and we hear the noise of machinery, but we escape its madness. Habit is the narcosis of city life. However, the surrealists were able to know these things. Their art is a reminder of the primeval truth that has been forgotten through custom. They witnessed the beheading of the sirens, and the conversion of men into mechanical dolls. They were able to do this because instead of living the reality of dehumanization, they stepped back and contemplated it as a nightmare. Hence their self-conscious and ironic attitude toward art. They adopted the dehumanizing principle of life, but did not remain serious at the same time. As a result, their work reflects an essentially tragic situation, but captures it in a grotesque and mocking way.

This deformation of tragedy would be cruel in real life, but in art it becomes a formal method. Since the basic tenet of the surrealist's credo is the absurdity of existence, his art is free of tragic

sentiments. He considers reason to be merely one of the many functions of spirit, and he is committed to exalting the irrational. This
is done not by subjectivism, as among the Romantics, but by dis-
carding the law of causality. The relationship between cause and
effect is nullified, and the rule of reversibility is installed in its place.
Thus, various states of mind and matter can be interchanged without reference to logic or sensorial experience. What Ortega called
the higher algebra of metaphor becomes, in surrealism, the calculus
of madness. This is true not so much in the use of obscure language
or absurd syntax, as in the abandonment of meaning as a criterion
altogether. Linguistic significance is preserved, but the larger meaning of relationships among phenomena and things is destroyed.
Most important, there is a dissociation of feeling from events. As
Alberti conceived it, the universe is a chaos of occurrences described
absurdly by a scientific diction. The old image of God as a law-giver
and mover becomes, in Jarnés' imagination, one of a capricious boy
spinning his game of tops.

Thus, the surrealist's notion of absurdity is gratuitous. Unlike
the existentialist's absurdity, it is not controlled by a moral im-
perative. True, surrealism employs a logic of the absurd, but this is
a formal requirement that does not transcend the work itself. In
other words, surrealism merely uses the fact of absurdity, but does
not try to overcome it. Indeed, we might say that the surrealists precipitated the crisis of the absurd, but then left it to the existentialists for resolution. The literature of Spanish surrealism is, therefore, dislocated from time, emotion, causality, and the senses. The
surrealists themselves were isolated from their French counterparts
and alienated from the cultural reality in Spain. Thus, their marginal status in history corresponded to the aesthetic dislocation of
their literature. They could see reality, but their bisected eye regis-
tered a disjunctive image. And this accounted for the difference between the aesthetic absurd and the ethical attitude toward absurdity
that came later.

Chapter Twelve

French and Spanish Surrealist Modes
(Conclusion)

In the preceding chapters, I have tried to show that the treatment of the surrealist mode in Spain is best undertaken without recourse to a priori definitions. Nothing is gained by thinking in terms of automatic writing, the unconscious, or Freudian concepts. Nor is it helpful to seek parallels with the French school, even though they exist, and even though the Spaniards were aware of what the French had accomplished. The surrealist mode in Spain was, by and large, like its Gallic counterpart: an aesthetic which was new and experimental, to be sure, but one which also had roots in the literary and intellectual history of the nation. Many of its antecedents can be found in the tradition of the Spanish grotesque, and perhaps even in the dehumanizing techniques of Gongorism.[1] It is characterized by absurdity, deformation, and nightmarish mood, qualities never before cultivated with such technical complexity and self-consciousness. Clearly, we are better served by the principle of autonomy in Spanish surrealism than by any set of categories established by the better-known Parisian school.

The reason for this is that the Spanish writers who employed surrealist methods did not act as a group obeying a single credo of artistic practices. They were not interested in repudiating bourgeois social values, or in promoting the Marxist revolution. Nor did they publish manifestos and statements of purpose. There was, in short, no external cohesion that could compare to the relative solidarity existing in France at the same time. Internal cohesion, of course, is another matter. A number of psychological and aesthetic concepts common to all may be deduced from their work, and I have tried to do just this in the previous chapter. But generally speaking, the surrealist mode in Spain grew out of many individual approaches to the problem of reality. In fact, given the variety of experimental literatures attempted by vanguard writers, most works combined the surrealist sensibility with other styles or techniques. And, as we have seen, the thematic content of these works had a range of interests that exceeded the scope of most other "isms."

None of this should discourage the use of the word "surrealism" in connection with the Spanish vanguard. With the exception of Guillermo de Torre, critics have freely applied the term to one aspect of its literature or another, and several anthologies bear witness to the existence of a surrealist poetry in Spain. In this book, the attempt was made to identify the principles behind the surrealist mode, not only in poetry, but in prose as well, as they developed from the post-Romantic crisis. That we have found a variety of practices ought not to surprise us, but the fact that we have also brought together a consensus of themes and ideas should sustain us in our belief in a genuine Spanish surrealism. The task for the future is to extend this introductory investigation to other members of the Generation of 1927 and, eventually, to Latin America. At any rate, if a final confirmation of the surrealist mode is necessary, perhaps it can be had by reviewing the critical and scholarly theories of French surrealism, and comparing them with the findings of this book about Spain.

By and large, the wide range of interests typifying Spanish surrealism corresponds in diversity to the eclectic interests of the original French group. Scholars have not only found it difficult to reconcile the conflicting views of the people gathered around Breton but they have had to contend with contradictions within the thought of individual writers too.[2] In spite of its many categorically stated theories, French surrealism is far from being homogeneous, and its numerous polemics testify to its varied nature. Accordingly, critical studies of the movement have also differed in approach and emphasis, often paying attention to artists who are not normally associated with surrealism even in a precursory way. Nevertheless, this body of criticism has given the French school a special identity, and it is important for us to see how that identity resembles or differs from the one portrayed for Spain in this book.[3]

We can perhaps best begin by noting what J. H. Matthews has ruled fundamental to any introduction to French surrealism. First is the fact that the movement grew out of Dadaism, and that it differed sharply from the latter in its revolutionary ethos and social commitment. Then too, the surrealists had an instinct for the marvelous, and its interest in magic was part of a general search for revelation, a search which was expressed in its apocalyptic writings. Thus, if surrealism discredits the everyday world, it intensifies certain aspects of behavior in that world: obsession, desire, eroticism. Most important, however, as Matthews documents so well, is French literary surrealism's intimate link to painting. By means of imagery, psychological insight, and parallel statements of theory, writers and painters joined forces to create the surrealist mode.

This description of surrealism is particularly true of France, but it represents the general surrealist mode as fully as the British Romanticists represent the European Romantic phenomenon. There is, of course, some common ground with Spain, especially with regard to psychological insight. But the historical framework of French surrealism, along with the aesthetic statements of purpose made outside the context of the works of art, belong to France, not to Spain. We will find, however, that there are more areas of similarity than of disagreement. On the other hand, we will also find that if there are uniquely French traits in surrealism as an international phenomenon, there are exclusively Spanish ones as well. Thus, the surrealist mode in Europe contains elements which can be found in Spain but not in France, and vice versa. Let us begin, then, with the differences between the French and Spanish surrealist modes.

The most important difference, at least on the surface, is the position vis-à-vis Romanticism. The French surrealists, most notably Breton, freely acknowledged their debt to certain Romantic forebears. Following this admission, critics have made much of the literary antecedents and Romantic tendencies of surrealism. In fact, Herbert Read regards both the French and the English movements as representing the last stage in the Romantic reaction against classicism. For Read, Romanticism means creation, liberation, and introversion, all values which are exalted by the surrealist revolt and its psychology. He does not, therefore, distinguish between the lyrical subjectivism of the Romantics, and the detached, almost clinical methodology of the surrealists. On the other hand, Read maintains that the artistic goals of both schools were the same. It is, of course, true that the French surrealists were rebellious individualists who wished to liberate art from the restrictions of conventional expression. But this is an external fact of history. Their attitude was a Romantic one, to be sure, but it was held by men in a social context, and it does not necessarily speak for the aesthetic characteristics of the works of art themselves. Here, the criteria have less to do with the historical framework of those creations than with their inner workings and psychological disposition. The question, therefore, is whether the most traditionally Romantic traits persist in surrealist literature: the love of nature, the tragic pose, the subjective outpourings of a sensitive heart. With these criteria in mind, it is difficult to postulate the affinity between Romanticism and surrealism. The issue, however, has not as yet been dealt with by the French critics, who have preferred to stress the historical continuity of the two movements instead.[4]

Insofar as the Spanish surrealist mode is concerned, it perpetuated few of the attitudes that characterize Romanticism. Not only was the quality of violence altered by a new sense of alienation but a cold, unfeeling dislocation of the emotions replaced the sentimentalism of the past. It is impossible to situate either a Byron or a Bécquer within the emotional spectrum of the Spanish surrealists.[5] The latter, moreover, lost all interest in Nature. Gone are the landscapes, the communion with natural life, the rustic solitude, and the religious stirrings prompted by Nature. In their place are the broken images of Romantic motifs: deformed moons, mechanical roses, mutilated birds. Dream and reverie change abruptly into nightmare, and whatever was predestined and tragic is now chaotic, grotesque, and absurd. In great measure, this divergence from Romanticism is easily corroborated by the paintings of Ernst, Tanguy, Dali, and De Chirico. One wonders, in fact, to what extent the definition of European surrealism might fruitfully be revised to stress the evidence observed from the visual arts all over Europe, rather than from what the French literary statements proclaim.

The second major difference between the two surrealist modes involves mysticism and the search for the Absolute. According to Anna Balakian's thesis, the French surrealists must be understood in terms of their mystical roots. This is not to confuse the surrealist experience with mystical states, for, as Alquié reminds us, only surrealism regards the subjective and the objective as being identical. But the striving for an ineffable and mysterious reality beyond this world belongs to the tradition of occult and supernatural experiences described by many French writers in the past one hundred years. The Spaniards, on the other hand, reveal nothing of this mysticism. They were, to be sure, deeply concerned with the nature of reality. But the surreality which resulted from their investigation was not, as in the French case, the product of a direct quest or desire. They did not deliberately set out to find a new reality which would fuse all levels of experience: external and internal, real and imaginary, conscious and unconscious, natural and supernatural. On the contrary, the Spaniards produced a surreality in their art as a result of specific reactions to their cultural environment. Their psychological response to reality was translated aesthetically into a surrealistic vision that contained all of the above-mentioned fusions. But there was no mystical determinism involved.

Here again, with regard to French surrealism, one has the feeling that scholarship has highlighted what is traditional in the movement at the expense of what is new. Even Anna Balakian senses this, for she stresses the new alienation of the senses rather than direct sensation. Moreover, she emphasizes, not primary experience, but the new uses of memory, and also such antihuman, antiemotional measures as the suspension of natural law and the destruction of conventional language. These developments are certainly essential to Spanish surrealism, especially in the way the latter treats causality and sense perception. Part of the dehumanizing technique in Spain consists of an aseptic, achromatic handling of the sensory world. The artist is in a laboratory, and he looks upon both living things and objects as interchangeable phenomena that serve to stimulate his own psychic processes. Therefore, the laws of sensation and cause-and-effect are revoked in order to produce a new surreality. This sensory repression is carried out by the precision instruments of technology, which are made to do the bidding of a liberated imagination. At the same time, both the repression and its instruments are used to illustrate the notion that Fact and Reality are myths of the scientific age.

Romanticism and mysticism, then, are two areas which separate the French surrealists from the Spaniards. But aside from these, there are many areas of agreement. The most important of all is the complex of psychological processes which have come to be called "Freudian." These processes are now the acid test of a work's claim to being regarded as surrealistic. Most critics, and Eduardo Cirlot perhaps most lucidly, have pointed out innumerable forms of psychological exploration: free association, hypnosis and hallucination, dreams, and hypnagogic states. In all of these psychic states, surrealists have attempted to both express uncensored subconscious thoughts and to release the Unconscious from the mechanisms erected by the reality principle. The result is an art filled with strange images, sometimes obsessive, and sometimes given to "black" humor. As critics like Alquié maintain, the French surrealists consciously adapted the methods of psychoanalysis to their own purposes. They used automatic writing, for example, to replace other expressive means of investigation in the same way that Freud had substituted free association for the older technique of hypnosis. Similarly, the French tried to present an oneiric reconstruction of

the world by using the dream processes of condensation and displacement. In these and in other methods, the overriding purpose
was to find, as Alquié suggests, a path to knowledge and salvation.
Modern psychoanalysis offered an escape from the tyranny of laws
imposed by the material world, and it tried to free the individual
from the social taboos of current morality. This was precisely the
goal of the surrealist, to free himself from everything that represses
and dams up, so that the total liberty of human nature could be
regained.

Turning to Spain, the same processes are found to have been
in operation. The only difference is that psychoanalytical concepts
were not used consciously for the sake of personal or social liberation. Ideas and techniques of this nature were simply part of a general fund of aesthetic possibilities which the artist could select and
cultivate. It is true that both Freud and Jung were known to the
Spaniards, but there was no need to acknowledge them as mentors.
The artistic use of modern psychology was not only "in the air," it
was part of the contemporary idiom and assimilated into the general intellectual awareness of the nation. If one wished to use it,
it was available, and when it was used, the reasons varied with the
personal vision of each artist.

Nevertheless, if the goals of the French and Spanish surrealists
differed in this area of psychology, their repertoires of techniques
were identical, except for automatic writing. On the other hand, the
motifs in Spanish surrealism were characterized by a higher degree
of violence and neurosis. Critical paranoia as a method had its
thematic counterpart in the paranoiac content of the works themselves. Fear, nightmare, and escapism dominate much of the literature, and even the eye motif—narcissistic or masochistic, sliced or
slicing, passive or persecutory—expresses the psychic derangement
of the surrealist atmosphere. There is, of course, a benign and even
whimsical deformation along side the pathological kind. However,
if one were asked for an example of surrealism, Lorca's *Poet in New
York* would be thought of before anything by Gómez de la Serna.
In Spain, violence holds the ascendency over benign fantasy.

Another aspect shared by the two surrealisms is the theme of
love. The French were, to begin with, considerably impressed by
the Marquis de Sade because of, as Torre indicates, the virtually
limitless possibilities he opened in the area of eroticism. Many other
critics have also pointed out how Sade represented the lack of concern for morality, and the release of instinctual behavior, both of
which were in keeping with surrealist theory in France. Breton went
a step further, however, according to Alquié, and defined love as

something more than sexual desire. Love-passion was supposedly the chief preoccupation of the surrealists, but its real importance lay in the focus it gave to life's most meaningful goal: transcendence and unification. Love, therefore, was the source of hope, although, paradoxically, it invited the surrealist to surpass the Feminine in a mystical rush of desire for the Ideal.

Surrealist painting, on the other hand, reveals anything but a reverential attitude toward women and love. The works of Dali, Ernst, and Magritte portray sex in all of its violence, with the Freudian implications of erotic dream motifs ever present. Spanish surrealism is comparable in its sexual violence, since the symbolic value of its imagery is also rich with Freudian meaning. However, the themes of women and love do not elicit much interest from the Spaniards, although sex does. The profound cultural reasons for this go beyond the scope of this book, and I will not try to interpret them now. What is clear, however, is that the eroticism of the Spanish surrealist is primarily pathological in its symptoms. Most obvious is the fact that the castration theme is deeply ingrained in the literature. Second is the tendency to regard sexuality as evil, both in its homosexual and its heterosexual forms. The converse of this tendency is the need to idealize love by repressing the erotic element, although occasionally the latter is sublimated into another form instead. What is interesting about this repression, and the sexual violence which is its opposite, is that they both contribute to the atmosphere of the surrealist mode. That is, they complement the formal techniques which aim at creating a distorted or otherwise disturbing mood.

A third characteristic common to surrealism on both sides of the Pyrenees is social awareness. In France, as Matthews demonstrates, the surrealists' decisive break with Dadaism was precipitated by a political disagreement. In Breton's case, his coming of age as an artist was speeded by his confrontation with war. Later, of course, Breton, Aragon, and Eluard, among others, held Marxist views and were, for a time, members of the Communist party. But more important than political affiliation was the problem of reconciling social commitment with artistic creation. Here, the alternatives could be reduced to two: either the artist proclaimed his absolute freedom, and thus rejected political claims, or else he committed his art to the service of politics, and thus rejected the mystique of Art. The French surrealists did both, and their disagreement eventually broke the movement's solidarity.

From another standpoint, the social issues in France had metaphysical overtones. The surrealists longed for what Alquié calls the primal fusion, an integrated view of reality which was lost to them when they inherited the modern world's objective vision. They realized the damage that science and technology could do to their dream of integration. Indeed, their praise of childhood stemmed from the fact that a child's perspective allowed many lives to be lived at the same time. Mechanized society, on the other hand, did not permit such flexibility within the limits of reality. Thus, reactions such as Breton's hatred of the machine reflected a sense of social alienation which ran deeper than the political opposition that existed at the surface of surrealist activity.

This reaction to technology had its parallel in Spain, but with different implications, as we will see in a moment. In general, Spanish surrealist literature shows a good deal of social awareness underlying its themes. This is remarkable, in view of the nearly total abstention from politics on the part of Spanish writers. In fact, we might even say that Spanish surrealists were apolitical, but that their works, paradoxically, contain much direct and indirect social criticism. Except for Valle-Inclán, none of the writers had a specific historical or political position in mind while they composed their surrealist works. This does not mean, however, that their themes and settings do not reflect an awareness of contemporary society. On the contrary, problems such as political corruption, class deprivation, and cultural decadence are all visible in their works. But there is no indication that art is being used as a platform for social messages. Moreover, it is only after their surrealist phase that Spanish writers become politically involved. What is important, then, is not so much a specific program in Spain's surrealist mode, as the depiction of sociological problems in the life of a modern culture.

Beyond these major areas so typical of the surrealist expression in Europe, there is only one other point which most critics would agree upon as being essential. This is the matter of what kind of a reality the surrealists were trying to produce in their works. According to Alquié, who has reconstructed a working "philosophy" of surrealism, the movement intended to destroy the distinction between subjectivity and objectivity. Its ideal was the union of the real and the imaginary, and indeed, these two realms were regarded as being one and the same. The problem was that the conventions of the waking world as opposed to sleep, and external reality as opposed to the inner life, tended to split that unity into separate levels of existence. Hence the cult of voluntary hallucination in the place of genuine madness. The surrealists employed every device that could free the mind of its rational categories. By means of what Alquié calls a "causality of desire," they willed a new reality whose truth was poetic rather than scientific, universal rather than particular. The instrument of that desire was the surrealist imagination, which faced the ordinary world and "derealized" it. In other words, the conventional boundaries of perception were broken down, and every conceivable approach to experience became permissible.

In practice, the Spanish surrealists came close to the situation just described. From conditions that range from submergence within the self to light fantasy and gross deformation, there was no discernible difference between reality and surreality. Each was contained in the other, as sentiments, qualities, and values all became interchangeable. Moreover, commonsense experience was contradicted, and sensorial discord was matched by the absurdity of meaningless objects that acquired expressiveness. Nothing was free of illogic. One finds then, that the animation of mannequins and mechanical dolls, or the dehumanization of people and feelings, lends credence to a new reality whose only law is reversibility. Included in this reversibility are pure chance, abrupt changes, and disjunction in chronology and spatial dimensions. What is more important, the elements of this surreality are not as significant as the relationships between them established by the mind. Although objects do gain an unprecedented independence from the world of men, the fact that they take on human characteristics while people become ambiguously human makes their independent existence unimportant. These factors, coupled with the absence of the law of causality, force the general mood and setting into a state of flux.

It can be said, therefore, that Spanish surreality is a single continuum in which the categories of fact, fantasy, delusion, image, and object are all obliterated. As a result, an infinite number of situations can and do arise, from grace and innocence to grotesquerie and bestiality. Infantilism and animalism are the two extremes of the surrealist world, and between them, provision is made for fairy tales, myths, narcotic constructs, and nightmare, all modified by the aesthetic principles that have been described. This, in short, is the general environment and atmosphere in which events take place or feelings are expressed, the stage setting or backdrop for the surrealist situation.

Within the framework of this surrealist reality, two unique contributions are found to have been made by Spain. These are what I have called the "georgics of technology" and "bioculturalism." Together, they grow out of the principle of reversibility, which allows imagination to mix everyday reality with the deepest psychological responses of contemporary man. Separately, they describe two stages in the development of surrealism. The first is the recognition that man must contend with the world of science and industry, a realization born of the social awareness mentioned earlier. Thus, the machine is converted into the perfect guarantor of formal beauty, with its technocratic symbolism being made to embody the spirit of the modern age. By extension, the surrealist sensibility is expressed by the use of a new rhetoric alluding to tools, materials, and chemicals. The pastoral mode is replaced by the technological, although the anguish at having lost Nature's grace is still visible.

This brings us to the second stage, the biocultural vision. Here, metropolitan life is seen as a strange hybridization of industrial and primitive elements. Not only is there uncertainty in determining the difference between fact and fancy, or cause and effect, there is a comparable confusion in the realms of organic and inorganic matter. Mineral, vegetable, and animal states occur in various metamorphoses, all designed to explore the chain of life that reaches back into prehistory. The atmosphere teems with life; yet sometimes it appears petrified, or else it reverts atavistically into unconscious but viable states of matter. A fetid and tumescent environment alternates with the mood of a clinical laboratory, where existence is analyzed from a biological point of view. In all of these situations, individual dreams reflect primal fantasies, and totemism contrasts with technical sophistication. Each scene, in its own way, lays bare the most elemental layers of culture. Thus, on one hand, the biocultural synthesis of modern life is useful sociologically in revealing the hidden truths of the species. And on the other hand, man's integration of the psychic and biological experiences within himself gives insight into the instinctual mechanisms that thrust civilization forward. Nature is transformed from a rustic harmony to urban chaos. And the new jungle is the city, its primitive vitality diluted by the cold scientism of civilized society.

In sum, Spanish surrealism discovers the link between every form of matter and existence, whether they are animate or inanimate, on one plane of reality or on another. This link is usually expressed in technological terms. What is ironic, however, is the fact that while technology means cultural progress, surrealism records how this progress is negated by a regression on the part of human beings. As a result, the surrealist vision describes technology and humanity alike as being dehumanized to the same degree.

All of this, of course, affects the language of surrealism, which is broken down, as well as set free, by a variety of techniques. Science is released from its utilitarian role, and its specialized vocabulary and methodology are appropriated for artistic ends. The rhetorical influence of technology is quite evident, whether we speak of chaotic images, strange metaphors, or the absurd logic of dreams. What is important, however, is not the concrete or abstract quality of imagery, nor the various relationships between image and object, or word and symbol—all questions which have held the attention of the French school and its critics. The main point is that the surrealist idiom reveals a historical perspective, even though surrealism as an aesthetic mode purports to transcend the category of history.[6]

In the last analysis, it is the language and style of a work that mark it as being surrealist. Often, as a consequence, critics can recognize a surrealist work almost instinctively, without recourse to literary history or aesthetic theory. Where word relationships are incongruous and metaphors clash in the special ways that we have been observing, there we have the surrealist mode. This is why many scholars have felt free to bring marginal figures into their discussions of French surrealism. Needless to say, this is entirely justifiable, for it assumes the principle that an "ism" is best defined in terms of its internal workings. In this respect, we must agree with Wallace Fowlie, who distinguishes between the historical meaning of the word "surrealism," and its wider philosophical and aesthetic meaning. Fowlie is also correct in asserting that the word deserves a place beside the terms classicism and Romanticism. Indeed, what he says about surrealism being antirealistic is true on an international scale, and we would do well to conclude with this idea.

If surrealism is linked to Romanticism, the bond consists of a common desire to find within the individual self, on all levels of consciousness, the rules and forms of life and art. But the difference is that the surrealist has a schizoid temperament. His basic condition is one of estrangement from reality and from himself. As Fowlie puts it, what is introspection in Proust is dissociation of personality in surrealism. Of that there is ample evidence in this book. The results, of course, are antithetical to realism, and they extend to the very essence of language, structure, and theme. It is well to recall Valle-Inclán's epithet for the character described as a dehumanized man, for it sums up the rhetoric and psychology of the surrealist mode in Spain as a whole: the "rigid mobility of an automatic doll . . . a private life of coiled wire." This is alienation with a vengeance, but it brings into play the incongruity of seeking Romantic introspection in a mechanized age.

Notes

Introduction

1 There is Manuel Durán's brief survey of poetry, with bibliography, *El superrealismo en la poesía española contemporánea* (Mexico, 1950). Vittorio Bodini's anthology *I poeti surrealisti spagnoli* (Torino, 1963) has an excellent, wide-ranging introduction, including an important section on French sources, and individual discussions of each poet's surrealism. Another good anthology is by José Albi and Joan Fuster, *Antología del surrealismo español* (Alicante, 1952).

2 Nor were there surrealist magazines. Guillermo de Torre identifies only one, *La Gaceta de Arte* (Santa Cruz de Tenerife, 1932–36), in *Historia de las literaturas de vanguardia* (Madrid, 1965), p. 576.

3 For Torre's position, see note 5. Dámaso Alonso: "Cuando se haga la historia de nuestro período creo que ha de resultar claro que la palabra superrealismo (*surréalisme*) conviene a muchas otras manifestaciones de la literatura actual. Para evitar le posible confusión llamo 'hiperrealismo' a esta tendencia general contemporánea dentro de la cual el 'superrealismo' sería sólo un subgrupo." *Ensayos sobre poesía española* (Buenos Aires, 1946), pp. 356–57. Alonso places *Sobre los ángeles, Poeta en Nueva York,* and *Espadas como labios* in the same category with *La voz a ti debida,* calling them all "neo-Romantic."

Note further, some of the comments made by other critics and contemporary poets. Jorge Guillén: "There were only two 'isms' after the preliminary *ultraísmo: creacionismo* . . . and *surrealismo,* which never crystallized as a movement and served rather as an invitation to freedom of the imagination" (*Language and Poetry* [Cambridge, 1961], p. 208). Ramón Gómez de la Serna: "El surrealismo es ya un concepto universal y desde luego una palabra eficaz y señaladora. . . . No es necesario saber

fijamente lo que es 'surrealismo' porque la verdad es que no es un punto
en un mapa sino un tren que corre, que hoy estaba aquí y mañana estará
mucho más lejos, no se sabe dónde" (*Ismos* [Buenos Aires, 1943], p. 309).
Luis Cernuda: "Aunque francés de origen, el superrealismo llegó a con-
vertirse en movimiento internacional, y eso, más que a influencia literaria
se debió quizá a que respondía a una rebeldía de la juventud, a un estado
de ánimo general entre la mocedad por aquellos años . . . Los curioso es
que el superrealismo sólo hallara en España expresión en el verso, pero
no en la prosa; y además, que no todos los poetas del grupo cuyos
comienzos estudiamos [la Generación de 1925] experimentaron dicha
influencia superrealista" (*Estudios sobre poesía española contemporánea*
[Madrid, 1957], p. 192). Cernuda believes that surrealism was the fourth
and last stage in that generation's development, and that the group was
subdivided into Guillén and Salinas, on one hand, and Lorca, Alberti,
and Aleixandre, among others, on the other. Although not knowing
French works directly, the latter came under the influence of Juan Larrea's
surrealismo by way of *creacionismo,* which was to Spanish surrealism what
Dadaism was to French surrealism (pp. 189–96). Leopoldo Rodríguez
Alcalde: "Los poemas del surrealismo español presentan, en general,
mayor coherencia que los textos surrealistas franceses. En los españoles se
agudiza la concepción del surrealismo como reflejo del mundo en el poeta,
como versión lírica de éste, que, mediante la imagen, describe su personal
universo" (*Vida y sentido de la poesía actual* [Madrid, 1956], p. 203); see
also pp. 63–77. Carlos Bousoño: "La escuela suprarealista española, de
alguna manera hemos de llamarlo para entendernos (Lorca, con *Poeta en
Nueva York;* Alberti, con *Sobre los ángeles;* Cernuda, con *Un río un amor;*
y Aleixandre con su segundo libro, *Pasión de la tierra*), nació con inde-
pendencia de la escuela francesa de análoga tendencia y sólo después, en
marcha ya el movimiento hispano, puede hablarse de contactos entre una
y otra" (*La poesía de Vicente Aleixandre* [Madrid, 1956], p. 167). Vicente
Gaos, characterizing the Generation of 1927 in terms of "antirrealismo y
antirromanticismo": ". . . el poeta se afana en una doble tarea de de-
formación y abstracción; se rompen los vínculos lógicos, se va a una
estilización geométrica de la realidad . . ." (*Antología del grupo poético
de 1927* [Salamanca, 1965], p. 12). Gaos then calls surrealism in Spain,
with its "intrascendencia," "la más importante de las nuevas tendencias"
(p. 14). Hugo Friedrich discusses all the traits of surrealism without using
the term itself: "der inkongruente Stil un die 'neue Sprache'"; "Ent-
humanisierung"; "Sprachmagie und Suggestion"; "das Absurde; der
'Humorismus'"; "diktatorische Phantasie," etc. (*Die Struktur der modern
Lyrik* [Hamburg, 1956]).

4 In this regard it is important to remember the insoluble dispute
between A. O. Lovejoy and René Wellek on the nature of Romanticism.
Lovejoy's position in the essay "On the Discrimination of Romanticisms"
runs as follows: (a) strictly speaking, the only movement having an indis-
putable title to the name Romanticism is Germany's, in the 1790's, since

it invented the term; (b) the term "Romanticism" should be used in the plural; (c) the Romanticism of one country may have little in common with that of another, and many critics not only differ on what the word means but admit that nothing in common has been concretely discovered; (d) critics should discriminate not only by nationality and language but by distinct thought processes too. *Essays in the History of Ideas* (Baltimore, 1948), pp. 228–53.

Wellek's counterargument can be summarized by this statement: ". . . we find throughout Europe the same conceptions of poetry and of the workings and nature of poetic imagination, the same conception of nature and its relation to men, and basically the same poetic style, with a use of imagery, symbolism, and myth which is clearly distinct from that of eighteenth-century neoclassicism." "The Concept of Romanticism in Literary History," *Comparative Literature,* I (1949), 147.

5 Guillermo de Torre is the only critic who insists on this unequivocal stand. For Torre, the revolution in Spanish poetry was spearheaded by *Ultraísmo,* and whatever experimentations came later were derivatives or "continuaciones y reflejos," but not part of surrealism, "cuya existencia en las letras españolas es más que dudosa." He discounts *Poeta en Nueva York, Sobre los ángeles,* and *Espadas como labios* as being anything more than "un superrealismo cuestionable." Only José María Hinojosa is recognized as authentically surrealist, while the title is conceded and then denied to Juan Larrea in the same breath. Torre also takes exception to D. Alonso's claim that the term fits other literary manifestations, and he refers to the "precise" surrealist vision of Breton and Eluard as his guide. This is not the place to evaluate Torre's position, which merits an essay in itself. It should be noted, however, that even he has been unable to avoid using the term in connection with Spanish poetry. In his essay on Miguel Hernández, he alludes to the Generation of 1927 as "pasando por ciertas infiltraciones superrealistas" (*Metamorfosis de Proteo* [Buenos Aires, 1956]), p. 97). He also attributes the formal aesthetic of *Poeta en Nueva York* to "la difusa influencia, entonces en el aire, de la estética superrealista" (*La aventura y el orden* [Buenos Aires, 1943], p. 101). And apropos of the young Dalí, he refers to "el influjo que el naciente superrealismo del pintor ejerció sobre [Lorca] (*Ibid.,* p. 100).

6 We must also contend with the meaning of the word *surrealism* as it is understood in mid-twentieth-century English. Note, for example, Webster's definition, third edition: *Surrealism:* "the principles, ideals, or practice of producing fantastic or incongruous imagery in art or literature by means of unnatural juxtapositions and combinations." *Surrealist, surreal* or *surrealistic:* "1—relating to or having the characteristics of surrealism— ~film, ~art, ~literature, ~painter. 2—of, relating to, or resembling mental free association." In contrast, Webster's entry for Dadaism is decidedly historical in definition: "the principles or practice of the arts and especially painting that flourished chiefly in France, Switzerland, and Germany from 1916 to 1920 and that were based on

deliberate irrationality, anarchy, cynicism, and negation of laws of beauty and social organization."

It is also pertinent to note the comments in certain dictionaries of literature. *The Oxford Companion to English Literature,* 3rd. ed. (London, 1946): *"Surrealism,* the name given to a recent movement among certain writers and painters. The former attempt expression by means of words set down without logical sequence; while the latter, led by the Spanish painter Juan Miró, give weird distorted forms to ordinary objects." *Dizionario universale della letteratura contemporanea* (Rome: Mondadori, 1959): "Un accento particolare ha il surrealismo in Spagna, dove il precedente di Góngora, a cui è spontaneo riferire il piú immaginismo barocchismo del Novecento, sta a indicare come la cultura ispanica sia tendenzialmenti portata a una sua deformazione o metamorfosi onirica del dato reale." *Diccionario de literatura española,* 3rd. ed. (Madrid, 1964): "Para los partidarios de esta tendencia [superrealismo], que se extiende pronto a España, donde encuentra bastante eco entre escritores de vanguardia, la creación artística ha de buscar 'algo' que esté por encima de la 'realidad'; para ello se aprovechan incluso las fuerzas creadoras subconscientes, los estados oníricos, y del choque entre las imágenes soñadas y la realidad circundante ha de surgir la obra de arte superrealista. En cierto modo, el superrealismo añade poco a movimientos semejantes en España, tales como el creacionismo."

7 For an excellent discussion of the relationship between surrealism and the grotesque, see Wolfgang Kayser, *Das Groteske in Malerei und Dichtung* (München, 1960), pp. 118–27. See also, Arthur Clayborough, *The Grotesque in English Literature* (Oxford, 1965), pp. 93–97.

8 Other works might have been chosen instead, especially by Juan Larrea, Antonio Espina, Juan José Domenchina, Ernesto Giménez Caballero, Luis Cernuda, Miguel Hernández, Camilo José Cela, and Azorín. It might well be argued that José María Hinojosa's *La flor de California* and Lorca's *Así que pasen cinco años* are required texts for a book of this type. My own judgment, however, was that these and similar works would be essential for a complete history of Spanish surrealism, but that they are of lesser importance in determining its aesthetic framework. Although they are all interesting, some of them reveal secondary aspects of the surrealist mode, or else have individual peculiarities, while others simply echo the works analyzed here with less artistic flair.

9 The English-speaking reader may want to consult the list at the end of the notes for sources and translations.

Chapter One

1 See Bodini's documentation, pp. xvii–xxii; and M. R. Warnier, "Apollinaire au Portugal et en Espagne," *Bulletin des Etudes Portugaises,* XXII (1959–60), 187–247.

2 "El superrealismo musical," *Alfar,* No. 47 (February 1925), 22–28.

3 "Neodadaísmo y superrealismo," *Plural,* I (January 1925), 3–7. Torre subsequently published "El suicidio y el surrealismo" in the *Revista de Occidente,* XIII (July 1935), 117–28.

4 "Realidad y sobrerrealidad," *La Gaceta Literaria* (October 15, 1928), p. 7.

5 "Nominalismo supra-realista," *Alfar,* No. 50 (May 1925), 3.

6 "La moderna pintura francesa," *La Gaceta Literaria* (October 15, 1927), p. 5.

Chapter Two

1 Kayser notes this fact (p. 12). He also comments on the link between the grotesque and surrealism, pointing out that surrealist theory rejected the grotesque while practicing it (p. 124). See also, Friedrich (p. 24) and Clayborough (p. 95).

2 This approach to Machado is not the orthodox one adopted by most critics, who normally study his metaphysics, existentialism, social realism, modernism, irony, etc. What I find of interest in Machado may occur infrequently, but it is neither rare nor uncharacteristic. At any rate, it is pertinent. As Lovejoy points out, one of the basic assumptions in the history of ideas is the importance of "the internal tensions or waverings in the mind of almost every individual writer—sometimes discernible even in a single writing or on a single page—arising from conflicting ideas or incongruous propensities of feeling or taste, to which, so to say, he is susceptible" (pp. xiii–xiv). And again, regarding our usual efforts to harmonize the thought of a writer: "precisely the most interesting and most noteworthy fact about him [is] the impact upon him of traditions of differing origins and opposite tendencies, or the dim emergence in his thinking of new ideas destined to be seized upon and made use of by his successors . . ." (p. xiv). There are many excellent studies of Machado in the mainstream of scholarship, some of which are cited in the notes below. See also, A. Sánchez Barbudo, *Estudios sobre Unamuno y Machado* (Madrid, 1959); S. Serrano Poncela, *A. M. Su mundo y su obra* (Buenos Aires, 1954); and for bibliography, A. de Albornoz in *La Torre,* XII (January-June 1964), 505–53.

3 *Poesías completas* (Buenos Aires, 1951), CXXXII. All quotations refer to the Losada editions, which will be abbreviated as follows: *Los complementarios:* C; *Abel Martín,* AM; *Juan de Mairena* (2 vols.): JM, JM-II.

4 See the following poems: LIV, XCIV, C, CVI, CVII, CVIII, and "La tierra de Alvargonzález: 'Los asesinos' iv."

5 This idea is elaborated by Ortega in his "Goya, distante de sus temas," *Goya* (Madrid: Revista de Occidente, 1958), pp. 23–24.

6 J. M. Valverde uses this passage about the troubador machine to demonstrate how M. regains his sense of reality. "Evolución del sentido espiritual de la obra de A. M.," *Estudios sobre la palabra poética* (Madrid, 1952), pp. 111–16.

7 In his discussion of "M. y la generación poética del '25," J. L. Cano refers to this fetichism as evidence of M.'s distance from the younger poets, and the fact that "a pesar de su buena voluntad, no llegó nunca a comprender lo nuevo en poesía, llamárase ultraísmo, creacionismo, surrealismo . . ." *La Torre,* XII (January-June 1964), 485. This judgment is incorrect (see below, notes 8 and 9).

8 M. was quite aware of the implications of his remarks from the standpoint of the history of aesthetic ideas. Elsewhere he refers to modern poets being divided into "dos sectas antagónicas: la de aquellos que pretenden hacer lírica al margen de toda emoción humana, por un juego mecánico de imágenes, lo que no es, en el fondo, sino un arte combinatorio de conceptos hueros y la de aquellos otros para quienes la lírica, al prescindir de toda estructura lógica, sería el producto de los estados semicomatosos del sueño. Son dos modos perversos del pensar y del sentir, que aparecen en aquellos momentos en que el arte—un arte—se desintegra o, como dice Ortega y Gasset, se deshumaniza" (AM, 95).

9 Although Machado voiced somewhat unsympathetic feelings toward "los estados semicomatosos de sueño," he cultivated them himself. See "Recuerdos de sueños, fiebre y duermevela" (AM, 67 ff.) and "Fragmentos de pesadilla" (C, 73 ff.).

10 For extensive information about the modernist aspect of Verlaine's influence, see G. Ribbans, "La influencia de Verlaine en Antonio Machado," *Cuadernos Hispanoamericanos,* Nos. 91–92 (1957), 180–201.

11 R. Gullón, writing about "Simbolismo y modernismo en Antonio Machado," sees the identity between the mockingbird and the spectator, but fails to explore its meaning in connection with either the poet or his art (*Direcciones del modernismo* [Madrid, 1963], pp. 128–53).

12 A hint of the deformations glimpsed by Machado in the "profound mirror of my desire" is given by R. de Zubiría in *La poesía de A. M.* (Madrid, 1955), pp. 107–12, but the issue is linked to the problem of time. For a general description of the imagery and symbolism involved in M.'s mirrors, dreams, and varied phantasmagoria, see C. Zardoya, "El cristal y el espejo en la poesía de M.," *Poesía española contemporánea* (Madrid, 1961), pp. 181–215.

13 See further, H. MacKenzie, *Byron's Laughter* (Los Angeles, 1939).

14 *Rousseau and Romanticism* (New York, 1955), pp. 241–42, 263–66.

15 The role of awareness is very important in the opinion of Serrano Poncela, who also distinguishes M.'s conscious activity from that of the surrealists: "Allá, en ciertas galerías sin fondo, los recuerdos se mueven como grandes peces tranquilos y difícilmente apresables. Fuera queda, un poco a la expectativa, el trivial y cotidiano sujeto que los demás consideran *el poeta* ofreciéndonos un perfil un poco grotesco. La disociación producida, ya nada se puede hacer más que aceptar el destino y entregarse a una serie de alquimias en el ámbito subliminal de la conciencia. . . . Queda sobreentendida que M. no poetizó siguiendo pautas surrealistas o simbolistas, desde lo que podríamos denominar un inconsciente provocado o estimulado. Su poesía traduce un estado *conciencial* de elaboración." "Borrosos laberintos," *La Torre,* XII (January-June 1964), 266. Of course, Eluard and Dali were just as self-conscious without being any less surrealistic. The difference lies in the extent of grotesqueness, not in an arbitrary definition of surrealism as an unconscious act.

16 The mental strain involved here is relieved, as Serrano Poncela explains, by a "límite autorreflexivo impuesto por la conciencia en vigilia que impide el desbordamiento hacia la anormalidad psíquica" (267). This article is also noteworthy for its allusions, however brief, to Freudian and Jungian elements in M.'s galleries.

17 As Torre phrases it, avoiding the term surrealism: "Negrismo, funebrismo, tremendismo y aun macabrismo son, en definitiva, los númenes solanescos." This is Solana's "visión de la intrarrealidad hispánica." "S. escritor," *Minorías y masas en la cultura y arte contemporáneos* (Barcelona, 1963), pp. 214, 216.

18 S.'s prose works have been resuscitated thanks to Camilo José Cela's *La obra literaria del pintor S.* (Madrid, 1957), and to his subsequent edition of the *Obra literaria* (Madrid, 1961). During the vanguard period, one of the first writers to consistently recognize S. was Antonio Espina: "S.," *España,* No. 288 (November 6, 1920), 8–9; "S.," *La Gaceta Literaria* (November 15, 1927), p. 5; "J. G. S.: Dos pueblos de Castilla," *Revista de Occidente,* X (October-December 1925), 261–63; "Cuadros de S.," *Revista de Occidente,* XVIII (October-December 1927), 269–72.

The best English introduction to S.'s painting is A. Kerrigan's "Black Knight of Spanish Painting," *Arts Magazine* (May-June 1962), pp. 16–20. Aspects of his prose are treated in W. Flint's "Wax Figures and Mannequins in S.," *Hispania,* XLVI (1963), 740–47. An excellent brief article in Spanish is X. de Salas' "La pintura de S.," *Leonardo,* VI-VII (1945), 305–11.

19 Torre links this reality to surrealism in his comparison of S. and Dali ("Realismo y superrealismo," *El Sol* [March 8, 1936]).

20 *La España negra* (Madrid, 1920), p. 81, henceforth abbreviated EN. Other abbreviations: MC—*Madrid callejero* (Madrid, 1923); I—*Madrid: Escenas y costumbres, primera serie* (Madrid, 1913); II—*ibid, segunda serie* (Madrid, 1918). Since the *Obra literaria* is slightly altered, I have used the original editions.

21 M. Sánchez Camargo, *Solana* (Madrid, 1945), p. 254.

22 For an extraordinary essay on S.'s psychopathology, see J. J. López Ibor, "S., existencialista carpetovetónico," *Papeles de Son Armadans*, III, No. 33 bis (1958). This issue is completely dedicated to S. Besides Camargo's biography, which has plates, a very readable and useful book is R. Gómez de la Serna's *J. G. S.* (Buenos Aires, 1944). Other good studies with reproductions are Camargo's *S. Pintura y dibujos* (Madrid, 1953) and E. M. Aguilera's *J. G. S.: Aspectos de su vida, su obra y su arte* (Barcelona, 1947).

Chapter Three

1 Aleixandre's critics have found it necessary to qualify his surrealism because he was not influenced by the French school. P. Salinas calls him a neo-Romantic, observing that his internal logic keeps him from being a surrealist. Salinas also declares: *"Espadas como labios y La destrucción o el amor significaron la plena incorporación del surrealismo a la poesía castellana. Mas el surrealismo de A. no era tanto un surrealismo de escuela o de fórmulas como una posición poética afirmada sobre un fondo personal . . . romántico"* ("V. A. entre la destrucción y el amor," *Literatura española siglo XX* [Mexico, 1949], p. 217).

D. Alonso writes: "*. . . esta poesía de V. A., como toda la poesía superrealista, en lo que más o menos está emparentada, forma parte de un vasto movimiento literario y científico, que no sé si calificar de hiper-realista o hipo-realista . . . encuentra su paralelo y hasta cierto punto su base, en los intentos psicológicos de los años últimos, el psicoanálisis. . . . Es una necesidad de la época, repito, y esto explica el hecho de que V. A. pudiera escribir un libro superrealista de poemas en prosa (publicado en 1935), sin intención ninguna de 'hacer superrealismo' y sin conocer directamente la escuela francesa"* (*Ensayos sobre poesía española*, pp. 356–58). However, Alonso was more willing in 1935 to admit that A.'s poetry was "*más o menos emparentada con el surréalisme francés y su pretendido automatismo*" ("V. A. *La destrucción o el amor*," *Revista de Occidente* [June 1935], p. 340).

2 *Poesías completas* (Madrid, 1960), p. 344.

3 The only full-length study of these works is C. Bousoño's *La poesía de V. A.* (Madrid, 1956). He finds that the "ingredientes suprarrealistas visibles" in *Pasión de la tierra* stem from the visionary tradition of Spanish literature, and A.'s knowledge of Rimbaud and Joyce. See especially his discussion of imagery and Freudian dream symbolism, pp. 167–78.

4 On the suspension of time and other dimensions of reality for the sake of linguistic imaginativeness and in order to cultivate the sensual word, see L. F. Vivanco, "El espesor del mundo en la poesía de V. A.," *Introducción a la poesía española contemporánea* (Madrid, 1957), pp. 341–83. This essay is one of the best written on A.

5 However, as Rodríguez Alcalde remarks, "El surrealismo español, que paradójicamente cuenta con más insignes figuras que el propio surrealismo francés, no fue nunca fiel a un estrecho concepto de la escritura automática, pues incluso V. A., que en *Espadas como labios* o en *Pasión de la tierra* parece seguir con entusiasmo las normas surrealistas, ha dicho categóricamente: 'No he creído nunca en lo estríctamente onírico, en la escritura automática, en la abolición de la conciencia creadora'" (*Vida y sentido de la poesía actual,* pp. 202–3).

6 For a different approach to the imagery of self-destruction as it fits into the development of A.'s poetry from surrealism to pantheism, see C. Zardoya, *Poesía Española Contemporánea,* pp. 439–598.

7 A. himself says of this work: "Es poesía 'en estado naciente,' con un mínimo de elaboración. Hace tiempo que sé, aunque entonces no tuviera conciencia de ello, lo que este libro debe a la lectura de un psicólogo de vasta repercusión literaria (Freud), que yo acababa de realizar justamente por aquellos años" (*Mis poemas mejores* [Madrid, 1956], p. 30).

Chapter Four

1 The comment by A. del Río on this new stage is still pertinent: "Lorca had deviated from the dominant folkloric and traditional elements to explore . . . a type of poetry characterized by an intellectual consciousness which Spanish criticism may have woefully underestimated" (*Poet in New York,* tr. by B. Belitt [New York, 1955], p. xii).

2 Virtually everyone has commented on the friendship between L. and Dalí, but hardly anyone has tried to analyze the ode in biographical terms. See J.-L. Schonberg, *F. G. L. L'homme-l'oeuvre* (Paris, 1956), pp. 75–79.

3 For a general discussion of the object in poetry, see W. Kellermann, "Die Welt der Dinge in der spanischen Lyrik des 20. Jahrhunderts," *Deutsche Vierteljahrsschrift,* XXVII (1953), pp. 102–36. On another level, Friedrich links the role of geometry to the art of dehumanization (p. 123). On the other hand, Guillén maintains: "If there is to be poetry, it will have to be human. How could it be otherwise? Inhuman or superhuman poetry has perhaps existed. But a 'dehumanized' poem is a physical and metaphysical impossibility, and the phrase 'dehumanization of art,' coined by our great philosopher, Ortega y Gasset, rang false from the very beginning. 'Dehumanization' is a completely inadmissible concept . . ." (*Language and Poetry,* p. 209).

4 This has a parallel with what happened during Breton's early years: he was attracted to Tzara's Dadaism, yet he held on to the controlled formalism of Mallarmé and Valéry. J. H. Matthews, *An Introduction to Surrealism* (University Park, 1965), p. 32.

5 In order to keep this fact in mind, note Del Río's comment on the ode to Dali: "Hay, en cambio, adivinaciones profundas del misterio último de las cosas, expresado más bien a través de las intuiciones de la subconsciencia. En ello hallamos la raíz de una de las fases más importantes de su arte. Esta oda al cubismo aséptico y geométrico—escrita en 1926— es en rigor el primer anuncio de los elementos surrealistas que luego veremos en gran parte de su poesía. Surrealismo el de L. más auténtico que el de ningún otro poeta de su generación" (*Vida y obras de F. G. L.* [Zaragoza, 1952], pp. 89–90).

6 This view would not apply to surrealism, according to Díaz Plaja, who regards the movement as "una reacción contra el intelectualismo abstracto de los cubistas. En este sentido el movimiento tiene un carácter neorromántico: postula un mundo fantástico, sin amarras con lo real, y un señorío absoluto del yo en oposición a cualquier exigencia externa de índole estética, social o moral . . . Es precisamente un 'retorno a lo humano' . . . que llega tras una exaltación del mundo impasible de la mecánica" (*F. G. L. Su obra e influencia en la poesía española* [Buenos Aires, 1954], p. 157). This statement appears plausible, although the last sentence would prove to be unfounded if it were applied to the context of the ode to Whitman. See Chapter Five.

7 A similar reason is offered by Díaz Plaja, who contrasts life against death in the framework of a Dionysiac attitude to Nature. He holds that artistic consciousness demands some restraint on the "total abandono del poeta a la embriaguez del subconsciente. . . . Por eso la obra central de F. G. L. es ecléctica," i.e., in order to maintain its human quality (p. 159).

8 Díaz Plaja thinks that "para Dali es posible la más irrazonada disposición de los objetos en el cuadro a condición de que cada uno de ellos sea trasladado con toda fidelidad al lienzo" (p. 150).

Commenting on what L. refers to as Dali's "amor a lo que tiene explicación," and his "miedo a la emoción," Díaz Plaja calls this "el retorno a la visión fría y desnuda de las cosas. Su fórmula más estable es el realismo mágico o posexpresionista (Roh), y aquí cabría situar la obra de Dali. Y nótese que ésta—y la poesía que la loa—no es en modo alguno cubista; y que sin desconocer la lección de geométrico rigor y de disciplina que la pintura contemporánea debe al cubismo, asistimos a un momento en que dicha lección se ha trasformado ya en ciencia infusa" (p. 151).

9 Del Río recognizes that the ode is in part a theoretical exposition of cubism, but then he says: "Y sin embargo, lo apasionado, el fondo dionisíaco y sensual de su carácter palpita también como a traición. . . . Nada abstracto ni puramente intelectual . . ." (pp. 88–89).

10 Dali's influence on L.'s surrealism has been pointed out repeatedly, but never with any proof. Actually, the painter's work before 1927 is not surrealistic, but cubist, and occasionally representational. L.'s surrealism, according to Torre, came from "la difusa influencia entonces en el aire"

of the French aesthetic (*La aventura y el orden,* p. 101). However, Torre reverses himself in his *Historia . . .,* crediting Dali with having an "impact" on the poet (p. 573).

Chapter Five

1 For a comprehensive view of the metaphors controlled by L.'s "afán surrealista," "deshumanización," and other techniques, see C. Zardoya, "La técnica metafórica de F. G. L.," *Poesía española contemporánea,* pp. 337–96.

With regard to the nightmarish city, Gómez de la Serna observes, while speaking about surrealism in general: "En lo que tiene de ensañado el surrealismo, estoy seguro que entra por mucho la emoción triste de París, su desesperación, su indiferentismo tentacular, su burguesía estranguladora" (*Ismos,* p. 291).

2 The opinion of Del Río is that L.'s admiration extended to his artistic activity as well: "The numerous repetitions, the chaotic enumerations, the length of the lines, the prophetic tone, the constant use of the first person, the great imaginative fluency and the cosmic breadth show without doubt that he had absorbed also a good deal of Whitman's style and mannerisms" (p. xxxi).

3 A different emphasis to this idea is given by Del Río: "Whitman's dream of a healthy love for the pure human being has been corrupted by ignoble perversion, and his prophecy of a powerful America where a new humanity would overcome pain and injustice and would feel strong, like the rivers, has come to naught" (p. xxv).

4 J.-L. Schonberg reads this ode, as he does the one to Dali, quite literally in its biographical implications (pp. 212–13).

5 A different conclusion is arrived at by R. Saez: "Whitman's Apollonian beauty depends upon his figurative castration. We are reminded of the eunuch priests of Attis. That association leads us to contrast the Apollonian grace of Whitman with the Dionysiac frenzy of the fairies . . ." "The Ritual Sacrifice in L.'s *Poet . . .,*" *Lorca: A Collection of Critical Essays,* ed. by M. Durán (Englewood Cliffs, 1962), p. 125.

6 By now, there ought to be no question as to whether L. is a surrealist. It is interesting, however, to review what has been said in passing about this issue, even though the critics do not seem to have given surrealism much thought. The semantic question is summed upon by R. Gullón: "Se denominó surrealista a la poesía lorquiana de esta época por un fenómeno de mimetismo crítico, y por su semejanza con los productos de esa escuela, pero el calificativo únicamente podría aplicarse con rigor y precisión revisando previamente el concepto y estableciendo los límites de un surrealismo hispánico, diferente del definido por Breton, pues caracterizado por una presencia de la conciencia contraria a la 'ausencia de la razón' exigida por el pontífice de la secta. No es imposible fijar un

nuevo concepto del surrealismo al hispánico modo, en cuyo ámbito, junto a poemas de Cernuda, Alberti, Aleixandre, Neruda, y otros, cabrían algunos de L. . . . . " But Gullón does not attempt to do this in his essay ("L. en Nueva York," *La Torre,* V [April-June 1957], 165).

On the other hand, L.'s brother Francisco opposes the use of the term surrealism: "I could tell, having in some cases been the conveying vessel, what scant circumstantial knowledge he [L.] had of various foreign poets who are the base of contemporary poetic movements. His accent is modern because he was a modern man. That period of his verse called surrealist, poetry of subconscious or semiconscious associations, has been considered by some as an excursion to the very margins of his real path and by others as a tribute to a compelling necessity. Both statements are unfounded. Aside from the fact that I do not believe Federico was a surrealist *strictu sensu,* his *Poet . . .,* the book that best represents this period of his development, is nothing but the crystallizing of a phase already contained, as with the rest of his books, in his previous poetry and drama" (*Three Tragedies of F. G. L.,* tr. by J. Graham-Luján and R. L. O'Connell [New York, 1947], pp. 9–10). The poet's brother admits, however, that "the part he turned over to a process of unconscious cerebration was enormous. And it is not only for such works as *If Five Years Pass* that this statement holds true, but in great measure for all of them" (p. 25).

Regarding L.'s knowledge of literary movements, M. T. Babín points out that he was explicit about surrealism. L.'s own words were: "Esta evasión poética puede hacerse de muchas maneras. El surrealismo emplea el sueño y su lógica para escapar. En el mundo de los sueños, el realísimo mundo de los sueños, se encuentran indudablemente normas poéticas de emoción verdadera. Pero, esta evasión por medio del sueño o del subconsciente es, aunque muy pura, poco diáfana. Los latinos queremos perfiles y misterio visible. Forma y sensualidad" (*La prosa mágica de G. L.* [Santander, 1962], p. 40).

As for terminology, Del Río is of two minds about the word surrealism. He points out the similarity between L.'s imagery and Dali's, but says: "There is no doubt that in form, content, and attitude a coincidence with surrealism exists, but Conrad Aiken was entirely right when he said that to call L. a surrealist was a mistake: 'For to be a surrealist,' he explains, 'is to be something else than a poet: surrealism is perhaps one of the many names, merely, for the substratum out of which poetry is made.' And he adds with great insight: 'L. devoured all the properties of surrealism, stuffed his cheek with them, like a conjurer, blew them out of his mouth again as poems—but so he did with everything else that he fed on.'" (p. xxxv). On the other hand, Del Río also feels that "L. was at the time inclined towards surrealism" and that *Poet . . .* "is the first important work that the movement produced in Spain" (p. xxxiii). He goes on to speak of L.'s "subconscious intuitions," and he declares that "in a certain sense it could be said that L. was more surrealist than the surrealists." The difference was that the latter were materialistic whereas L. was spiritual (p. xxxviii).

The spiritual aspect of *Poet* . . . is also emphasized by E. Honig, who refers to L.'s "incoherent prophetic vision." He finds the poems "tormented and mutilated, but still sensually realistic. . . . It is easy to think of them as the fabrications of a mind which has lost its balance, as the outpourings of a surrealist gruesomely constructing an antihuman nightmare world." But, says Honig, "a fervid spiritual effort informs them" ("The Triumph of Sensual Reality," *Lorca: A Collection* . . ., p. 89).

Perhaps the most sensible observation about L.'s surrealism comes from D. Alonso, who chides historians for seeking literary influences. They forget, he says, the everyday fact, "por muy misterioso que sea, de las emanaciones difusas, de eso que está en el aire. Es evidente que los elementos oníricos son lo que da trasmundo y misterio a la poesía de Federico desde sus primeras canciones, mucho antes de todo superrealismo" ("Una generación poética," *Poesía española contemporánea* [Madrid, 1952], p. 188; see also note, p. 189).

7 R. Bosch explains the link between L. and surrealism by studying "El choque de imágenes como principio creador de G. L." Referring to L.'s early imagery, he writes: "Se piensa aquí en el surrealismo en un sentido amplio, como interpretación fantástica de la realidad en términos de más allá de la realidad por medio de la imaginación irracional que reúne elementos extraños y heterogéneos. En este sentido, hay un surrealismo natural y congénito en L., y un surrealismo exacerbado e histórico, especialmente en su *Poeta* . . ." (*Revista Hispánica Moderna*, XXX [1964], 43n; see also 37n).

Chapter Six

1 Apropos of social criticism, Del Río quotes from Conrad Aiken's review in *The New Republic:* " 'There has been no more terribly acute critic of America than this steel-conscious and death-conscious Spaniard, with his curious passion of the modernities of nickel and tinfoil and nitre, and for the eternities of the desert and the moon. He hated us, and rightly, for the right reasons' " (p. x). And again: " 'He probably did not realize what it all meant, ignorant as he was of economic laws and history, but the signs and portents were there for him to perceive and express in an incoherent and semi-conscious way' " (p. xiii).

2 On this point, G. Correa makes the following remark: "Los Negros representan aquí la búsqueda de lo genuino primitivo, de la savia pristina que ha de revitalizar algún día la sangre débil de los blancos ineptos y metalizados. Su origen primero en las asoladas tierras del Africa adquiere la categoría de un mitológico paraíso" ("Significado de *Poeta* . . .," *Cuadernos Americanos*, XVIII [January-February 1959]), 227.

3 With regard to the general orientation of this chapter, I do not want to leave the impression that I am interpreting L. ex post civil rights movement. L. himself made his position clear when he returned from New York. Referring to the Negro, he said: "Con su tristeza se han hecho

el eje espiritual de aquella América. El negro que está tan cerca de la naturaleza humana pura y de la otra naturaleza. ¡Ese negro que se saca música hasta de los bolsillos! Fuera del arte negro no queda en los Estados Unidos más que mecánica y automatismo." "Yo creo que el ser de Granada me inclina a la comprensión simpática de los perseguidos. Del gitano, del negro, del judío . . ., del morisco, que todos llevamos dentro." ". . . el gran barrio del negro de Harlem, la ciudad negra más importante del mundo, donde lo más lúbrico tiene un acento de inocencia que lo hace perturbador y religioso." "Yo quería hacer el poema de la raza negra en Norteamérica y subrayar el dolor que tienen los negros de ser negros en un mundo contrario; esclavos de todos los inventos del hombre blanco y de todas sus máquinas, con el perpetuo susto de que se les olvide un día encender la estufa de gas, o guiar el automóvil . . ." (M. Laffranque, "F. G. L. Nouveaux textes en prose," *Bulletin Hispanique,* LVI [1954], 263–65, 271.

4 Del Río sees this degradation in somewhat theological terms: "Here the equation of pain, spiritual vacuity and primitive passion astir in the mechanical jungle is organized around two meaningful motifs of medieval tradition and religious overtones: Paradise Lost and The Dance of Death. The Negro, snatched from the real jungle but still 'nostalgic of pristine blue' and deprived of 'the lore of the trunk and the bypath," becomes the symbol of confused humanity in Pandemonium. He is the victim of civilization, while at the same time he preserves intact, under the dark eclipse of the skin, the impulses and strength of man unmarred by original sin" (p. xix).

5 What is important is the terminology of this problem, and its implications. Thus far, critics have not progressed beyond Díaz Plaja's summation: "la Gran Ciudad nos presenta en su más agudo vértice dramático . . . el choque gigantesco de lo natural y lo mecanizado . . . lo libre biológico y la mecánica implacable" (p. 163).

6 A quite different interpretation of the blood theme is given by R. Saez: "The absence of a ceremonial ritual to celebrate the animal sacrifice of nature, results in the diseased congestion of unspilt blood, occasionally bursting cataclysmically, which in turn dictates the disconnected form and nightmare imagery of the poem" (*Lorca: A Collection* . . ., p. 109).

7 An interesting Jungian interpretation is offered by Correa, who at one point refers to the mythological creatures that spring forth from the city's depths while man struggles for sunlight: "Surge entonces el arquetipo de la lucha contra el dragón y el del héroe niño que ha de librar y redimir a la humanidad de las terribles amenazas. Es el momento liberador de la conciencia que se afirma sobre el panorama oscuro de la subconciencia. La figura libertadora se convierte en un héroe cultural. Pues bien, este estado agónico entre la subconciencia y la conciencia se reproduce en la estructura arquetípica de *Poeta* . . . . Al penetrar en la caverna oscura y laberíntica de la ciudad, el poeta ha descendido al abismo de su propia

subconciencia, donde las fuerzas amorfas y oscuras de la creación poética se debaten en lucha aterradora para producir la luz liberadora y armoniosa de la obra creada" (p. 233).

Chapter Seven

1 *Hidden Faces,* tr. by H. Chevalier (New York, 1944). The Spanish version, expurgated, is *Rostros ocultos* (Barcelona, 1952).

2 For an excellent, if unsympathetic, essay on Dali in general, see G. Orwell's "Benefit of Clergy," in *Collected Essays* (London, 1961). See also E. Wilson's mixed review of the novel, "S. D. as a Novelist," *The New Yorker* (July 1, 1944).

3 R. Descharnes, *The World of S. D.* (New York, 1962).

4 For general surveys of D.'s artistic techniques in painting and prose, see G. de Torre, "S. D. en tres tiempos," *Minorías y masas en la cultura y arte contemporáneos,* pp. 271–303; R. Gullón, "S. D. y el surrealismo," *La Torre,* I (October-December 1953), 131–45; R. Gómez de la Serna, "Definición de D. y sus bigotes," *Temas,* V (March 1953), 60–75; A. Zúñiga, *Palabras del tiempo* (Barcelona, 1952), pp. 46–51; J. T. Soby, *S. D.* (New York, 1946).

5 *La Gaceta Literaria* (October 15, 1928), p. 7.

6 *L'Amic de Les Arts,* II (September 31, 1927), 90–91.

7 Furthermore, see these works by D.: *Conquest of the Irrational* (New York, 1935); *The Secret Life of S. D.* (New York, 1942); *Diary of a Genius* (New York, 1965).

8 Additional information on D.'s career and interests can be found in: F. Cowles, *The Case of S. D.* (Boston, 1959); A. M. Dali, *S. D. visto por su hermana* (Barcelona, 1949); and M. Utrillo, *S. D. y sus enemigos* (Sitges, 1952).

Chapter Eight

1 See E. Dehennin, *La résurgence de Góngora et la génération poétique de 1927* (Paris, 1962), pp. 143–79.

2 On the other hand, the quality of Alberti's emotional distance in *Sobre los ángeles* is noted by Vivanco: "Su poesía es de ángel rebelde, pero no a la manera romántica—o idealista ingenuo—, sino rebelándose también contra su propia rebeldía, es decir, manteniéndose distanciado de la lucha, para crear con ella su mundo poético absoluto" (p. 246).

3 L. Monguió explains why A. cannot be considered a surrealist. Surveying the French movement, he says that Breton advocated "the poetic exploitation of the irrational." He then declares, "I should like to go on to insist that the poetry of A. is wholly devoid of the irrational

and surreal in this sense. It is a fact, however, that the poetry of Europe of that period is permeated with a quality of free association he did not hesitate to employ, on occasion, for his own purposes. The operative words in this case are 'employ' and 'purpose,' rather than 'abandon' and 'surrender,' indispensable to the surrealist mystique" (*Selected Poems of R. A.,* tr. by B. Belitt [Berkeley, 1965], p. 20). It is questionable whether "abandon" and "surrender" are indispensable, except for a very primitive definition of surrealism. The "operative words" would seem to be "free association," since all artists, surrealists included, "employ" techniques with a "purpose."

4 *Poesías completas* (Buenos Aires, 1961), p. 243.

5 The only full-length essay on this collection, although with a different emphasis, is G. W. Connell's "The End of a Quest. A.'s *Sermones y moradas* and Three Uncollected Poems," *Hispanic Review,* XXXIII (1965), 290–309.

6 An outstanding essay on this point, especially in view of its date, is E. Proll's "Surrealist Elements in R. A.," *Bulletin of Hispanic Studies,* XVIII (1941), 70–82. Of the *Sermones . . .,* he writes that it "enters further into the realm of Surrealism, but lacks concentration, and contains a large amount of *preciosité* and mere fooling. The length of the sentences tends to make the book tiresome, and one even grows weary of fulgent images and abstract jests. . . . Elements of the social realist phase which follows are already to be found" (p. 80).

7 An allusion to this disjunctiveness is made by Vivanco, but he fails to develop its implications. Instead, with respect to the increasing surrealistic tendencies in *Sobre los ángeles,* he finds enacted "una escapada hacia lo alto en que la imaginación posee ya tanta plasticidad autónoma que no puede concentrarse en símbolo unitario" (p. 248). See, too, C. B. Morris, *R. A.'s 'Sobre los ángeles': Four Major Themes* (Hull, 1966).

8 This passage about the electric shock is quoted in passing by R. Bosch to illustrate his theory of "El choque de imágenes como principio creador de García Lorca" (p. 42). Comparisons of Alberti and Lorca have been frequent in Spanish criticism. Viewing their respective surrealisms, Del Río has maintained that "surrealismo el de Lorca [es] más auténtico que el de ningún otro poeta de su generación, que el de Alberti, por ejemplo, en quien no fue sino una forma más de su continuo cambiar de estilo con la habilidad de un gran virtuoso de la poesía" (*Vida y obras de F. G. L.,* p. 90).

Chapter Nine

1 P. Salinas' essay is a landmark in criticism on this subject. It establishes the historical setting and describes the general characteristics of the *esperpento,* thus preparing the way for later studies of a more detailed nature ("Significación del esperpento, o Valle-Inclán, hijo pródigo del 98,"

Literatura española siglo XX, pp. 87–114). See too E. Speratti Piñero, *La elaboración artística en Tirano Banderas* (Mexico, 1957); M. Fernández Almagro, *Vida y literatura de V.-I.* (Madrid, 1943); G. Díaz Plaja, *Las estéticas de V.-I.* (Madrid, 1965); and A. Risco, *La estética de V.I.* (Madrid, 1966).

2 None of the Spanish critics has thought of V.-I. as a surrealist. He is so designated, however, by M. Esslin in *The Theater of the Absurd* (New York, 1961), pp. 286–87.

3 Cf. Ulrich Weisstein, "Expressionism: Style or 'Weltanschauung'?" *Criticism,* IX (1967), 42–62.

4 For an introductory description of the "teatro satírico" and the "musa grotesca," see A. del Saz, *El teatro de V.-I.* (Barcelona, 1950), pp. 37–53, and G. Heinrich, *Die Kunst Don R. M. del V.-I.* (Rostock, 1938), pp. 71–95. On the grotesque in general in V.-I.'s work, there are several studies, my own included, in *R. del V.-I.; A Critical Appraisal of His Life and Works* (New York, 1968).

5 The nature of tragedy and its transformation by V.-I. is ably discussed in A. Zahareas, "La Desvalorización del sentido trágico en el esperpento de V.-I.," *Insula,* No. 203 (October 1963), pp. 1, 15. See also Torre, "V-I o el rostro y la máscara," *La difícil universalidad española* (Madrid, 1965), pp. 113–62.

6 Since the reader may have any one of so many popular editions of the novel, I will quote according to *Parte, Libro,* and section, in that order, instead of by page number: (III, 3, i).

7 A methodical study of the *esperpento,* its definitions, critical interpretations, and structure, is presented in C. Iglesias, "El *'esperpento'* en la obra de V.-I.," *Cuadernos Americanos,* XVIII (May-June 1959), 247–63; (July-August 1959), 212–33. The author breaks down techniques into categories like the vivification of static objects, the humanization of animals and things, the dehumanization of man, etc.

8 The political background of the action here is well documented by Zahareas, who then discusses its literary function in "The Esperpento and Aesthetics of Commitment," *Modern Language Notes,* LXXXI, No. 2 (1966), 159–73.

9 The best essay on the historical meaning of the *esperpento* and V.-I.'s position in Spanish culture is one by R. Sender, "V.-I. y la dificultad de la tragedia," *Cuadernos Americanos,* XI (September-October 1952), 241–54. This provocative discussion of the Spanish mind is reprinted with the same title by Gredos (Madrid, 1965).

Chapter Ten

1 The only survey of Gómez de la Serna's works is R. Cardona's *Ramón* (New York, 1957). For biography, see G. Gómez de la Serna,

Ramón, obra y vida (Madrid, 1963) and L. Granjel, *Retrato de Ramón* (Madrid, 1963). There is nothing pertinent written on Jarnés or Arderius.

2 On this question of reality, see J. Marías, "Ramón y la realidad," *El oficio del pensamiento* (Madrid, 1958), pp. 253–58.

3 On the significance of games in surrealist practice, see Matthews, *An Introduction to Surrealism,* pp. 110–11.

4 M. Thalmann finds this to be true of the German Romantics, who cultivated the fairy tale in order to use its comic, grotesque, and absurd elements for deforming the bourgeois world. Judging precision clocks, business relationships, and proven laws to be invalid, they liberated themselves from these restrictions through the fairy tale. "These abstractions [of time and geographical location] are not childlike simplifications; they are products of experience in which the person who is disquieted by the relativity of phenomena finds peace" (*The Romantic Fairy Tale* [Ann Arbor: The University of Michigan Press, 1964], p. 122).

Chapter Eleven

1 The script for *Le Chien andalou* can be found in Julien Levy's *Surrealism* (New York, 1936).

2 The bibliography on Jiménez is so vast that I cannot take account of it here. Needless to say, it all deals with what is characteristic of J.: his Modernism, pantheism, style, and aesthetics. My own approach is to find what is atypical in J.'s work in order to locate his position vis-à-vis surrealism. Most of the scholarly criticism, therefore, is not relevant here. I have found, however, two hints of what I am trying to get at. The first is Gullón's attempt to link Modernism with a "descenso a los infiernos," a phrase which includes Negro and other indigenous art forms, as well as irrationalism and Freudianism. See *Direcciones del modernismo*, pp. 74–76.
The second point is that J. J. Bajarlía places Jiménez between modernist Rubén Darío and vanguardist Vicente Huidobro, although for reasons (form, ethics) that differ from mine. He also reaffirms F. de Onís' statement in the latter's *Antología de la poesía española e hispanoamericana* (Madrid, 1934): "si por Rubén Darío entra definitivamente la poesía hispánica en el modernismo, por J. R. J. sale definitivamente de él, viniendo a ser los dos polos en torno a los cuales gira toda la poesía contemporánea" (*El vanguardismo poético en América y España* [Buenos Aires, 1957], pp. 27–28).

3 *Pájinas escojidas. Verso,* ed. by R. Gullón (Madrid, 1958), p. 88.

4 This differs from the view of D. Alonso, who has some interesting remarks to make about the Generation 1920–36 in *Poetas españoles contemporáneos:* "Lo primero que hay que notar es que esa generación no se alza contra nada . . . No tiene tampoco un vínculo político. Ninguno de

estos poetas se preocupaba entonces de cuáles fueran las ideas políticas de los otros; varios hasta parecían ignorar que hubiera semejante cosa en el mundo" (p. 172).

Then, with regard to Alberti in the years following 1922: "No hay caso más curioso que el de R. A. No sólo era A. el más inconsciente, desocupado y despreocupado gustador de la vida, sino el espíritu más rebelde a toda disciplina, con una manera de anarquismo estrictamente literario. ¡Nadie le podría haber imaginado como pieza de una especie de conventualidad política, de una disciplinada estructura de hierro!" (pp. 172–73).

On the other hand, Bodini plays up the political awareness of the Generation of 1927 in his anthology. At one point he calls Alonso a "letterato puro" who misses the political implications of what Alberti, Lorca, and others did and said after 1929. Of L., Bodini writes: "C'è una congiura di parte degli amici e dei nemici (e per questi ultimi lo si può comprendere) per tener Federico fuori dalla politica, al di sopra di essa" (p. xlvi).

As for L., Del Río reports that "L. sentía el malestar de España y el malestar del mundo, pero a diferencia de otros intelectuales, su desasosiego nunca tomó forma política, limitándose a una instintiva solidaridad con los humildes y al deseo de una España mejor" (p. 50).

On Machado's politics, see R. A. González, "Las ideas políticas de A. M.," *La Torre*, XII (January-June 1964), 151–70. For a general essay on social criticism written during the vanguard era, see Corpus Barga, "Política y literatura," *Revista de Occidente*, XIII, No. 144 (June 1935), 313–30; No. 145 (July 1935), 92–116; No. 146 (August 1935), 182–99.

Chapter Twelve

1 Further remarks on Góngora's influence can be found in D. Alonso, "Góngora y la literatura contemporánea," *Estudios y ensayos gongorinos* (Madrid, 1955), pp. 532–79; F. Ichaso, *Góngora y la nueva poesía* (La Habana, 1927); E. Dehennin, *La résurgence de Góngora et la génération poétique de 1927* (Paris, 1962); J. J. Bajarlía, *Notas sobre el Barroco* (Buenos Aires, 1950). Bajarlía's idea is that the baroque poetry of Góngora and Marini prefigures surrealism, an idea rejected by E. Cirlot, *Introducción al surrealismo* (Madrid, 1953), pp. 257–58, but upheld by Friedrich, pp. 112–13.

2 One of the most recent studies on the weakness of the definition of surrealism, and the lack of cohesiveness in Breton's thought is R. Champigny's "Analyse d'une définition du surréalisme," *PMLA*, LXXXI (1966), 139–44.

3 Among the many works on surrealism, I have selected the following cross-section as a basis for my discussion: F. Alquié, *Philosophie du Surréalisme* (Paris, 1955); A. Balakian, *Surrealism: The Road to the Absolute* (New York, 1959); E. Cirlot, *Introducción al surrealismo;* W. Fowlie, *Age*

of Surrealism (Bloomington, 1960); J. H. Matthews, *An Introduction to Surrealism* (University Park, 1965); M. Raymond, *De Baudelaire au Surréalisme* (Paris, 1933); H. Read, "Surrealism and the Romantic Principle," *The Philosophy of Modern Art* (London, 1952).

4 For a critique of Read's position, see P. C. Ray, "Sir Herbert Read and English Surrealism," *Journal of Aesthetics and Art Criticism,* XXIV (1966), 401–13. M. Raymond believes that surrealism rediscovers the state of nature, the mystical experience of the "great Being" of Rousseau. Gaos, however, states the difference between Romantic and modern poetry succinctly: "Lo que decía el poeta [romántico] solía decirlo referido a sí mismo. El poeta vanguardista combate el subjetivismo romántico, elude la confusión personal, desaparece tras el poema, que es lo que de veras importa" (*Antología del grupo poético* de 1927, p. 13). See further J. Díaz Fernández, *El nuevo romanticismo* (Madrid, 1930).

5 Torre cites statements by Crevel and Eluard that deny the influence of Romanticism on the surrealists, but he refutes them and upholds the Romantic position (*Historia . . .* pp. 394–99).

6 For a different treatment of surrealist language, see G. Sobejano, "El epiteto surrealista," *El epiteto en la lírica española* (Madrid, 1956), pp. 459–78, and O. Svanascini, "La metáfora en el superrealismo," *Boletín de la Academia Argentina de Letras,* XVIII (1949), 61–147.

Sources and Translations

Selected Poems of Rafael Alberti, tr. by B. Belitt (Berkeley, 1965).
Federico García Lorca, *Poet in New York,* tr. by B. Belitt (New York, 1955).
Juan Ramón Jiménez, *Selected Writings,* tr. by H. R. Hays (New York, 1957).
Juan Ramón Jiménez, *Three Hundred Poems,* tr. by E. Roach (Austin, 1962).
Eighty Poems of Antonio Machado, tr. by W. Barnstone (New York, 1959).
Castilian Ilexes; versions from Antonio Machado, tr. by C. Tomlinson and H. Gifford (London, 1963).
Antonio Machado, *Juan de Mairena,* tr. by B. Belitt (Berkeley, 1963).
Contemporary Spanish Poetry, ed. by E. Turnbull (Baltimore, 1945).

Especially recommended for background reading in English are the works of these authors listed in the bibliography: Barea, Bowra, Campbell, Cohen, Durán, Honig, Putnam.

Bibliography

Aguilera, Emiliano M., *José Gutiérrez Solana: Aspectos de su vida, su obra y su arte*. Barcelona, 1947.

Alberti, Rafael, *El poeta en la España de 1931*. Buenos Aires, 1942.

Alberti, Rafael, *Poesías completas*. Buenos Aires, 1961.

Albi, José and Fuster, Joan, *Antología del surrealismo español*. Alicante, 1952.

Albornoz, Aurora de, "Bibliografía de Antonio Machado," *La Torre*, XII (January-June 1964), 505–53.

Aleixandre, Vicente, *Mis poemas mejores*. Madrid, 1956.

Aleixandre, Vicente, *Poesías completas*. Madrid, 1960.

Alonso, Dámaso, *Ensayos sobre poesía española*. Buenos Aires, 1946.

Alonso, Dámaso, "Góngora y la literatura contemporánea," *Estudios y ensayos gongorinos*. Madrid, 1955, pp. 532–79.

Alonso, Dámaso, *Poetas españoles contemporáneos*. Madrid, 1952.

Alonso, Dámaso, "Vicente Aleixandre. La destrucción o el amor," *Revista de Occidente*, XIII (June 1935), 331–40.

Alquié, Ferdinand, *Philosophie du Surréalisme*. Paris, 1955. English tr., *The Philosophy of Surrealism*. Ann Arbor, Mich., 1965.

Arconada, César M., "El superrealismo musical," *Alfar*, No. 47 (February 1925), 22–28.

Arderius, Joaquín, *Los príncipes iguales*. Madrid, 1930.

Azorín, "El superrealismo es un hecho evidente," *Obras completas*, IX (Madrid, 1954), 101–4.

Azorín, "Una obra superrealista," *Obras completas*, IX (Madrid, 1954), 159–61.

Babbitt, Irving, *Rousseau and Romanticism*. New York, 1955.

Babín, María Teresa, *La prosa mágica de García Lorca*. Santander, 1962.

Bajarlía, Juan Jacobo, *El vanguardismo poético en América y España*. Buenos Aires, 1957.

Bajarlía, Juan Jacobo, *Notas sobre el barroco*. Buenos Aires, 1950.

Balakian, Anna, *Surrealism: The Road to the Absolute*. New York, 1959.

Barea, Arturo, *Lorca. The Poet and His People*. London, 1944. (tr. *Lorca. El poeta y su pueblo*. Buenos Aires, 1957.)

Barga, Corpus, "Política y literatura," *Revista de Occidente*, XIII (June 1935), 313–30; (July 1935), 92–116; (August 1935), 182–99.

Baumgart, Hildegard, *Der Engel in der modernen spanischen Literatur*. Geneva, 1958.

Bergamín, José, "Nominalismo supra-realista," *Alfar*, No. 50 (May 1925), 3.

Bergamín, José, "El pensamiento hermético de los Artes," *Cruz y Raya*, I (1933), 41–66.

Bodini, Vittorio, *I poeti surrealisti spagnoli*. Torino, 1963.

Bosch, Rafael, "El choque de imágenes como principio creador de García Lorca," *Revista Hispánica Moderna*, XXX (1964), 35–44.

Bousoño, Carlos, *La poesía de Vicente Aleixandre*. Madrid, 1956.

Bousoño, Carlos, *Teoría de la expresión poética*. Madrid, 1952.

Bowra, C. M., *The Creative Experiment*. London, 1949.

Breton, André, *Poésie et autre,* ed. by Gérard Legrand. Paris, 1960.

Breton, André, *Position politique du surréalisme.* Paris, 1935.

Campbell, Roy, *Lorca. An Appreciation of his Work.* New Haven, 1952.

Cano, José Luis, "Machado y la generación poética del '25," *La Torre,* XII (January-June 1964), 483–504.

Cano, José Luis, "Noticia retrospectiva del surrealismo español," *Arbor,* XVI (June 1950), 334–35.

Cano, José Luis, *Poesía española del siglo XX.* Madrid, 1960.

Cano Ballesta, Juan, *La poesía de Miguel Hernández.* Madrid, 1962, pp. 128ff.

Cansinos Assens, Rafael, *El movimiento vanguardista poético.* Madrid, 1924.

Cardona, Rodolfo, *Ramón.* New York, 1957.

Carmody, Francis J., "Eluard's Rupture with Surrealism," *PMLA,* LXXVI (1961), 436–46.

Cela, Camilo José, *La obra literaria del pintor Solana.* Madrid, 1957.

Cernuda, Luis, *Estudios sobre la poesía española contemporánea.* Madrid, 1957.

Champigny, Robert, "Analyse d'une définition du surréalisme," *PMLA,* LXXXI (1966), 139–44.

Cifarelli, Antonio P., "Azorín e il surrealismo in terra di Spagna," *Letterature Moderne,* VII (1957), 751–54.

Cirici-Pellicer, A., *El surrealismo.* Barcelona, 1957.

Cirlot, Eduardo, *Introducción al surrealismo.* Madrid, 1953.

Cirre, José Francisco, *Forma y espíritu de una lírica española.* México, 1950.

Clayborough, Arthur, *The Grotesque in English Literature.* Oxford, 1965.

Cohen, J. M., *Poetry of the Age.* London, 1960.

Collins, G. R., *Antonio Gaudí*. New York, 1960.

Connell, G. W., "The End of a Quest. Alberti's *Sermones y moradas* and Three Uncollected Poems," *Hispanic Review,* XXXIII (1965), 290–309.

Correa, Gustavo, "Significado de *Poeta en Nueva York* de Federico García Lorca," *Cuadernos Americanos,* XVIII (January-February 1959), 224–33.

Cowles, Fleur, *The Case of Salvador Dali*. Boston, 1959.

Dali, Ana María, *Salvador Dali visto por su hermana*. Barcelona, 1949.

Dali, Salvador, *Conquest of the Irrational*. New York, 1935.

Dali, Salvador, *Diary of a Genius*. New York, 1965.

Dali, Salvador, *Hidden Faces*. New York, 1944. (tr. *Rostros ocultos*. Barcelona, 1952.)

Dali, Salvador, "La fotografia, pura creació de l'esprit," *L'Amic de les Arts,* II (September 31, 1927), 90–91.

Dali, Salvador, "Realidad y sobrerrealidad," *La Gaceta Literaria* (October 15, 1928), p. 7.

Dali, Salvador, *The Secret Life of Salvador Dali*. New York, 1942.

Dehennin, Elsa, *La résurgence de Góngora et la génération poétique de 1927*. Paris, 1962.

Del Río, Angel, Introduction to *Poet in New York*, tr. B. Belitt. New York, 1955. (tr. *Poeta en Nueva York*. Madrid, 1958.)

Del Río, Angel, *Vida y obras de Federico García Lorca*. Zaragoza, 1952.

Descharnes, Robert, *The World of Salvador Dali*. New York, 1962.

Díaz Fernández, José, *El nuevo romanticismo*. Madrid, 1930.

Díaz Plaja, Guillermo, *Federico García Lorca. Su obra e influencia en la poesía española*. Buenos Aires, 1954.

Díaz Plaja, Guillermo, *Las estéticas de Valle-Inclán*. Madrid, 1965.

Durán, Manuel, *El superrealismo en la poesía española contemporánea.*
México, 1950.

Durán, Manuel, "El surrealismo en el teatro de Lorca y Alberti,"
Hispanófila, No. 1 (September 1957), 61–66.

Durán, Manuel, ed., *Lorca: A Collection of Critical Essays.* Englewood
Cliffs, 1962.

Espina, Antonio, "Cuadros de Solana," *Revista de Occidente,* V (October–
December 1927), 269–72.

Espina, Antonio, "José Gutiérrez Solana: Dos pueblos de Castilla,"
Revista de Occidente, III (October–December 1925), 261–63.

Espina, Antonio, "Solana," *La Gaceta Literaria* (November 15, 1927), p. 5.

Espina, Antonio, "Solana," *España,* VI (November 6, 1920), 8–9.

Esslin, Martin, *The Theater of the Absurd.* New York, 1961.

Fernández Almagro, Melchor, *Vida y literatura de Valle-Inclán.* Madrid,
1943.

Flint, Weston, "Wax Figures and Mannequins in Solana," *Hispania,*
XLVI (1963), 740–47.

Fowlie, Wallace, *Age of Surrealism.* Bloomington, 1960.

Franconeri, Francesco, "Lorca, New York e il surrealismo," *Vita e Pensiero,*
XLVI, 192–99.

Friedrich, Hugo, *Die Struktur der Modern Lyrik.* Hamburg, 1956.

Gaos, Vicente, *Antología del grupo poético de 1927.* Salamanca, 1965.

García Lorca, Federico, *Obras completas.* Madrid, 1957.

García Lorca, Francisco, Prologue to *Three Tragedies of Federico García
Lorca,* tr. by J. Graham-Luján and R. L. O'Connell. New York, 1947.

Gasch, Sebastiá, "La moderna pintura francesa," *La Gaceta Literaria,*
October 15, 1927, p. 5.

Gómez de la Serna, Gáspar, *Ramón, obra y vida.* Madrid, 1963.

Gómez de la Serna, Ramón, "Definición de Dalí y sus bigotes," *Temas* (New York), V (March 1953), 60–75.

Gómez de la Serna, Ramón, *El incongruente*. Madrid, 1922.

Gómez de la Serna, Ramón, *Ismos*. Buenos Aires, 1943.

Gómez de la Serna, Ramón, *José Gutiérrez Solana*. Buenos Aires, 1944.

Gómez de la Serna, Ramón, "Ultimátum del surrealismo," *Clavileño*, VII, No. 39 (1956), 32–39.

González, Rafael A., "Las ideas políticas de Antonio Machado," *La Torre*, XII (January–June 1964), 151–70.

Granjel, Luis, *Retrato de Ramón*. Madrid, 1963.

Guillén, Jorge, *Language and Poetry*. Cambridge, 1961.

Gullón, Ricardo, *Balance del surrealismo*. Santander, 1961.

Gullón, Ricardo, *Direcciones del modernismo*. Madrid, 1963.

Gullón, Ricardo, "Lorca en Nueva York," *La Torre*, V (April–June 1957), 161–70.

Gullón, Ricardo, "Salvador Dalí y el surrealismo," *La Torre*, I (October–December 1953), 131–45.

Gutiérrez Solana, José, *La España negra*. Madrid, 1920.

Gutiérrez Solana, José, *Madrid callejero*. Madrid, 1923.

Gutiérrez Solana, José, *Madrid: Escenas y costumbres, primera serie*. Madrid, 1913.

Gutiérrez Solana, José, *Madrid: Escenas y costumbres, segunda serie*. Madrid, 1918.

Gutiérrez Solana, José, *Obra literaria*. Madrid, 1961.

Hardré, Jacques, "Present State of Studies on Literary Surrealism," *Yearbook of Comparative and General Literature*, IX (1960), 43–66.

Heinrich, Gunter, *Die Kunst Don Ramón María del Valle-Inclán*. Rostock, 1938, pp. 71–95.

Honig, Edwin, *García Lorca*. Norfolk, 1948.

Honig, Edwin, "The Triumph of Sensual Reality," in Durán, *Lorca* . . . , pp. 80–99.

Ichaso, Francisco, *Góngora y la nueva poesía*. La Habana, 1927.

Iglesias, Carmen, "El 'esperpento' en la obra de Valle-Inclán," *Cuadernos Americanos*, XVIII (May–June 1959), 247–63; (July–August 1959), 212–33.

Ilie, Paul, *La novelística de Camilo José Cela*. Madrid, 1963, pp. 197–208.

Ilie, Paul, "The Grotesque in Valle-Inclán," in *Ramón del Valle-Inclán: A Critical Appraisal of His Life and Works*. New York, 1968.

Jarnés, Benjamín, *Teoría del zumbel*. Madrid, 1930.

Jarnés, Benjamín, "El texto desconocido," *Revista de Occidente*, VIII (March 1930), 397–401.

Jean, Marcel, *The History of Surrealist Painting*. New York, 1960.

Jiménez, Juan Ramón, *Pájinas escogidas. Verso*. Madrid, 1958.

Kayser, Wolfgang, *Das Groteske in Malerei und Dichtung*. München, 1960.

Kellermann, Wilhelm, "Die Welt der Dinge in der spanischen Lyrik des 20. Jahrhunderts," *Deutsche Vierteljahrsschrift*, XXVII (1953), 102–36.

Kerrigan, Anthony, "Black Knight of Spanish Painting," *Arts Magazine* (May–June 1962), pp. 16–20.

Kovacci, Ofelia and Salvador, Nelida, "García Lorca y su Leyenda del tiempo (*Así que pasen 5 años*)," *Filología*, VII (1961), 77–105.

Kyrou, Ado, *Le surréalisme au cinéma*. Paris, 1953.

Kyrou, Ado, *Luis Buñuel: An Introduction*. New York, 1963.

Laffranque, Marie, "Federico García Lorca. Nouveaux textes en prose," *Bulletin Hispanique*, LVI (1954), 260–300.

La John, Lawrence, "Surrealism in Azorín's Theater," *Kentucky Foreign Language Quarterly*, X (1963), 20–25.

Larrea, Juan, *El surrealismo entre viejo y nuevo mundo*. México, 1944.

Levy, Julien, *Surrealism*. New York, 1936.

López Ibor, J. J., "Solana existencialista carpetovetónico," *Papeles de Son Armadans*, III, No. 33 bis (1958), pp. 29–50.

Lott, Robert, "Azorín's Experimental Period and Surrealism," *PMLA*, LXXIX (1964), 305–20.

Lovejoy, A. O., *Essays in the History of Ideas*. Baltimore, 1948.

Machado, Antonio, *Abel Martín*, Buenos Aires, 1953.

Machado, Antonio, *Juan de Mairena*. 2 vols. Buenos Aires, 1957.

Machado, Antonio, *Los complementarios*. Buenos Aires, 1957.

Machado, Antonio, *Poesías completas*. Buenos Aires, 1951.

MacKenzie, Harriet, *Byron's Laughter*. Los Angeles, 1939.

Marías, Julián, "Ramón y la realidad," *El oficio del pensamiento*. Madrid, 1958, pp. 253–58.

Martínez Cachero, J. M., *Las novelas de Azorín*. Madrid, 1960, pp. 224–33.

Matthews, J. H., *An Introduction to Surrealism*. University Park, 1965.

Monguió, Luis, Prologue to *Selected Poems of Rafael Alberti*, tr. by B. Belitt. Berkeley, 1965.

Morris, Cyril B., *Rafael Alberti's 'Sobre los ángeles': Four Major Themes*. Hull, 1966.

Nadeau, Maurice, *Histoire du Surréalisme*. 2 vols. Paris, 1945, 1946.

Nietzsche, Friedrich, *The Birth of Tragedy*, in *The Philosophy of Nietzsche*. New York, 1954.

Nora, Eugenio, *La novela española contemporánea*. Madrid, 1962. Vol. II, Parte 1, pp. 151–87; Vol. II, Parte 2, pp. 12–22.

Oliver, William, "Lorca: The Puppets and the Artist," *Tulane Drama Review*, VII, No. 2 (1962), 76–95.

Ortega y Gasset, José, *Goya*. Madrid, 1958.

Orwell, George, "Benefit of Clergy," *Collected Essays*. London, 1961, pp. 209–19.

Otero Seco, Antonio, "Sobre Valle-Inclán y el esperpento," *Asomante,* XX (1964), 15–27.

Peña, M. de la, *El ultraísmo en España*. Avila, 1925.

Poggioli, Renato, *Teoria dell'arte d'avanguardia*. Bologna, 1962.

Pradal, Gabriel, "La paloma y el leopardo o lo humano y lo inhumano en la obra de Federico García Lorca," *Cuadernos Americanos*, XVI (July–August 1956), 193–207.

Proll, Eric, "Surrealist Elements in Rafael Alberti," *Bulletin of Hispanic Studies*, XVIII (1941), 70–82.

Putnam, Samuel, ed., *The European Caravan*. New York, 1931.

Ray, Paul C., "Sir Herbert Read and English Surrealism," *Journal of Aesthetics and Art Criticism*, XXIV (1966), 401–13.

Raymond, Marcel, *De Baudelaire au Surréalisme*. Paris, 1933.

Read, Herbert, "Surrealism and the Romantic Principle," *The Philosophy of Modern Art*. London, 1952, pp. 105–41.

Ribbans, Geoffrey, "La influencia de Verlaine en Antonio Machado," *Cuadernos Hispanoamericanos*, Nos. 91–92 (1957), 180–201.

Risco, Antonio, *La estética de Valle-Inclán*. Madrid, 1966.

Rodríguez Alcalde, Leopoldo, *Vida y sentido de la poesía actual*. Madrid, 1956.

Rof Carballo, J., "Máscara de la mujer en la pintura de Solana," *Entre el silencio y la palabra*. Madrid, 1960, pp. 298–330.

Roger, Juan, *El surrealismo francés*. Madrid, 1956.

Sábato, Ernesto, *Hombres y engranajes*. Buenos Aires, 1951, pp. 108–15.

Saez, Richard, "The Ritual Sacrifice in Lorca's *Poet in New York*," in Durán, *Lorca . . .* , pp. 108–29.

Salas, Xavier de, "La pintura de Solana," *Leonardo*, VI–VII (September–October 1945), 305–11.

Salinas, Pedro, *Literatura española siglo XX*. México, 1949.

Sánchez Barbudo, Antonio, *Estudios sobre Unamuno y Machado*. Madrid, 1959.

Sánchez Camargo, Manuel, *Solana*. Madrid, 1945.

Sánchez Camargo, Manuel, *Solana. Pintura y dibujos*. Madrid, 1953.

Sandoval, M. de, *Lo inconsciente y lo involuntario en las obras literarias y poéticas*. Madrid, 1920.

Santos Torroella, Rafael, *Genio y figura del surrealismo*. Barcelona, 1948.

Saz, Agustín del, *El teatro de Valle-Inclán*. Barcelona, 1950, pp. 37–53.

Schonberg, Jean-Louis, *Federico García Lorca. L'Homme-L'Oeuvre*. Paris, 1956.

Sender, Ramón, "Valle-Inclán y la dificultad de la tragedia," *Cuadernos Americanos*, XI (September–October 1952), 241–54. (Republished with same title, Madrid, 1965.)

Serrano Poncela, Segundo, *Antonio Machado. Su mundo y su obra*. Buenos Aires, 1954.

Serrano Poncela, Segundo, "Borrosos laberintos," *La Torre*, XII (January–June 1964), 265–84.

Sobejano, Gonzalo, "El epiteto surrealista," *El epiteto en la lírica española*. Madrid, 1956, pp. 459–78.

Speratti Piñero, Emma, *La elaboración artística en Tirano Banderas*. México, 1957.

Svanascini, Osvaldo, "La metáfora en el superrealismo," *Boletín de la Academia Argentina de Letras*, XVIII (1949), 61–147.

Thalmann, Marianne, *The Romantic Fairy Tale*. Ann Arbor, 1964.

Torre, Guillermo de, "Así que pasen cinco años," *Fiel de la balanza*. Madrid, 1961, pp. 171–99.

Torre, Guillermo de, *Historia de las literaturas de vanguardia*. Madrid, 1965.

Torre, Guillermo de, *La aventura y el orden*. Buenos Aires, 1943.

Torre, Guillermo de, "Limitaciones y noblezas del superrealismo," *Problemática de la literatura*. Buenos Aires, 1951, pp. 290–99.

Torre, Guillermo de, *Literaturas europeas de vanguardia*. Madrid, 1925.

Torre, Guillermo de, *¿Qué es el superrealismo?* Buenos Aires, 1955.

Torre, Guillermo de, "Realismo y superrealismo," *El Sol* (March 8, 1936).

Torre, Guillermo de, "Salvador Dalí en tres tiempos," *Minorías y masas en la cultura y arte contemporáneo*. Barcelona, 1963, pp. 271–302.

Torre, Guillermo de, "Solana, escritor," *Minorías y masas* . . . pp. 213–18.

Torre, Guillermo de, "El suicidio y el surrealismo," *Revista de Occidente*, XIII (July 1935), 117–28.

Torre, Guillermo de, "Valle-Inclán o el rostro y la máscara," *La difícil universalidad española*. Madrid, 1965, pp. 113–62.

Utrillo, Miguel, *Salvador Dalí y sus enemigos*. Sitges, 1952.

Valverde, José María, *Estudios sobre la palabra poética*. Madrid, 1952.

Valle-Inclán, Ramón María del, *Tirano Banderas,* cuarta ed. Buenos Aires: Colección Austral, 1948.

Vela, Fernando, "Freud y los suprarrealistas," *El Sol* (July 31, 1936).

Vela, Fernando, "El suprarrealismo," *Revista de Occidente*, II (December 1924), 428–34.

Videla, Gloria, *El ultraísmo*. Madrid, 1963.

Vivanco, Luis Felipe, *Introducción a la poesía española contemporánea*. Madrid, 1957.

Warnier, M. R., "Apollinaire au Portugal et en Espagne," *Bulletin des Etudes portugaises*, XXII (1959–60), 187–247.

Weisstein, Ulrich, "Expressionism: Style or 'Weltanschauung'?" *Criticism*, IX (1967), 42–62.

Wellek, René, "The Concept of Romanticism in Literary History," *Comparative Literature,* I (1949), 1–23; 147–72.

Wilson, Edmund, "Salvador Dali as a Novelist," *The New Yorker* (July 1, 1944).

Zahareas, Anthony N., "La desvalorización del sentido trágico en el esperpento de Valle-Inclán," *Insula,* No. 203 (October 1963), pp. 1, 15.

Zahareas, Anthony N., "The Esperpento and Aesthetics of Commitment," *Modern Language Notes,* LXXXI (1966), 159–73.

Zardoya, Concha, *Poesía española contemporánea.* Madrid, 1961.

Zubiría, R. de, *La poesía de Antonio Machado.* Madrid, 1955.

Zum Felde, Alberto, *Estética del novecientos.* Buenos Aires, 1927.

Zúñiga, Angel, *Palabras del tiempo.* Barcelona, 1952, pp. 46–51.

Index